Music Therapy in Health and Education

of related interest

**Music Therapy, Remedial Music Making and Musical Activities
    for People with Developmental Disability**
Frans Schalkwijk
ISBN 1 85302 226 8

Making Music with the Young Child with Special Needs
A Guide for Parents
Elaine Streeter
ISBN 1 85302 187 3

Handbook of Inquiry in the Arts Therapies
One River, Many Currents
Edited by Helen Payne
ISBN 1 85302 153 9

Group Work with Children and Adolescents
Edited by Kedar Nath Dwivedi
ISBN 1 85302 157 1

Music Therapy in Health and Education

Edited by Margaret Heal and Tony Wigram

Foreword by Anthony Storr

Jessica Kingsley Publishers
London and Philadelphia

Acknowledgements

To Denize Christophers and Alison Collyer for their help in typing the chapters.
To Ben Gerits, Chairman of Stichting Muzietherapie, who kindly allowed us to
reproduce a print of his wood cut on the front cover.
To the authors, for the fascinating insights into therapy their contributions provide.

To our clients.

All royalties from this book go to the Juliette Alvin Memorial Fund towards the
training of music therapists and research in the field.

First published in the United Kingdom in 1993 by
Jessica Kingsley Publishers Ltd
116 Pentonville Road
London N1 9JB

Copyright © 1993 the contributors and the publisher
Foreword copyright © 1993 Anthony Storr

British Library Cataloguing in Publication Data
Music Therapy in Health and Education
I. Heal, Margaret II. Wigram, Tony
615.8

ISBN 1-85302-175-X

Printed and Bound in Great Britain by
Biddles Ltd., Guildford and Kings Lynn

Contents

Families

Adults

Part 2: Research
Literature Review

Applied Research

Foreword

At the end of the Second World War, when I was about to begin my training as a psychiatrist, music therapy scarcely existed. Although bitter disputes went on between Freudians, Kleinians, and Jungians, all psychotherapists using techniques derived from psychoanalysis would have agreed that the word was paramount. Patients in therapy were expected to be verbally fluent; and although analysts might not say very much to their patients, what they did say was thought to be highly significant. In so far as patients changed for the better, their improvement was attributed to increasing insight, brought about by the analyst's interpretations of the verbal material which the patients provided. Interpretation of transference, of the patient's emotional attitude to the analyst, became increasingly important as pointing the patient's way to forming new and better relationships with other people. But the patient's relationship with the analyst remained one which was based on verbal interchange. Analytical psychotherapy, therefore, was only possible with patients who were articulate, at least moderately intelligent, and preferably from the same kind of more or less educated background from which most psychoanalysts came.

Gradually, the arts began to play a limited part in psychotherapy. Following the lead of Jung, some analysts encouraged their patients to draw and paint, and it was soon realised that these productions might indicate the patient's state of mind and changing moods more vividly than words were able to do. Moreover, paintings are less ephemeral than words. A series of paintings can provide a record of emotional progress, which it is often valuable to look back upon. Some patients have allowed their psychotherapeutic sessions to be tape-recorded, but I don't know how many patients have gained much from replaying tapes. Paintings provide a summary; tape-recordings are often too diffuse to be useful. Paintings also have another function. Disturbed people feel threatened by the strength of emotions which they cannot control. By painting their despair or rage they are expressing these dangerous affects; making them into phenomena which are no longer so threatening because they are 'out there' and can be studied more objectively.

Art therapy became recognised as respectable before music therapy began to flourish; and it is tempting to suppose that this sequence was partly determined by the personalities of the two most important originators of psychotherapeutic schools, Freud and Jung. It is deeply regrettable to record that neither founding father had any use for music. Freud's nephew tells us that his uncle despised music and regarded it solely as an intrusion. When Freud was a boy, his parents removed his sister Anna's piano from their apartment because the sound of her practising disturbed the *Wunderkind*. What a monstrous deprivation to inflict upon an innocent girl! As Peter Gay suggests in his biography of Freud, the Freuds must have been one of the very few middle-class European families without a piano.

In his autobiography, Jung revealed that he could not abide polyphonic music. Although Jung professed an interest in Wagner, it was Wagner's use of myth rather than Wagner's music which engaged his attention. Although I respect both Freud and Jung, their failure to appreciate music constitutes an insuperable barrier to my being whole-heartedly enthusiastic about either. Shakespeare was right.

> The man that hath no music in himself,
> Nor is not mov'd with concourse of sweet sounds,
> Is fit for treasons, stratagems, and spoils;
> The motions of his spirit are dull as night,
> And his affections dark as Erebus:
> Let no such man be trusted.[1]

If Freud had appreciated music as much as he enjoyed sculpture, and if Jung had been as interested in music as he was in alchemy, music therapy might have established itself even earlier. Perhaps analysts, like the Inuit, would have learned to settle their disputes by song contests instead of employing character assassination and verbal abuse. But, in spite of the limitations of Freud and Jung, music therapy is now flourishing in many parts of the world, as the various chapters of this book amply demonstrate.

Music therapy is obviously appropriate in cases where verbal communication is impaired or impossible. Participating in music not only affords an opportunity for expressing and mastering disturbing emotions, but also opens up new channels of communication between therapist and patient. Anyone who has played chamber music or sung in a choir knows that music reinforces emotional ties with others; and this is as true of the simplest forms of music-making as it is of more sophisticated varieties. For autistic children and other patients whose disabilities make it difficult for them to communicate with their fellows verbally, music can be a life-saver, preventing regression into the hell of total isolation.

---

1   William Shakespeare, *The Merchant of Venice*, Act V, Scene 1, 1.83–88.

It isn't really surprising that music provides an alternative to speech as a means of communication. When mothers talk to their infants, the meaning of the words which they employ is unimportant; but the changes in pitch, stress, rhythm, speed, and volume which characterise a mother's utterance convey a message of concern and love to which the infant responds with gurgling pleasure. Darwin thought that music began as an elaboration of mating calls; but I think it more likely that it is an elaboration of mother–infant vocal exchanges which foster attachment by strengthening the bond between them. In similar fashion, music promotes group solidarity between adults by synchronising physical responses in different individuals.

The therapeutic uses of music are not confined to patients who cannot use language normally. Everyone who plays an instrument or who listens to music for pleasure knows that music has potent effects upon mind and body. Music can alter our moods, reduce fatigue, facilitate muscular movement, stir our memories. Chapter 15 of this book, *Applications of Music in Medicine*, lists a wide variety of therapeutic uses of music, from reducing pain to decreasing the length of labour and promoting the healthy development of infants in intensive care units. The physical and emotional effects of music are undoubted; but much more research is needed before we fully understand how these effects are brought about. Modern neurological techniques are beginning to reveal the effects of music upon the brain. Electro-encephalographic studies suggest that music creates a unique level of coherence of electrical activity in separate parts of the brain. Musicians and neurologists are beginning to talk to one another; and I confidently expect that, within the next ten or fifteen years, we shall understand a great deal more about music's effects upon the brain.

The idea of using music therapeutically is not new. Pythagoras, after he had emigrated to Croton in Italy around 531 B.C., founded a religious society. The Pythagoreans developed a science of musical psychotherapy in which a daily programme of songs and pieces for the lyre made them bright and alert on rising, and purged them of the day's cares when they retired to bed.

Plato reports Socrates as saying that:

> Musical training is a more potent instrument than any other, because rhythm and harmony find their way into the inward places of the soul, imparting grace, and making the soul of him who is rightly educated graceful.[2]

---

2   Plato, *The Republic of Plato*, third edition, translated by Benjamin Jowett, (Oxford: Clarendon Press, 1888), Book III, p.88.

In *Protagoras*, Plato refers to teachers of music who teach boys poetry set to the music of the lyre. When rhythm and harmony become implanted in their souls, the boys become less wild and:

> through being better rhymed and attuned, good at speaking and in action; for a man's whole life calls for good rhythm and good attunement.[3]

And in the *Timaeus* Plato wrote:

> All audible musical sound is given us for the sake of harmony, which has motions akin to the orbits in our soul and which, as anyone who makes intelligent use of the arts knows, is not be used as is commonly thought, to give irrational pleasure, but as a heaven-sent ally in reducing to order and harmony any disharmony in the revolutions within us. Rhythm, again, was given us from the same heavenly source to help us in the same way; for most of us lack measure and grace.[4]

Today, when at last more attention is being given to the effects of music upon human beings, we have almost reached the depth of insight displayed by the Greeks in the 5th century B.C.

Anthony Storr
Oxford, April 1993

---

3   Quoted in M.L. West, *Ancient Greek Music*, (Oxford: Clarendon Press, 1992), p.248.

4   Plato, *Timaeus and Critias*, translated and introduced by Desmond Lee, (London: Penguin Books, 1977) p.65.

Introduction

From conception we are cradled in a watery world of sound and movement. This first symphony of life, the regular ebb and flow of mother's heart and lungs punctuated by a sometimes gurgling tummy, the muffled sounds of the outside, and our own evolving pulse, may well be our prototype for later uses of sound and the strong emotional reactions which we have to it.

Within the first few days of life, long before words, an infant begins to interact with those around him, using sound and movement to experience and negotiate relationships. As adults we continue to use sound to express how we are feeling. At the most basic level we may sigh or slam a door when we are annoyed, or honk our car horn as we find ourselves locked in a traffic jam. We may use sounds in a more organised and creative way such as whistling, humming, or tapping our fingers or feet.

Music therapy in practice explores our experience of sound, emotion and behaviour. In some cases this occurs within the context of a client-therapist relationship as it develops over time. Alternatively, it may involve more objective observation of the effects of the application of music. The music can be live – either improvised by the client and/or therapist, or precomposed – or may involve tape recordings. This diversity arises from what can be an uncomfortable, yet enriching, marriage of art and science.

Nowhere is this diversity more evident than in the field of music therapy research. Some practitioners focus on the processes that occur during music therapy, as examined through the development of the music, the therapeutic relationship, or a mixture of both, while others are more concerned with the outcome of a particular music therapy intervention. In addition, some researchers have evaluated the application of sound and music as a supplement to mainstream medicine. Music therapists actively seek to take their place within a multi-disciplinary team setting and collaborate closely with other professionals. Music therapy, however, is recognised as a unique intervention in which noticeable change and development occur.

As members of a relatively young profession we are striving to develop new models for understanding clinical practice. This often involves cross-fertilisation with other schools of thought: psychoanalysis and analytical psychology; psychotherapy; behavioural, cognitive, developmental, humanistic and new paradigm psychology; aesthetics and philosophy; music analysis; ethnomusicology; sonology; education; and physiology and medicine.

Over the last forty years, as music therapy has grown, the scientific world and the organisations that employ music therapists have become increasingly interested in both the nature and process of music therapy, and in clear evidence of its outcomes and effectiveness. Music therapy has also excited much interest and attention from the medical profession, paramedical professions, and education services, and also, inevitably, the media. Much is beginning to be published about the practice of music therapy.

In April 1992 three hundred music therapists from twenty-three countries gathered at King's College, Cambridge to participate in the conference 'Music Therapy in Health and Education in the European Community'. This was sponsored by the British Society for Music Therapy and the Association of Professional Music Therapists. From the proceedings of this event, twenty-two papers have been chosen, to reflect the breadth and scope of music therapy practice in the world today, and adapted for publication.

These chapters have been divided into two areas, namely clinical practice and research – a useful, although at times artificial, division. They have been ordered according to the chronological ages of the subjects, rather than by the setting of the work, the dominant problem of the client group, or the approach employed.

The clinical practice section begins with a description of work with children. It is appropriate that the first chapter is written by Clive Robbins, a pioneer in music therapy with over thirty-two years of clinical experience. In 'Creative Processes in Music Therapy' he sensitively details the musical and emotional development of two children with mental and physical handicaps as they travel with him as co-therapist, and a primary therapist on their therapeutic journey. The second chapter, 'A Case of Severe Infantile Regression Treated by Music Therapy and Explored in Group Supervision', is written by a group of psychiatrists under the supervision of Pier Luigi Postacchini. It describes the treatment of a young girl with a controversial diagnosis of Rett's Syndrome.

The adolescent section opens with a chapter by Jos De Backer on 'Containment in Music Therapy'. From a psychodynamic stance, he explores the function of musical improvisation as a container of chaotic feelings for psychotic, borderline and mentally handicapped clients in individual and group therapy sessions. Claire Flower's contribution, 'Control and Creativity: Music Therapy with Adolescents in Secure Care', provides us with an insight into the effect that being in a secure unit may have on the musical and therapeutic relationship. She makes particular reference to the issues of loss of freedom and imposed control. This is followed by Amelia Oldfield's lucid description of the value of music therapy with families in a psychiatric unit in 'Music Therapy with Families'.

The adult section starts in the field of psychiatry. In her chapter 'Music Therapy in the Psychodynamic Treatment of Schizophrenia', Hanne Mette Kortegaard considers how clinical improvisations in music therapy sessions exist in the 'inner worlds' of the schizophrenic patient and the therapist, and in the intermediary space between them.

The next two chapters describe group and individual supervision of music therapy work in psychiatry. Giuseppe Berruti and his colleagues, in 'Description of an Experience in Music Therapy Carried Out at the Department of Psychiatry of the University of Genoa', illustrate the value of music therapy in opening channels of communication with psychotic patients in a hospital setting. Esmé Towse and Claire Flower, as supervisor and supervisee respectively, examine 'Levels of Interaction in Group Improvisation'. This thoughtful discussion considers when and why music therapists might choose to improvise in sessions, and whether or not this is always the most helpful therapeutic intervention.

Gianluigi di Franco writes from a more philosophical point of view in 'Music Therapy as a Methodological Approach in the Mental Health Field'. He compares clinical aspects of the psychiatric hospital and the day hospital and examines how these may affect music therapy practice.

Fiona Ritchie, who works psychodynamically with highly institutionalised adults who have a mental handicap, shares her experience in 'Opening Doors: the Effects of Music Therapy with People who have Severe Learning Difficulties'. Also employing a psychodynamic approach is Ann Sloboda, who follows with 'Music Therapy with a Man who has an Eating Disorder'.

In 'Music: a Mega Vitamin for the Brain', Denise Erdonmez draws on the literature of music psychology and neuropsychology to enrich her clinical practice for clients with diseases of the central nervous system or those who have suffered a stroke. This is followed by 'Music Therapy's Role in the Diagnosis of Psychogeriatric Patients in the Hague', Josée Raijmaeker's description of a music therapy programme which observes the emotional, cognitive and interactive functioning of the elderly as part of a multi-disciplinary diagnosis.

The research section includes a literature review and a selection of applied research. Tony Wigram, in 'Music Therapy Research to Meet the Demands of Health and Education Services: Research and Literature Analysis', outlines some of the work already recorded. This is followed by Cheryl Dileo

Maranto's chapter, 'Applications of Music in Medicine', in which she highlights the value of music as an aid to conventional medical treatments.

A section of applied research begins with Anthi Agrotou's 'Spontaneous Ritualised Play in Music Therapy: A Technical and Theoretical Analysis'. In this innovative piece she distinguishes spontaneous ritualised play from that of pathological ritualism, before going on to describe how they might manifest themselves as clinical phenomena. Ruth Bright with her research into 'Cultural Aspects of Music Therapy' presents compelling arguments that prolonged experience and exposure to the music of any given culture is necessary in order for the therapist to perceive the emotional content of music from that culture. Jeff Hooper examines the effect of music therapy on a withdrawn subject who exhibits stereotyped behaviours, in 'Developing Interaction Through Shared Musical Experiences: A Strategy to Enhance and Validate the Descriptive Approach'.

This is followed by two chapters which describe the joint work of a researcher and a music therapist. Pierette Muller, a research psychologist, in association with Auriel Warwick, a music therapist, present the results of a doctoral study: 'Autistic Children: The Influence of Maternal Involvement in Therapy'. This scholarly work outlines the hypotheses, methodology, and system of measurement employed to examine the musical interaction between mother, child and therapist. Henk Smeijsters and José van den Hurk, music psychologist/researcher and music therapist respectively, then demonstrate a creative approach to the difficulties of evaluating ongoing psychodynamic work, in 'Research in Practice in the Music Therapy Treatment of a Client with Symptoms of Anorexia Nervosa'.

Julie Sutton in 'The Guitar Doesn't Know This Song: An Investigation of Parallel Development in Speech/Language and Music Therapy' reviews the results of her ongoing research in schools and special units in Belfast. The final chapter of the book, 'Observational Techniques in the Analysis of Both Active and Receptive Music Therapy with Disturbed and Self-Injurious Clients' by Tony Wigram, explores an observational method of evaluating research in vibro-acoustic therapy and more interactive music therapy.

As is evident from this book, music therapy embraces a broad spectrum of treatments and approaches, with the unifying element being sound or music. This diversity reflects the nature of music itself.

Margaret Heal and Tony Wigram

Part 1

Clinical Practice

CHAPTER 1

The Creative Processes are Universal

Clive Robbins

United States of America

Music therapy is a varied, enormous, and at this time, far from fully explored field. It is only through a diversity of approaches that clinical practice, research and theory can evolve to investigate this great field of human endeavour throughout its breadth, width and depth. Diversity is inevitable: different nationalities preserve different social values and needs, and distinct life styles. Concepts of social responsibility are evolving; music therapy itself is at different stages of development in different countries. As creative individuals, music therapists themselves have different abilities and insights, and are comfortable in different modes of practice, and so contribute to the development of the field in a variety of individual ways. It is, therefore essential to accept, and more, respect the diversity of viewpoints and approaches among music therapists. It is mandatory to get beyond the insularity of personal prejudices.

Currently, Europe faces a challenging situation, one unique in its history. An American reference would seem to be appropriate. Particularly from the middle of the nineteenth century to the middle of the twentieth, the United States was known as a 'melting pot' in which different cultures, nationalities, and life-styles came together to form new blends of human character, ability and potential. Perhaps nowhere is the effect of the melting pot more evident to musicians than in the colourful and vital productions of 'Tin Pan Alley' and the American musical theatre. In a creative confluence that spanned the first four decades of this century, classical music, opera, European operetta, British music hall tradition, folk song in different ethnic styles, ballad, negro jazz, blues and gospel, various popular and regional dance styles, and so forth, became freely and variously combined in America to produce a wealth of popular music, much of which continues to live in the musical repertoire of the Western world and influence other cultures. (It is interesting to consider how many of the gifted musicians who created this music, mostly in New York City, were European or Russian immigrants, or the children of such immigrants.) With the removal of borders and lessening of border mentalities, Europe now is becoming a melting pot which, with all its cultural richness and potential for creative interaction, must influence the evolution of European music therapy. For me, 'melting' carries the inference of warmth and mobility: warmth of interest, acceptance, commitment; mobility of thinking, sharing, planning; all prerequisites for productive collaboration.

After a generation of music therapy experience, particularly creative improvisational experience, I find it impossible to escape the belief that the human being and music are deeply interrelated, and that music therapists need to adopt a big concept of music, or at least to leave space in their personal relationship to music for this concept to expand. Throughout history, mankind has created music for self-expression, for socio-political and religious rituals, and for artistic and cultural experience. The inspirational processes and compositional techniques of music have been channeled into many social purposes. Now, in music therapy, there is a new purpose – the contemporary act of music being created specifically to influence an individual's condition or state. In creative music therapy the same artistic processes that have produced and continue to produce the social repertoire of music are at work. One is aware of an equal artistic integrity in action, now clinically focussed on meeting an individual human being's needs, whether adult or child. The conclusion is inevitable: here in this individual-ized realization of music is the next stage in the evolution of the deepening relationship between mankind and music. I venture to assert that much of the essential value of the role of music in human life in the future will lie in the creative realization of music in therapy. This is in the destiny of music, and music therapists now and in the future are going to carry this develop-ment forward. Music therapy researchers will find themselves unfolding the mysteries of mankind's rich and comprehensive relationship to the world of music. Paul Nordoff once remarked: 'The world of pathology is immense, but the world of music is just as immense and can contain it all.' In the vast range of music of all styles, idioms and origins bequeathed to us by human evolution, in the innovative styles of today and all the current possibilities offered by electronic technology, music therapists have access to immense resources. The key question is: how do we best train music therapists to use these resources, not only appropriately, but creatively?

Obviously, as a profession, we have a long way to go and we must start from where we are as individuals. I believe that it is timely and important for music therapists to have the perspective of such an artistic and therapeutic world view of their profession. We must realize that creative clinical practice in music therapy has already become an intimate and living component of the universal processes of musical creation. With the aid of video-based documentation of music therapy sessions, let us look at some of these dynamics as they become manifest in musical improvisation in a clinical setting. This will give me the opportunity to ground this article in clinical work, and to bring in work with two children with very different needs. At times we must remind ourselves of the obvious: music therapy happens between patient and therapist. Patients are as much part of the dialogue as therapists. Also, our patients are our greatest teachers; they challenge us and demand that we change and expand to meet their conditions and needs. It is they who reveal many deeply personal aspects of human musicality.

Nicole

The first child is Nicole, who began music therapy at the age of four. The primary therapist is Carol Robbins, I am the co-therapist. Nicole was born in the twenty-fourth week of gestation and was not expected to survive. Surgery was necessary on the eighth day, and again, a week later. When she came off the respirator at three months, she was found to be blind. The first fourteen months of her life were spent in hospital: her mother was with her every day, all day. During her second year she was repeatedly re-admitted, and her mother felt it was difficult for Nicole to trust her. By the time she began music therapy, Nicole had had twenty-five operations; most of her small intestine had been removed. Because she could not take food by mouth and it was necessary to monitor closely her intake of nutrients, she had been fed since birth by a gastrostomy tube for continuous daytime feeding, supplemented by intravenous feeding via a Broviac catheter for up to fourteen hours at night. At the time music therapy begins, Nicole can partially imitate words and name a number of objects, but does not use speech communicatively. Autism had been diagnosed at fourteen months. As her mother reports, 'She would just live in her own little world, just tune you out.' Nicole shows little initiative, and is averse to using her hands for anything that does not lie within her narrow circle of interests. She is unsteady on her feet, and waits passively to be led. She has always liked music. She is a sensitive listener who knows when the batteries in her cassette recorder are getting low, long before anyone else can detect it. She hums and, in her own way, sings melodies she is currently interested in. It is because Nicole's response to music seems the most 'normal' aspect of her life, that her Mother sought music therapy for her.

Session one

I lead Nicole into the room, quietly saying 'Here we are' to reassure her. Carol takes this up and gently sings, repeating 'Here we are in music.' I take the little out-of-tune ukulele she has carried in and leave her standing at the treble end of the piano. She immediately reaches out to find the keyboard and begins to play with her right hand; her playing is tentative, but she starts on the beat, in tempo, and at the beginning of a phrase. She turns to face the keyboard and uses both hands, playing mostly with the right. Carol accompanies her. Nicole uses her middle fingers, but also explores playing clusters with the flat of her hands and her knuckles. Her face is serious and intent. She briefly imitates quavers. As her playing gains in sureness, Carol improvises a little more forcefully to meet and support her, carefully following when she plays more slowly. The song returns with a brighter, more active melody to match her increasing confidence.

Here we are in music, Here we are today.

Here we are in music, Nicole.

Copyright © 1992 by Carol Robbins

How important improvisation is in moving carefully into the unknown and in exploring contact! Throughout, the music's mood was suited to the child's mood as suggested through behaviour, posture and facial expression; the tempo was determined practically by what was appropriate to her way of playing. After the session, which was twenty-seven minutes in length, we analysed the video recording and thoroughly documented all that happened; any significant music was transcribed for reference in subsequent sessions.

The song 'Here we are in music' arose in a spontaneous musical response to meet a perceived need. It appeared as a structurally simple song, a five note melody consisting of major seconds, fourths and fifths in a moderate tempo. Its message was exactly about the moment, it asked nothing, nor demanded any particular response.

Session two

(i) Nicole stands at the treble as Carol holds her left hand and plays the melody of 'Here we are in music!' with the middle finger. Nicole, relaxed and cooperating happily, smiles with recognition; with her right hand she plays along with the second phrase, exactly in the melodic rhythm. Carol supports the playing with a left hand accompaniment. She reaches over Nicole's shoulder, takes her right hand, and plays the melody an octave higher. Again, Nicole joins in rhythmically with her disengaged hand. Her face registers enjoyment as the song is played.

(ii) A few moments later Nicole plays freely and confidently with her right hand as the song is repeated. Her playing rises and falls step-wise over an octave and a half range. I whistle the melody as she plays. Again, her face shows discovery and delight.

Nicole was becoming intrigued with playing the piano both rhythmically and tonally. The repetitions of 'Here we are in music,' intermixed with improvisation, provided a defined, dependable and enjoyable framework of experience in which she could continue to explore the keyboard. The discovery that the song could be played on the piano keys and that she could be involved in playing it evidently surprised and delighted her. My whistling of the melody seemed to add another aspect of pleasure to the active musical relationship that was growing between us.

Session three

(i) As she is led into the room, Nicole shows no sense of spatial orientation relative to the sound of the piano. When she is brought to the piano she becomes active immediately. Her responses to 'Here we are in music' are lively and have clear musical intention: she plays in the melodic rhythm then fills in between the phrases by joining in with Carol's accompaniment rhythms. She shows an understanding of the form of the song and also the style in which Carol is playing: spontaneously, she participates in a lively rhythmic ornamentation between repetitions. Both hands are used energetically and in free coordination. At times, her independent playing creates counter melodies.

(ii) Christmas is approaching, and Nicole's mother has reported that, in her own way, Nicole has been singing 'Jingle Bells'. When Carol brings this song into the session, Nicole plays the melodic rhythm and begins to rock from foot to foot. She pauses, poised on one foot, perhaps to listen, but Carol pauses with her, only recommencing playing when she does. Nicole quickly recognizes this, and begins to make pauses in her rocking and playing deliberately, thus stopping and starting the music. She enjoys this musical game and the control it gives her.

Everything that was happening was demonstrating to Nicole that in all this living music, there was someone attentive to her, playing and singing for and with her, and responding to her. That her discoveries progressed so quickly, that she felt free to explore, all indicated her bold confidence in this mobile, stimulating situation.

(iii) Rocking from foot to foot and smiling broadly, Nicole plays with her left hand while holding on to the piano case with her right to maintain balance. Behind her, I play two hand chimes that harmonize with the music (a further dimension is being added to Nicole's musical experiences, one that will perhaps increase her motivation to play hand chimes herself). The improvisation is in 4/4 and has a clear structure; Nicole plays phrases at random that fit in rhythmically. When Carol adds emphasis to the rhythmic structure with a short vocal phrase, Nicole responds immediately on the piano with an answering phrase that is well placed rhythmically and has a distinct melodic outline. As they repeat their phrases, an antiphonal give-and-take arises and in the repetitions Nicole's phrase becomes melodically developed. She goes on to repeat her phrase with Carol's singing.

Nicole was discovering that her playing made melody. At this stage, her melodic explorings were based on repetitions of clearly formed rhythmic phrases. As she spontaneously moved these phrases over the keyboard, she experienced melodies being created. To provide her with a simple musical basis for melodic exploration, one essentially free from harmonic demands, Carol went on to improvise with a drone bass, a primal form of accompaniment often found in folk music.

(iv) Nicole plays uncertainly as she listens to the unfamiliar drone bass. To encourage her, Carol offers a simple melodic idea. Nicole feels the tempo of the underlying pulse and begins stepping from side to side with lively determination. She initiates a rhythmic phrase that begins on the second beat of the measure and is based mostly on five notes that rise and fall melodically. She plays with attack and there is control and intention in the way she waits through the rests between her phases; she knows what she wants to do. As she repeats the phrase her playing takes on melodic character. Gradually, Carol increases the drive and intensity of the improvisation, first by singing lightly and rhythmically, then by adding lively tremolo chords in the right hand. Nicole responds to the new stimulation and plays firmly, her face expressing her concentration and her satisfaction in the co-activity.

(v) The joint improvisation continues with Nicole still stepping vigorously from foot to foot. She plays a repeating rhythmic phrase with complete confidence, her melodic explorations becoming freer and wider in tonal range. As a feeling of climax becomes imminent, I join in the improvisation, playing cymbals rhythmically. As she hears the cymbals, first one then another, she seems to experience a stimulating affirmation to her playing, for her face becomes radiant with joy. She is all energy, rhythm and rapture as she is carried into the climax of the improvisation. In her excitement she cannot hold on to her rhythmic phrase and plays along freely. When the crescendo passes and my accompaniment quietens to a soft drum rhythm, she recovers her phrase and continues her interactive playing with Carol.

Nicole's musical activities were securely based on her sense of the basic beat, the pulse of the music. Moreover, she felt how the pulse was organized into metre. This enabled her to repeat her rhythmic phrases accurately within the measure structure. In turn, this dependable sense of rhythmic structure was forming the basis for her exploration of melodic phrases. In following one melodic phrase with another, she was exploring melodic development.

For a music therapist, clinically directed creative improvisation is obviously a versatile means of searching out a means of contact with a child, and of developing such a contact. But the improvisational approach has a yet more significant potential: it gives the child the opportunity to improvise. For Nicole, the possibility of improvising in a responsive supportive situation presented unique opportunities to discover and explore both music and herself, to unfold abilities, to grow, experience purposefulness, intelligent communication and close musical companionship. There existed no other means of therapeutic intervention capable of bringing her such highly interactive, shared, purposeful experiences, no other means of so deeply and effectively engaging her in a dynamic process of self-actualization.

(vi) I am sitting a few feet from the piano; Nicole stands supported between my knees, a large cymbal to her left and a drum to her right. She holds a mallet in each hand and beats the instruments exploratively. Carol begins playing 'We Wish You a Merry Christmas', another song Nicole has been singing. She beats parts of the melodic rhythm on the cymbal, listens, then taps the beaters together. We hear quavers and more of the melodic rhythm. As Carol begins a repetition, I lead her right hand to the drum; immediately and with precision she beats the melodic rhythm of the first two phrases then transfers her beating to the left hand on the cymbal. She attempts to continue beating the melodic rhythm but is not yet sure of the cymbal's position. As the song is repeated, she listens and variously beats the basic beat with hands independently and alternately, and also parts of the melodic rhythm. When the song is repeated more slowly with a simple sparse accompaniment, I whistle the melody; her head raised, Nicole listens intently. She smiles and sways with pleasure at the familiar song presented in a novel way, and emphatically beats the cymbal, knowing exactly its position, with the three concluding notes. A further repetition is played grandioso in a slower tempo; once more she responds to a different style, and again concludes the song by beating the cymbal assertively, this time beating the melodic rhythm of the entire last phrase.

Music therapy offers a particularly potent modality for bringing children's musical memories into expression and communication. Many developmentally disabled children are known to respond positively to music where other means of comprehending and sharing experience are confused or limited. Nicole apparently had an extensive repertoire of songs in her memory. Drawing on such a remembered song, when this was clinically appropriate, as a vehicle for musical expression and activity served to enlarge her skills and connect her 'personal musical life' with her ongoing sense of success and self-esteem within therapy. This was obviously an enriching experience for her. Such activities strengthen the child–therapist relationship. For children who listen so intently to music it is also important to play remembered songs in different styles.

Movement was brought into the work with Nicole late in the fifth session. This began as an exploration with two purposes. (1) How would she move freely to music? Would she enjoy it, move rhythmically, or even be confident enough to initiate movement when left unguided in an open space? (2) Her sense of orientation in space appeared to be poorly developed. We noticed, for example, that when she entered the therapy room, she gave no indication of locating the piano by its sound. Could her great pleasure in music help her gain a sense of spatial orientation: specifically, to hear the piano and therapist's voice as a central auditory reference, thus giving her a sense of location in the room?

Session five

As Carol sings and plays to provide supportive music, I lead Nicole back and forth across the room. Gradually, I loosen my hold on her hand and, as it becomes possible, disengage my hand from hers. She shows reluctance to release my hand, but twice walks a few steps unguided. The second time, she comes to a standstill in the center of the room. The music pauses; she adopts her habitual head-down, passively waiting stance. Carol begins to improvise light and lively music in 6/8. I dance a few steps past her, hoping she will hear my steps and feel their rhythm through the floor. For eight measures she listens to the rhythmic, dancey music. At the same instant that Carol uses her voice and style of playing to energize the dance, Nicole begins to move sideways from foot to foot, her steps placed on the emphasized beats.

From a tentative beginning, her self-initiated dance becomes bolder. Gradually, she increases her movement until it resembles her side to side stepping at the piano. A huge smile appears and she begins to bend her knees to lift her feet ever higher. Carol slows and adapts her playing, giving emphasis to Nicole's steps. As Nicole has nothing to hold on to, her balance is precarious but she continues, determined to move as freely as she can with the music. I take her left hand to support her; she starts to sway strongly from side to side. I find I have to hold both her hands to cope with the tremendous amount of energy she begins to pour into a left–right swinging of her entire body and head. Stepping rhythmically from foot to foot, she throws her body as far as she can from one side to the other. Her face shows utter joy and release matched in spirit by the joyfulness in Carol's stimulating singing and playing. We are both very much aware of the strength of Nicole's individuality, and the power of her will to express herself in music. When I bring her back to the piano after the dance, she immediately joins in playing the 6/8 rhythm.

It is important not to undervalue *joy*. Joy is more than fun, more than just having a good time. There is something transcendent about the purity of joy, something that relates to an original realization of one's full humanness. For a child as developmentally disabled as Nicole, joy in discovering self-expression or in achieving musical creation with a therapist can be momentous. Such events bring a release from feelings of confusion, restriction, inadequacy and dependency, and from negative expectations, to generate a living, positive sense of selfhood that is fundamentally optimistic. In Maslow's terms, this experience, the 'cognition of being', results from a 'peak experience'. Such experiences build morale, the child becomes more fulfilled and also more resilient in coping with the challenges of life. Joy is an essential nourishment.

The uses of improvisation with Nicole in these first five sessions demonstrate the importance of undertaking musically specific research. Obviously, her responses were intimately related to the kinds of musical experiences created, and to the musical techniques that established her skills and experiences and then extended them. One still reads so many music therapy research reports, both in product research and in process research, that are musically nonspecific. We learn that music therapy took place, but are told nothing musical about it, only that it was done by a music therapist or music therapy student. The music is left faceless, anonymous. It is as if music itself didn't matter, that all music was the same, and all uses of music in therapy were equivalent. How can a researcher meaningfully study and measure the behaviour of a patient when the clinical musical behaviour of the therapist is disregarded, especially in a clinical situation that is so potentially interactive?

In my experience, the development of music therapy is best served by a romantic vision, not one that in any sense relates to the sentimental, but to the wonder, enthusiasm and fortitude that connect to a great creative enterprise. The nature of music itself requires that music therapists preserve an element of romanticism in their attitude to their profession. We must love music intensely and identify with music and with all it can be in human life. The first expression of this love and identification is a commitment to high standards of clinical practice and competence. We must be rigorous in our work, methodical in our analyses, fully clinically accountable. But, we must remember that the power of music in therapy stems from the reality that music is an art, that music therapists are privileged to mediate this art to meet many areas of need and experience. I see a romantic attitude as necessary to a therapist's creativity and resourcefulness. It nurtures hope, caring, compassion and insight. It can also protect therapists from the encroachments of bureaucracy, and from reductionist approaches in research. Romanticism enfolds wonder, the root source of both scientific enquiry and creative endeavour. On this note let us look at our second child and at the creative processes involved in her course of therapy, particularly at the evolution of songs in therapy. This is a dual study; it examines the responses of both child and therapist, and shows how intimately a child's growth in therapy is linked to musical and personal growth in the therapist. Nowhere is this more clearly evident than in the training of music therapists.

Karyn

Karyn, aged nine, is described as atypically autistic, with developmental delay and a speech and language disorder. She shows considerable intelligence in some areas, and appears to have taught herself to read; the extent of her comprehension is unclear. Yet she is distractible and her impulsive behaviour can be provocative and infantile. She tends to be echolalic, perseverative, and to cling to routine. She has always responded to music: her mother reports that she sang before she spoke, and 'knows a thousand songs'. Despite her sensitivity, her musical responses can be rambunctious and scattered.

Karyn's primary therapist, Walter Stafford, is an Afro-American, who, at the time of this course of therapy, is a trainee at the Nordoff-Robbins Music Therapy Clinic, New York University. As a child, he showed a natural talent for playing the piano. He grew up playing jazz and popular music, received classical training, and was for many years a church organist. He earned his Masters in Music Therapy in 1972, and became employed as a music therapist in a geriatric setting. He has also always played professionally for hotels, clubs, receptions, recitals and similar functions.

Karyn had been in music therapy the previous year with other trainee therapists, but her experiences, although promising, were inconsistent due to poor attendance and the primary therapist's illness. The sessions had to be discontinued in the spring.

When Walter became Karyn's new primary therapist the following autumn, he was faced with a complex, demanding situation: he was training in what for him was a totally new approach to music therapy with an unfamiliar patient group; he had inherited another therapist's child and co-therapist. At first, his approach was very much influenced by the previous therapist's work and he found himself in the position of following her role by presenting Karyn with much the same repertoire of activities and popular music. Although he had some success in holding her attention with impro-vised variations of these musical materials, the sessions remained essentially imitative and so lacked individual creative integrity. Consequently, Karyn's behaviour – a confusion of musical response and disorder, evasion and impulsiveness – made it difficult for him to find a clinical focus for his work with her.

After the fourth session, I was asked to become Walter's co-therapist. It became my responsibility to mediate between child and therapist, to help bring them together in music-making. This required being adaptable in the context of ongoing clinical situations to facilitate Karyn's response, while providing Walter, as necessary and appropriate, with clinical promptings and guidance that he could then take up freely and creatively.

We worked experimentally, developing activities that served to explore Karyn's abilities and needs. Energy, humour and playfulness were important in fostering concentration and consistency in her responses. A greeting song was evolving from session to session; as Walter began to 'get the measure' of Karyn, the song came into a form and style that was more suited to her.

Session eight

Walter greets Karyn with a lively song: 'Hello Karyn!' She beats along, yet is distractible, often looking away from him. She is slightly more attentive when the song is repeated in a slower tempo. She makes no attempt to join in the singing. I repeatedly direct her attention to Walter, at times inserting his name into the song. I am also poised to check her impulses to beat the cymbal (these are mostly habitual and provocative), limiting its use to musically meaningful places. When rhythmic patterns are improvised, her attention is stimulated. She responds accurately but her concentration is short-lived, her beating impulses become repetitive and she loses the musical connection. As 'Hello Karyn!' is repeated she beats with more awareness.

During these early sessions we were also feeling a need for a more thoughtful song, and were developing a theme that closely linked Karyn's name with ours and with making music together.

Session nine

Karyn is seated on the piano bench beside Walter, I am beside her to her right. She plays freely in the treble as a theme on 'Karyn and Walter, Karyn and Clive' is improvisationally developed. She plays clusters with the side of her right fist and with several fingers of both hands together, then plays single notes with her left hand with more care and intention. She is obviously listening and there are moments of sensitive musical response: she briefly imitates quavers in Walter's accompaniment in a way that shows her awareness of the melody; she plays thoughtfully, mostly in the tempo of the song.

By the next session, Walter had found the melody and form he felt to be right for the song.

Session ten

Karyn is seated between us, listening as 'Karyn and Walter, Karyn and Clive' is sung to her. The song has a warm hymn-like quality, a feeling akin to the devotional mood of a Spiritual:

Copyright © 1992 by Walter Stafford

Her attention is held; there is just a brief moment of distraction. She plays lightly and only a little in the treble. At the end of the song she plays the tonic note, recognizes this and repeats it several times.

That Walter was continuing to gain the musical measure of Karyn was evident in the melody of the song he created for her, and also in the commitment with which he sang it. The full warm presence of his voice was saying to her: 'At this moment, there is nothing more important than what we are doing, I am completely here with you Karyn.' His increasing confidence enabled her, in turn, to place a deeper trust in all her musical and personal experiences with us.

Session twelve

Walter is extending 'Hello Karyn!' into an energetic improvisation in the same style. Using two sticks, Karyn beats vigorously with hands together. She smiles with pleasure, intent on her crisp, controlled beating. She is totally attentive to the music and looks toward Walter as he makes a slight diminuendo and ritard. She follows him closely, then goes to hit the cymbal – I intervene to make her wait for a more meaningful moment. Walter extends the improvisation; Karyn, exclaiming with happiness, beats with him. After a ritard she accurately anticipates the concluding cadence, halves the tempo of her beating, and joins him in finishing the music with a firm sense of completion. Her participation is impressively successful. I congratulate her by exclaiming 'Great!... Wonderful!' This leads into several repetitions of the phrase 'wonderful music' which she partially imitates. Walter joins in with the phrase and freely accompanies its repetitions.

'Wonderful music' became a new theme to be developed in subsequent sessions, but what struck me when the idea was first introduced was Walter's accompanying music – pure cocktail piano! And what were its qualities? Enticing, light, pleasurable, warmly supportive, and with a playful fantasy. There was a therapeutic potential in this music which I was intrigued to see being realized.

At every stage in the course of therapy, Walter, in common with all trainees in creative music therapy, was facing a continuing musical challenge: the need to develop and apply wider freedoms of improvisation, particularly in tempo and style. His years of playing as a provider of background entertainment, and the continuous repetition of earlier popular music in his work with elderly patients, had combined to set him into playing in constant tempos. He had been long accustomed to establishing a tempo for a piece and keeping it throughout, reinforcing the beat physically by tapping a foot while elaborating melody and harmony. The improvisation training classes introduced other resources and styles of playing which were unfamiliar to him, but which, in the context of ongoing clinical experience, came to be recognized as directly applicable to meeting Karyn's needs. Habituated styles of playing were displaced as directive freedom and clinical resourcefulness developed hand in hand. Walter became increasingly adept at bringing musical resources spontaneously and creatively into his work.

She was ready for what he could bring her. Her attentiveness and control advanced further early in the next session when he led from her greeting song, which had now attained its complete form, into work on rhythmic structure.

Session thirteen

(i) Walter begins to involve Karyn in a musical game, antiphonally playing and beating rhythmic patterns. She eagerly beats each pattern as it is played and waits with sticks poised above the drum, listening for the next. She is receptive and accurate. She loses concentration briefly when a three beat pattern (quaver, quaver, crochet) triggers a repetitive reaction and, habitually, she reaches out to beat the cymbal at random. This is easily discouraged, and her keen interest in perceiving and imitating each new pattern keeps her attention purposefully focussed. The unpredictable rhythms of the patterns, plus the subtle variations of tempo, and the melodic and harmonic variety with which they are played make the antiphonal playing into a captivating musical game for her.

'Hello Karyn!' returns, now with the feeling of celebrating her successful work. She beats with big emphatic movements of her arms, smiling broadly and exclaiming with happiness as she sways her body with the music. She sings and mouths some of the words. When the melodic rhythm becomes twice as fast she spontaneously doubles the tempo of her beating. The rhythmic game returns and she is immediately attentive. Walter plays a three beat pattern; Karyn responds, and again seems to be conditioned to repeating this particular pattern, but her motivation to continue the give-and-take causes her to inhibit this behavioural tendency. Walter repeats the pattern with a sudden diminuendo and a ritard. Karyn responds with great care, sensitively reproducing the rhythm, dynamic and tempo. As the patterns continue she is unable to maintain the soft dynamic, but continues beating them accurately, including one with a dotted rhythm. Much of the time, she watches Walter as he plays, then, as she beats her response, she turns to me with a smile, sharing her feelings of achievement with him.

'Hello Karyn!' is played and sung once more. Her radiant face and rapturous body movements express her satisfaction and joy.

Later in this session we took up the 'wonderful music' theme, adding other exalting words with the same rhythm as 'wonderful'; we tried out 'marvellous', 'beautiful', 'glorious', and some additional lines.

(ii) Walter expressively sets the new words and feels his way toward a melodic form for a song. Karyn sits at the piano between us; as I wish to encourage her listening and possibly her singing, I gently hold her hands to still the impulse to play. The music is richly romantic and seems to hold her mood. At no time is she distracted, and there are moments when she softly sings in response.

In the following weeks this theme continued to evolve as Walter searched for the right form for Karyn. Our relationship with her became closer; she joined more freely in singing all the songs. She was obviously identifying with them and they were becoming increasingly self-expressive for her. In singing them, she lived her pleasure and fulfilment in our making music together. 'Hello Karyn!' acquired three verses, one for each of us, and the time came when she took the important step of wholeheartedly including us in the greeting. She wished to return to us the feeling of being welcomed into the session.

Session sixteen

(i) Karyn strides confidently into the room, stepping in time to 'Hello Karyn!' She takes the drumsticks put out for her and beats with the song. As the first verse ends, she firmly calls out 'Walter!', points to him, then sings the second verse, 'Hello Walter!' to him. She beats as she sings. She shows some verbal confusion and does not have all the words, but this does not stop her, her commitment is unmistakable. At the end of the verse, she turns to face me, calls out 'Clive!' and sings the third verse directly to me. We reply by singing the first verse back to her; she joins in with us.

It was obvious how 'Hello Karyn!' with its brightness and lively rhythmic flow was just right for her.

By now she was showing a widening interest in freely playing pitched instruments such as resonator bells or a metallophone. This provided a contrast to the drum and cymbal and offered her opportunities to continue realizing and enjoying her tonal sensitivity.

(ii) Karyn plays a two-octave alto diatonic metallophone with a mallet in her right hand. The improvisation is a variation of her greeting song, played in a steady tempo and in an even dynamic without accents. She plays on the basic beat, moving freely over the bars. As a descending melodic line takes her into the lower tones she smoothly changes the mallet to her left hand, without losing connection with the piano improvisation. There is an element of coincidence in the way her playing produces notes that fit with the melody and harmony of the improvisation, but she shows some degree of awareness of the concurrences as they happen. She appears to be directing her playing with a feeling – searching to prolong or find more of these tonally satisfying moments.

We were to see more of this side of Karyn's musical growth both on the metallophone and at the piano.

Session nineteen

(i) Walter and Karyn are seated at the piano, Karyn in the treble playing with both index fingers pointing down to the keys. She is involved in creating a melody. She plays on the basic beat in a moderate tempo, passing the playing from one hand to the other as her sense of melodic movement prompts. She is deeply absorbed as she concentrates on the notes she plays and how they sound with the calm, steady accompaniment. There is a feeling of phrasing in the slight variations in dynamics in her playing. She is also extending phrases, obviously becoming aware of melodic possibilities and thoughtfully exploring them. Her playing is entirely independent except for a moment when I direct her to lower notes. In a sensitive melodic invention, she puts quavers into two passages in successive measures.

Her mood was so receptive and our musical relationship so close that when she finished playing I felt it right to encourage her directly to sing.

(ii) I am suggesting to Karyn that she sing, but she indicates the metallophone. With some humour I ask 'Where's your voice?' Partly imitating, partly teasing, she repeats the question to Walter. The mood is playful. I indicate her mouth and say 'It's in here! I want to hear it sing "Karyn and Walter, Ka—"' She interrupts me, interjecting 'Clive!', indicating that the three names belong in the song. As Walter plays an introduction, I prompt: 'Ready?' 'Go!' she responds, then waits quietly as the music leads into the song. She sings softly with great care, using a light soprano voice we have not heard before. She requires only minimal prompting. Halfway through the song she begins to rock gently forward and backward. As she repeats the song, the amplitude of the rocking increases slightly. To bring a thoughtful closure to the mood of her singing, Walter and I add a coda by repeating the last line twice.

Karyn's mother was currently observing the sessions on closed circuit television, gaining much reassurance from them. She was moved by the depth of Karyn's involvement and commented warmly on the closeness of our relationship. She stressed that music therapy was a totally positive experience in her daughter's life, and was deeply relieved that the temper tantrums and crying from frustration that were frequent in school and other areas of her program were never seen in music therapy. She reported that Karyn's ability to express herself was improving and she was showing more confidence. She also said, 'I love what goes on in these sessions. As I watch Karyn in music, I know in my heart that everything is going to be OK!' The more Walter developed clinical freedom in playing for Karyn, the more his personal musical history surfaced. In the following session, when she was keen to play the metallophone, he responded with a style of music characteristic of Bach. The emergence of this new clinical resource and its relevance to Karyn at this time reflected their interrelated paths of development: she moves him to grow and as he grows, she moves into the space he creates for her.

Session twenty

(i) Karyn plays freely over the range of the metallophone to music in the style of Bach. Her playing is on the basic beat, partly at random and partly directed as she feels tonal connections between the notes she plays and the improvisation. It is obvious that she feels the tonal centre of the D minor key. As Walter adds his voice she smiles with pleasure and softly sings along with him. He ceases singing and emphasizes the melody in the treble of the piano for four measures; her playing has the character of a counter melody. When his playing moves to a lower register, Karyn spontaneously begins to bring out a melody on the metallophone emphasizing the melodic element with quavers. Her playing has a genuine affinity with the character of the music.

The Bach improvisation continued, with Karyn still fitting sensitively into the style.

(ii) She now plays by leaving the mallet pressed against the bars after striking them, thus damping their sound and producing a detached, staccato effect. The improvisation is such that much of her playing fits well tonally. The moment Walter begins a ritard, she appears to sense that the end of the music is approaching for she puts in a glissando which she has not done before. She joins him carefully in making the ritard, then, as she hears the closing cadence, plays a concluding phrase uncannily in the style of Bach – a descending phrase ending on the third. She adds another glissando and gives a little applause and cheer. I thank her as I take her beater and ask 'What shall we do now?' Spreading her arms in a gesture of openness, her face relaxed and eager, she replies 'Wonderful!'

With anticipation, she expressed her wish for the romantic theme which had begun its development in her twelfth session and came to completion in the eighteenth.

(iii) She sits at the piano between us. The moment the introduction begins, she extends both hands for me to hold as I have held them in several previous singing times. She sings softly and tentatively, partially know-ing the song, and shadow-singing what she is not yet sure of. To sustain this degree of emotional closeness for over two minutes is something of a challenge for Karyn, and there are several signs of nervousness. But her life of musical feeling is held by the song, by its words and by the beauty of its melody. It is important that the song is appealing and comforting in its tenderness, yet it has a warmth and strength that offer support. The words, too, must echo some of her own thoughts and deepening feelings about music:

Copyright © 1992 by Walter Stafford

She sings the repeat with more confidence and concludes the song with soft sustained applause.

In 'Wonderful,' Walter held and expressed the essence of Karyn's identification with her experiences in music therapy, and also the quality of the relationship the three of us shared. The song was truly inspired by Karyn in exactly the same process whereby a character in a libretto inspires a composer with a song or an aria. From session to session, as in a studio, there was a working through; ideas were tried and discarded, clearing the way toward the realization of a theme that had existential truth and definition. Similarly, the improvisations for Nicole, for her piano playing and dancing, were directly inspired by the uniqueness of her being as manifested in the whole gestalt of her ongoing response. The living music reflected – lovingly imaged – the living child, moment by creative moment.

The creative processes are inherently therapy processes – and therapy processes are intrinsically artistic processes – and they are indeed universal.

With thanks to: Ken Aigen, Morva Croxson and Carol Robbins for their suggestions.

CHAPTER 2

A Case of Severe Infantile Regression Treated by Music Therapy and Explored in Group Supervision

Pier Luigi Postacchini, Massimo Borghesi,
Brigitte Flucher, Loredana Guida, Marzia Mancini,
Piera Nocentini, Laura Rubin, Sergio Santoni
Italy

Introduction

This work is the result of a music therapy supervision group run by Dr Postacchini. The students were from the music therapy course at the Assisi Cittadella. The case of Alice, treated in therapy by Marzia Mancini, had a complex diagnosis characterised by a serious regression in speech, behaviour and basic autonomy, and also by degeneration of movement. This psycho-motor regression had a controversial diagnosis of Rett Syndrome.

In the case material there are important elements which demonstrate the contributions made by students during the course of supervision work. Particular attention was given to analysis of Alice's senses (sight, hearing, taste, smell and touch) in relation to her motor skills. The confused use made by the child of learning skills where hand, voice and looking were inter-changed was examined, as well as the use of muscle tone as an expression of Alice's symbolic relationship with the objective world. For example, at times she showed a taut muscular condition, while at other times she was relaxed in response to the world around her. The work focused on Alice's changed muscle tone, posture, use of vision and breathing, in relation to the quality of the therapeutic relationship.

Case discussion

Alice is a lovely five-year-old girl that our group 'adopted' four years ago. Little was actually known about her. She showed speech and behavioural problems. Her tender years, the undefined diagnosis, the lack of any therapeutic intervention with her, and her apparent rejection of music were all elements which motivated us. Marzia, who worked on musical expression in the nursery which Alice attended, began to collect more detailed information. From talking with her parents, the teachers and the psychologist who had observed the child for a certain period, she learned of Alice's real difficulties. At two and a half years, following an apparently normal development, Alice showed speech regression, crying episodes and a tendency to isolation.

The information revealed a picture of confusion. There was no communal planning among doctors, psychiatrists and teachers for Alice. The child had been examined in very specialised centres because the mother had not been reassured by anyone. The different diagnoses (brain damage, autism, Rett Syndrome) and the suggestions for future drugs or therapeutic treatment had not given the parents confidence and had therefore not been carried out. No one had really taken on the job of caring for the problematic situation of the child.

Initial observations

In February 1989 Marzia began observations on Alice in her home environment and at school. From her observations it appeared that:

(1) Alice showed very complex stereotyped movements; often she used the left hand clutched to hit the palm of the right hand, a movement which gives a particular rhythm with two different timbres. Alice's parents would admonish her for this movement, although in affectionate and playful terms.

(2) she moved with rigid legs spread open as though she were not aware of space.

(3) she had no speech but produced a wide range of sounds; vocalisations which cover different sound ranges, giggles, chattering of teeth.

(4) she had a vague, absent look, which at times could be extremely intense: she looked straight into another's eyes in a penetrating manner (one teacher defined it as a challenge).

(5) she was disturbed by very loud noises, frightened by the door bell, but also alert to the sound of tissue paper crumpling. She liked nursery rhymes and she could enjoy rhythmical games with her playmates, but her attention lasted for few minutes.

In May 1989 Marzia began proper music therapy for Alice inside the school, at first in a rather noisy atmosphere and then later in a more tranquil setting, a small room. Marzia tried to discover Alice's sound capability, surrounding the child with a few much loved objects: music toys, little drums and cymbals.

Clinical material

1. Rhythms

When the music therapy sessions began Alice was characteristically in an isolated state, absorbed in listening to herself and in producing stereotyped movements of her hands.

From these almost continuous stereotypes we extracted two types of rhythm: an isochronal scansion, quite fast, produced by the left hand which from under hits the right, and a more elaborate rhythm obtained by rotating the right hand over the left, a rhythm which is ternary or binary depending on whether the hand in movement stops in the air. The sounds obtained were dull and weaker in intensity. Marzia sought to create a relationship based on a mirroring of the child and her stereotypes. Within this system the intensity of the therapeutic relationship increased, particularly when the rhythms produced became meaningful, for example the introduction of a new element, a song often sung at the nursery. Alice liked this song a lot, probably because she saw that the rhythms she expressed coincided. The therapist's song was accompanied by the child's isochronal scansion, perfectly synchronised.

At this point the relationship became more intense and trusting: Alice could let go of her autistic object – a bell with a light tinkling sound – and adopt the intermediate instrument, a cymbal, through which the relationship developed. Her gesticulation became more showy and her vocalisation more evident, often in tune. Her voice became an important part of the relationship, excited vocal elements with notable variety of timbre that clearly expressed joy and excitement.

2. Movement

Movement of the lower limbs was remarkably improved when compared with the initial stage which was characterised by considerable rigidity.

Alice could run short distances. This result was obtained in a brief period of time. However, it was necessary to analyse the quality of this movement to assess the situation and consider new objectives. Let us examine one session.

At the beginning her walking was rigid, but it loosened up during the encounter; her knees bend imperceptibly. The muscles were strained, especially in the lower part of the body. Eye and lower limb coordination underwent an evolution: for example, Alice trod on the cymbal, looked at it then dragged it along with her foot. During this session she kicked a ball twice, intentionally. She was able to bend over. Every so often she threw her arms backwards; her upper limbs were in fact more mobile than the lower limbs. She clapped her hands more forcefully and with more conviction.

Now seemed to be the moment to introduce other stimuli/situations – sand, dry leaves, polystyrene – to create tracks for movement games for Alice to acquire new skills. From this new work, sound was not to be excluded, but would be part of the play. Alice needed to let herself go in a rich and gratifying situation of multi-sensory stimuli. Without realising it, she was able to relax and to improve her balance and her walking. She needed to perceive not only space in front and behind her but also above and below her.

3. Space and seeing

When we first met Alice she looked only at objects, people and activities which interested her. For a brief period her gaze would meet another's before fading and her eyes would look into space. She was often interested in her hands and observed their sound and rhythmic movement. As she watched them, her eyes did not function visually but rather in a tactile, auditory way.

Careful listening and intentioned activity could bring more decision and expression to her gaze. For example, in a reassuring and companionable situation Alice could meet her companions' look.

Her hands had a sound function and were used to explore the mouth. They were seen as both part of her and as an external object. Sometimes she looked at them surprised. They seemed to represent an intermediate area between the internal and external world. Through this third area Marzia entered into a relationship with Alice, accompanying and reflecting the beat of her hands.

With her sound stereotypes, Alice was part of the social/sound space. At first, the work surroundings were not well defined. It began in a semi-open area, metaphorically located between the social space of the nursery and the therapeutic space. Alice participated in both: she was attracted by external noises, but recognised the particularity of the setting within which the privileged relationship was developing.

The increasing closeness between Alice and Marzia coincided with a change of room, to one which was smaller and more intimate. For the first time Alice immediately shared with Marzia the same toy, a cymbal, in a space/sound game.

The sound exchange was still much characterised by alternating and by the temporary division of the same space. This was made more vivid with new rhythms and timbres. Alice fluctuated between her search for an intimate space to be shared with Marzia (for example, ever narrowing the circles she made around her until she finally stopped face to face and gazed intensely at Marzia) and in finding a personal space away for herself (for example, moving some distance away in runs). In this personal space the experience of her meeting with Marzia was played out, and Alice prepared new encounters as she tested the external space.

4. Voice

Alice expressed herself in a global way that involved, principally, the movement of her hands, of her gaze and of her voice, alternating between obviously significant relaxed and taut tonic states. This alternating was particularly evident in her vocal production and its intensely linked breathing.

At the beginning of the encounters, Alice hardly ever used her voice. Her few vocal expressions were weak, subdued, hesitant. With the passing of time, as she increased her control of space, so her voice 'came out', particularly when she was more comfortable in the relationship. As openness in a relationship is variable, so was the tonic quality of her voice, which ranged from rather deep, throaty laborious sounds – a direct expression of an overall taut tonic state – to other very acute sounds which were resonant and confident, linked to relaxed tonic states.

The meaning behind the voice quality became even clearer when related to other events which occurred inside Alice's mouth, i.e., the sound of her teeth and of her laborious breathing. The former took on a communicative significance and, when reinforced by mirroring, favoured the emission of relaxed vocal sounds, creating a bridge between the initial closed, abdominal sounds, and moments of greater dispnea, and other sounds where the breathing became normal. At the same moment there was a change, too, in the production of relationally significant phonemes. In particular, the phoneme 'hii', which Alice pronounced often in an interrogative tone, became a clear 'chi' ('who') complete with consonant, which prior to this had been produced in with different vowel openings and multiple tonic nuances. Sometimes, for example in the presence of a colleague doing the video recording, this 'chi' was enriched by a verb to become without any doubt 'chi è' (who is it?).

It was comforting to observe how the enrichment of her repertoire in favour of vowels, which allowed her easier voice modulation, enabled Alice to transform the gliding sounds made with a vibrating 'mmh' into short melodic sequences, using intervals of an ascending or descending minor third and major sixth.

This initial study of the relationship between voice and emotive tonic states may perhaps enable us to make more convincing hypotheses regarding the level of symbolic function reached by the child.

Conclusion

The supervision group enriched and supported the case work. It focused on examining the changes in Alice's rhythm, movement, use of vision in space and use of sound in relation to the development of the therapeutic relationship. She seems to have evolved from a pre-symbolic mode of communication to one that is at times more symbolic and less regressed.

References

Benenzon, R., and Wagner, G. (1985) *Atti del 5th Congresso mondiale di Musicoterapia, Genova 1985.* Torino: Omega.

Bertolini, M. (1984) *La formazione del sè come elemento di separazione tra soma e mente. In La nascita psicologica e le sue premesse neurobiologiche.* Roma: Yes Mercury.

Milani Comparetti, A. (1982) 'La motricità fetale nel processo ontogenetico psico-biologico', in Zulli P., Ianniruberto A., and Catizone F.A., *Motricità e vita psichica del feto.* Roma: C.I.C.

Postacchini, P.L. (1989) 'Percorsi dell'integrazione', in *Musicascuola n.14.* Nicola Milano Editore.

Postacchini, P.L. and Ruggerini, C. (1984) 'Un approccio strutturale al problema dell'handicap', *Quaderni di musica applicata n.5.* Assisi: P.C.C. Edizioni.

Stern, D.N. (1985) *The Interpersonal World of the Infant.* New York: Basic Books.

CHAPTER 3

Containment in Music Therapy

Jos De Backer
Belgium

Introduction

Little has been written about the use of 'containment' in psychoanalytically oriented music therapy, although it seems to be one of the essential aspects of the therapeutic relationship. This seems especially true with 'ego weak' patients: psychotic and borderline, as well as patients with learning difficulties. This chapter will analyse the aspects of containment more fully.

Let us begin with the image of an ego weak twelve-year-old boy who is at present undergoing therapy. David is the eldest of three children and the only boy. His parents brought him for therapy because of his extreme learning and behavioural problems at school. He was hyperactive and had difficulty concentrating. This resulted in David being very impulsive and aggressive, especially when the efforts required of him exceeded his capability. At home his parents felt unable to provide a good grounding. This was complicated by the fact that they regularly went abroad for business reasons. His intellectual ability is damaged, but this seems to be not only constitutional but also exaggerated by emotional problems.

Initially, I saw him during therapy as a boy who had problems with his feelings and fantasies; he was impulsive and regularly destroyed the sessions. Moreover, the sessions were mostly chaotic and he could hardly make or maintain contact with me. This gave me an impression of disintegration.

The first series of therapy was laborious. David's behaviour was impulsive and full of confused messages. It was impossible for me to understand either him or the situation and I continually lost contact with him. He had a tendency towards destruction. I also felt desperate and lost. At a certain moment I became aware of this projective identification (Klein 1946) and recognised my feelings as being swept along in his world of twisted experiences. I wondered what therapeutic stance would be acceptable to David.

The concept of containment

Bion (1962) describes the importance of the presence of a 'psychic container' in the development of a child. This container (the parents) absorbs the various stimuli and feelings spilling over from the baby, hangs on to these experiences, thinks about them, makes sense of them, and reacts accordingly. Because of this, the child does not feel lonely and experiences the feeling that the good object (the mother) is not overawed by these feelings but is able to give a form or shape to the chaotic, frightening experiences of the child. The frightening and confusing mental feelings can then be dealt with. Containment is an important experience in a child's development. When children have not experienced this because their mother has, for various reasons, been unable to assimilate and consolidate these feelings, the feelings remain unbearable and terrifying. They are too much for the child, who cuts off all contact. He then projects these feelings outside himself. This results in the child destroying his capacity for introspection as well as his perception of others.

Cluckers (1989) describes containment in the therapeutic relationship as follows:

> 'It is the creation of a psychic space in which each and every communication, however confused and painful, is received by the therapist, retained and mentally digested with the aim of removing any unbearable qualities from the patient's feelings. These feelings can then be given an acceptable form and placed in the patient's experience. The final aim is for this experience to enable the patient to accept his anxieties and learn to live with them; in other words, to understand and accept the containment function.'

Clinical material

As an example of the way in which containment can be included in music therapy, I will give you a fragment from a session with David when his parents were away for a few days. David wanted to be the conductor and use me as the orchestra. He started by placing percussion instruments, a guitar, flute and kantele in a semi-circle in front of me. By gestures and mimicry he tries to indicate which instrument I have to play. Because of his fanatical efforts to exteriorise, he tries to make this clear to me, although he himself does not know which instrument he wants me to play. After a few chaotic attempts which are energetically and speedily alternated with rest periods, he is swamped in confused feelings, has lost touch with himself and me, and becomes angry. Shouting, he goes to the instruments and shows me how to play them.

This results in his playing being chaotic and alarming. He wants to play all the instruments simultaneously. This is impossible. He becomes more and more angry till he starts kicking the instruments and screams abusively at me. I am doing it all wrong. I thought, 'I have to find out what is happening within him'. He trembles with rage and impotence.

I express his feelings of anger, helplessness and loneliness, the fact that he feels misunderstood, that he is angry because of his failure to suceed. He then falls onto the mat, adopts the foetal position and starts to cry gently, whispering 'I can't do it' a couple of times. I sit next to him, start to hum softly, and then proceed to improvise a song expressing his helplessness and loneliness. It is one of those moments when he is himself and does not run around hyperactively fleeing from or in search of himself. He, the ever excited boy who fluctuates from one mood to another, rarely holding on to a feeling, can now accept a feeling and an experience. After ten minutes he sits upright on the mat and we sit there together peacefully. He is in touch with himself. It is a moment when I do not feel he is disintegrating. After a few minutes I pick up a kantele and play a note which slowly dies down. David reacts by striking another note. This dialogue continues for a while. After this, the session is over and David leaves peacefully and visibly happy.

The choice of being conductor reveals something of David's omnipotent and narcissistic position. His jealousy is clearly shown by the position in which he places me as simultaneous player of all the instruments. This is, of course, impossible. 'The therapist cannot do this.' This is exactly what David wants; to show me as being unable to achieve something, just as he cannot do something.

The choice of wishing to be the conductor clearly expresses his omnipotence, but at the same time his helplessness – the feeling of not having everything under control – his loneliness; all experiences with which a conductor is familiar. David is torn by these ambivalent feelings which he can neither understand nor bear and can only express by chaotic fragments lacking continuity. I do not immediately start correcting and restructuring in a pedagogical way, but remains receptive to David's experiences.

Pedagogic intervention would keep David's inner threatening experiences beyond the bounds of communication, and would make him feel that the therapist could neither stand up to him nor accept this primitive aggression and jealousy. To oppose this, I now create an intermediary inner mental space in which David's experiences and emotions can find room and in which David's anxieties and confused feelings become meaningful. I put them into words and returns them to David in an understandable and acceptable form. David then returns to his feelings of loneliness and helplessness. He regresses to an earlier phase in which his desire for love and security become apparent. The humming and singing are done at a regressive level; in the same way a mother comforts her child by taking it in her arms, whispering softly, singing or humming. This attitude is very close to reverie, an intuitive state of mind a mother needs to adopt in relation to her baby (Bion 1967).

David's sitting up is a transition to reality. This brings us into a phase where the ability to think and feel becomes possible and real communication can be attained. Whilst the aforegoing was entirely enacted in the field of projective identification, there now exists an authentic pre-verbal dialogue. He is master of his feelings which he need not transfer to me. This means I can exist and be there for him.

The subsequent sober musical dialogue is, by its clarity, sharply in contrast to the confusing cacophony of the first efforts. In this sober, constructive communication David is in touch with himself and me.

I would like to examine the transition from the foetal to the sitting position more carefully. David and I sit. We do not stand. I adopt the same regressive level. The phase between sitting and standing is analogous to that between the purely musical game and verbalising. As yet a verbal dialogue is not possible, only communication through games and singing. At this moment nothing can be said verbally, but can be expressed musically. Herein lies the strength of music therapy.

The use of music

The use of music in therapeutic relationships offers definite possibilities. In the psychic space created in the sessions, the patient is able to project his chaotic and confused feelings and experiences (which he can nether digest nor control), towards the therapist. This enables him to bear what seem uncontainable feelings (projective identification). Music therapy provides the possibility of expressing alarming and unbearable experiences by improvising on musical instruments.

In other words, in his impotence, the patient has the opportunity of expressing these experiences, thus avoiding the possible defence of silence. Also, the therapist can react via musical interaction. The expression of these feelings is in turn chaotic, confusing, alarming or aggressive. The patient is himself surprised by this eruption of feelings and does not know how the session will evolve. The music therapist does not remain passive through all this but tries to accompany and shape the musical outburst. He will, as it were, stretch a skin over the patient's experience – an acoustic skin – which binds and shapes the expression of chaos. For the patient this represents a first step; he no longer feels that these confused feelings and his experience of not being understood, are unbearable. All this takes place in an intermediary space described by Winnicott (1951) in the article 'Transitional Objects and Transitional Phenomena'.

Music offers the advantage that the patient need not be alone in his chaotic expression and experience. The music therapist has the means of being with him without having to exclude him. He achieves this not only by his attitude but by his empathetic accompaniment. This means the patient can, often for the first time, feel that someone accepts his experience, accompanies him without being swept along, and does not become alarmed. Someone who gives him the feeling that his expression is not 'destroying' anyone.

> 'Music is a third step in the therapeutic relationship which carries part of the unbearable burden of emotions, making some of them more acceptable by sublimation to a musical creation. The music says: "Listen, these emotions can be expressed and borne together". You can even play with them.' (Priestley 1983)

Since ego-weakness genetically finds its origin in the pre-verbal stage, it is obvious that music is very closely connected to this world of experience. What cannot be put into words (these chaotic feelings and experiences) can primarily be addressed and expressed through a non-verbal media. In a subsequent phase, this can be expressed verbally. This second step is indispensable if one wishes to go further than the symbolic level. To illustrate this, I will give you another example from David's therapy.

David has placed his arsenal of musical instruments, consisting of drums, congas, kettle drums and cymbals in front of himself in a semi-circle. He really wants to let fly. The off-loading is mostly short and fragmented. I accompany him at the piano. He starts to play forcefully and energetically. The playing is confused and chaotic – his facial expression strained. I can play along just as energetically, but in this improvisation offer him a basis to play rhythmically in the lower register through discordant chords. When David suddenly and impulsively stops playing, I switch to a more tonal melodic and restful tune in the middle register. At this point David responds by playing the cymbals softly. He adapts. When the urge becomes too strong, he again releases his feelings by playing chaotically and I accompany him again as I did at the beginning. This is again interrupted so that I start playing melodically and peacefully again and accordingly, David again switches to playing the cymbals softly, gets a hold on himself and is once more in touch with himself and me. The restful phases grow longer and longer.

Here it will be noticed that David can be symbolically retrieved in his confused and fragmented playing. Again and again he has the opportunity to externalise his projections to me without destroying the latter. This brings us to the expression 'splitting' (Klein 1929). The good and the bad parts are separated. He can now join these together; join good and bad elements in one person. After this game situation, David expresses his synthesis: death and life. This seems to be connected with his parents being dead for him when they are away on a business trip, at a moment when he has no idea of time. The presence and absence of his parents become symbolically possible through this musical game. Death is a chaotic and alarming game, life a peaceful and melancholic one. Thus, the presence and absence is not expressed in words, but symbolised in the musical game. Freud (1920) described this on the level of verbal symbolising in the 'Fort-da' (gone – there) game. Through symbolism one creates the possibility of the psychic acceptance of presence and absence. One learns to control presence and absence. In this way one is no longer a victim of these circumstances and no longer subject to the contingency of the parents' absence.

Control of the presence and absence syndrome is still being worked on in therapy, but simply being aware of it, being able to talk about it, play games around it, has been a big step for David.

Instruments

An aspect not to be neglected is the choice of instruments. It is important to suggest instruments which can bear and depict these confusing, chaotic and primary experiences. They must be strong and offer a certain support. Instruments which can be broken or blown to pieces should not be used, as they must present the possibility of expressing impulsive bursts of rage. The individual must not feel limited in his expression. The instrument must not curtail him.

Psychiatry

On the basis of group situations in psychiatry, I would like to show briefly that containment can be used not only in individual therapy but also in group therapy with ego weak people. I have taken an example of including

containment from music therapy sessions with young psychotic and borderline patients.

The patients and I are seated in a circle. The patients each have a conga
in front of them, and I a kettle drum. The task is as follows: I takes the part
of the container and strike a rhythmic continuous ostinato. The patients try
to find a rhythm, which, according to them, goes with it. As soon as everyone
has found a suitable rhythm, the patients can then send feelings rhythmically
and musically to me as they wish. They can adapt or express their anger,
aggression or sadness. I notice that several patients fluctuate a great deal in
their playing which means they are not always in control. In the ensuing
discussions, it is obvious that most patients realise I cannot be shaken, that
I am strong enough to hold my position and that I can accept all these
expressions. During the ensuing discussions it is important that these
experiences are put into words and that their expressions are given their
proper place and meaning.

The group can also act as container during which it plays a collective
basic rhythm. Over this the patients individually and musically express their
feelings. These can be very adaptive (seeking harmony) but also ambivalent
and primitive. Regularly, attempts are made, consciously or unconsciously,
to split up the group, break through the basic rhythm, or let it break down.
It is crucial that they realise that the group can be maintained and not
collapse. This can be different from patients' experiences of their family
collapsing or threatening to do so because of their illness.

Conclusion

Thus we see that containment plays an essential part in the therapeutic
relationship, in particular with ego weak patients. Being aware of, and
reflecting on, this therapeutic aspect permits us to have a deeper insight of
what happens in the music therapy process.

The two extracts from individual therapy show that the therapist can act
as a psychic container. The therapist can accept the chaotic, alarming
experiences and feelings which the patient cannot or dare not hold on to,
and which rob him of any continuity in his world of experiences. The
therapist accepts these experiences, mentally digests them and then returns
them to the patient in a form which is more bearable and understandable.

Within group music therapy both the therapist and group can function
as the container. Containment is one of the basic requirements of the
therapeutic relationship, and not the final goal. The specific contribution of
music therapy, as opposed to verbal therapies, lies in the fact that ego weak
patients can express their chaotic experiences and that the therapist can,

because of this specific medium, allow them to do so, and be there for them without leaving them isolated in their chaos. In his accompanying musical game the therapist can surround the chaos like a musical skin and hold it together. The characteristic of music as a medium is that it gives both patient and therapist the possibility of reaching a subconscious understanding and anticipated symbolic articulation which can serve as a basis for the development of speech.

References

Bion, W.R. (1962) 'A Theory of Thinking', *International Journal of Psychoanalysis*, 43, 306–310.

Bion, W.R. (1967) *Second Thoughts. Selected papers on psychoanalysis.* London: Maresfield reprints.

Cluckers, G. (1989) 'Containment in de therapeutische relatie: de therapeut als drager en zingever', in H. Vertommen en G. Cluckers (eds) *De relatie in therapie.* Universitaire Pers Leuven, pp.49–64.

Freud, S. (1920) 'Beyond the Pleasure Principle', in *Standard Edition of the Complete Psychological Works of Sigmund Freud, Vol XVIV.* London: Hogarth Press.

Klein, M. (1929) 'Personification in the play of children', in *Love, Guilt and Reparation and Other Works 1921–1945, The Writings of Melanie Klein Volume I.* London: Hogarth Press.

Klein, M. (1946) 'Notes on some schizoid mechanisms', in *Envy and Gratitude and other Works 1946–1963, the Writings of Melanie Klein Volume III.* London: Hogarth Press.

Priestley, M. (1983) *Analytische Musiktherapie.* Stuttgart: St Ernst Klett.

Winnicott, D.W. (1951) 'Transitional Objects and Transitional Phenomena', in *Playing and Reality.* London: Penguin.

CHAPTER 4

Control and Creativity
Music Therapy with Adolescents in Secure Care

Claire Flower
United Kingdom

Introduction

The world of the adolescent can be a strange and dangerous place. Turbulent emotions, the desperate battle to become independent, coupled with the tremendous urge to belong, all combine to make the journey towards adulthood a traumatic one for many. Working with adolescents who have experienced some sort of breakdown in this process can be both uncomfortable and deeply challenging.

In particular, working as a music therapist on an Adolescent Forensic Secure Unit, I have often struggled with the question of how much freedom and control to give to clients.

In outlining the adolescent's need for a clear sense of identity, Erikson (1963) mentions the confusion which may arise when the individual fails to develop an integrated image of him or herself. When the adolescent finds the struggle to assume an expected image too great, he may take on a negative identity, reacting against all expectations. Major elements in the search for identity are the many unspoken and contradictory roles which children may be expected to fulfil within family systems. Miller (1983) sees this as one of the main causes of delinquency. She describes the vicious circle which begins with the adolescent's experience of helplessness. Their need to regain some mastery of their situation leads them to disturbed and delinquent behaviour. This in turn leads care givers to take strict counter-measures, rendering the child helpless once again. The child's response to such a situation may be a further escalation of anti-social behaviour. This could take the form of vandalism, fire-setting or sexual offending. Such behaviour may evoke fear and anger in adults who may then be unable to respond to the needs behind the behaviour. Eventually, larger systems may become involved in imposing restraints on the child. In extreme cases secure care may be deemed appropriate.

Discussion

The Gardener Unit is a small secure unit for approximately 15 adolescents between the ages of 11 and 18. They are referred from a variety of sources and for diverse reasons. While many of them have exhibited behaviours which have made them a risk to society, in other cases the risk may be more of self-harm. The unit offers both assessment and treatment programmes, for an average of three months, carried out by a multi-disciplinary team which includes occupational, art and music therapy. Music therapy sessions took place in a large, airy room. A wide selection of instruments was available for clients, who received one individual 45 minute session each week.

From the outset I adopted a non-directive approach in my sessions. I was concerned that these individuals, who had very little choice about being in secure care, should have an opportunity to make choices, musically or otherwise. The only limitation was a rule that they damage neither any person nor any instrument in the room. I was initially afraid that my clients, so adept at breaking rules, would not respect this boundary. To my surprise, they usually did.

After an initial assessment period of six sessions, all clients had the opportunity to decide whether to continue with music therapy. They were also able to choose whether to tape record their sessions. This theme of choice was extended into our musical work: I took my lead from the clients themselves.

In early sessions, allowing clients this degree of control left me feeling uncomfortable; anything could happen. Often I felt the temptation to take the reins more strongly, banishing my own discomfort. I became aware that my experience of powerlessness reflected that of my clients. Allowing them an experience of being in control began to elicit unexpected responses. Clients who had aggressively argued that they wouldn't use a tape recorder, or certainly didn't want to continue sessions, changed their minds once the decision became theirs.

In this environment, it was possible for some clients to have the experience of play. For many, childhood had been traumatic, whether through illness or severe family breakdown. The importance of play and creative impulse as a vital part of healthy development may have been lost. This loss may have been significant. As Winnicott (1971) stressed:

> It is in playing, and only in playing that the individual child or adult is able to be creative and to use the whole personality, and it is only in being creative that the individual discovers the self. (p.54)

I hoped that through the innately creative experience of improvisation the individual would discover an ability to play and, through play, move towards a deeper sense of self.

Clinical material

Michael, a fourteen-year-old boy, had come to the unit facing serious charges of fire-setting. He was a thin, plain-looking boy, with a rather expressionless face and a markedly reserved manner. When I first invited him to music therapy he barely spoke to me, seeming terribly shy. I imagined that he might need encouragement to participate in sessions.

Nothing could have been further from the truth. In our first session he burst through the door and, without greeting me, made straight for the piano and began to play. He filled the room with continuous quavers. I joined him at the piano, trying to add a melodic line to his rhythmic moto perpetuo. As I started to play he stopped abruptly, only resuming his play when I stopped. I tried to join him again but the message was very clear. I retreated to a corner of the room for the remainder of the session, playing a sporadic percussion accompaniment to his torrential piano music.

After the session, my first thought was of how unusual it was for a client to make such an immediate and spontaneous use of improvisation. Other individuals seem to experience great difficulty in impulsive playing. For some this was undoubtedly due to normal adolescent inhibitions, but in others it seemed to reflect a deeper developmental deficit. As mentioned earlier, many individuals on the unit had known deprivation in the area of play and creative experience. For them the spontaneity of improvisation seemed too great a demand on their inner selves. Their limited imaginative play often meant that popular tunes were endlessly and painfully recreated on the piano.

One client, Peter, favoured the *Eastenders* theme tune. His use of a pre-composed melody seemed to serve an important function. It offered him a safe musical starting point from which he could begin to explore the potentially unsafe world of the music therapy session. It was rather like having a musical hand to hold. This put me in mind of Ainsworth's (1979) observations of mothers and toddlers in a new environment. Given a healthy attachment between mother and infant, Ainsworth pointed out that the child will cling to its mother for a time before gradually beginning to explore. It will then return to its mother occasionally for reassurance. The repeated playing of the *Eastenders* melody by Peter seemed to be an equivalent musical attachment, offering him a refuge from which to begin a wider exploration. In time he relinquished the use of the theme completely. It had been a springboard to greater musical creativity. In Michael's case, his improvisation was based on the repetition of short motifs, less free than I had realised.

From our second meeting onwards, Michael allowed me to play the piano with him and the sessions were filled with virtually uninterrupted improvisation. I became increasingly aware that in this flurry of music Michael left no time for silence or for talking. Although he now admitted my musical presence, he remained largely in command of the vast output, governing how the music started, how it finished, changes in tempo or variations in dynamics. Any musical initiatives that I attempted were summarily dismissed. This experience of losing my musical control was most unusual, leaving me with a sense of rejection. It made me wonder how often in the past Michael himself had experienced such rejection and powerlessness.

I was aware that Michael's father had physically abused him at an age when he was too weak to retaliate and too young to communicate his distress to others. Michael's mother, herself a victim of the father's abuse, was in no position to help him to express and thereby resolve the damage done to him. It became well hidden over the years. Now it seemed as though Michael was telling what had been done to him by doing the same to me in our music together. His former passivity, when abused by his father, was turning to activity. He was causing me to suffer, albeit musically, as he had done. The abused became the abuser. My survival and non-retaliation was a key to any success in our work together.

This was even more striking for me in my work with another client. Andrew had grown up within a very disturbed family system. He had also had to deal with being remarkably small for his age, and having a minor facial deformity. He came to the unit having indecently assaulted several women. It was on this that his music therapy work focussed. He developed a rather sinister game called 'Giant's Footsteps'. This involved Andrew assuming the role of the Giant and directing the music, while I played the part of the Dwarf. A variation on this was 'The Spider and The Fly'. The titles may have been different but the basic themes were the same. Andrew cast himself as the predator who would musically chase me until, with a loud bang on the drum, I was caught. Through these sometimes disturbing episodes it was clear that Andrew was reliving events which had been painful

to him. He was doing to me what had been done to him. It was no surprise
that Andrew wished to see someone else as the dwarf for a change.

Michael had not used such strong visual images, but his playing had still
evoked an intense feeling of helplessness in me. He ignored me and made
only a minimal response to my musical interventions. This was difficult for
me to deal with. Surely as the therapist I should be more in charge? Yet I
recognised that Michael needed me to experience what he had gone through
as a child. As he began to feel in control, changes came more quickly.

Following our initial three sessions, which had been exclusively centred
around the piano, Michael became interested in the drum. He surprised me
by requesting well-known marches for us to play together. Our sessions took
on a regular pattern. In the first half of each meeting we shared the piano,
while in the second half, Michael moved to the drum. Each arrangement had
its own quality. In our shared piano playing Michael usually initiated changes
in speed and loudness, seeming reluctant to follow me. On the drum he
played more sensitively, not only following changes in the basic beat, but
also copying subtle rhythmic patterns. His physical presence altered considerably during this drum and piano music. He sat more upright, used his body
freely and abandoned the tense, hunched position which he adopted at other
times. The drumming seemed important to Michael. At first I was not sure
why. In a later session Michael spontaneously told me that he liked to play
the drums because they reminded him of his father who had played in a
military band. Michael recounted proudly that it was his father's job to 'set
the rhythm'.

'That's a very important job', I commented.

'Yes', he said, 'It means he's in control, he's the boss'.

In spite of, or perhaps because of the abuse he had suffered, Michael idealised
his father, seeing him as a powerful man to be revered. Now, in his music,
Michael seemed to want to experience that power himself. I wondered who
was 'the boss' in our sessions. Maybe it was important to Michael that he
perceived himself as being in control, and that I saw him as such.

As our sessions progressed, Michael began to talk more, to allow more
silence and to employ a greater flexibility and creativity in his playing. His
exploration of the instruments and their capabilities increased, enabling him
to express feelings that were, at times, disturbed and chaotic. During a time
when Michael's move to another unit had just been finalised, he talked of
being excited but felt that he dare not show it in case he lost control of
himself. In the following improvisation, Michael played the drum and
cymbal while I played the piano. In this music he exercised a large degree

of control, but within this control was a newly discovered creativity. If Winnicott is to be believed, through this kind of play he began to make contact with his own true self. I felt relieved that early on I had not stolen Michael's musical and therapeutic experience by trying too hard and overwhelming him.

Awkward and inadequate as I felt at times, by being with my own helplessness I had perhaps allowed Michael the freedom to be strong and autonomous within our relationship.

Conclusion

For Michael, Peter, Andrew and other adolescents, creative self-expression can be a dangerous business. The chaotic depth felt is often too much to handle. Secure care offers a control that they might previously have lacked, both externally, within their families and internally, within themselves. Within music therapy it was my task to transform this often stifling institutional control into a more permissive therapeutic containment. This framework was inevitably used and abused in many different ways as clients played out their various dramas.

Winnicott advised parents that if they had done all they could to promote personal growth in their offspring, they could expect startling and, at times, disturbing results in their children. This thought often seemed particularly apt to me. My experience of being with Michael, Peter, Andrew and with other clients, as they struggled to express themselves creatively and to take control of their lives was not always comfortable, but then why should it have been?

References

Ainsworth, M.D.S. (1979) 'Infant–mother attachment', *American Psychologist, 34*, 932–937.

Erikson, E.H. (1963) *Childhood and Society.* (2nd Ed.) New York: Norton.

Miller, A. (1983) *For Your Own Good.* London: Faber and Faber.

Winnicott, D.W. (1971) *Playing and Reality.* London: Tavistock.

CHAPTER 5

Music Therapy with Families

Amelia Oldfield
United Kingdom

Introduction

One of the earliest and most common forms of musical interactions is that of a mother (or father) singing to soothe a crying infant. Although the main objective may be to stop the baby from crying, the music will also serve many other functions. The act of singing may have a calming influence on the mother and help her to feel closer to her baby. If she feels she is relieving her child's distress this will boost her confidence and help her to feel positive about her relationship with her baby. The baby may well react to the mother's heightened sense of well-being and this may in turn help the baby to relax and feel at ease.

Music can be used in many ways to improve or restore relationships between children and parents in a family. This chapter will examine the different ways in which music therapy has helped a number of families at a psychiatric unit in Cambridge.

The Croft Children's Unit, Cambridge

Children and families are referred through their GP, their school, social services or other agencies, to the Brookside Family Consultation Clinic and are then referred on to the Children's Unit. The primary aim of the Unit is to assess and treat children and families who are troubled by:

- emotional disturbance
- behavioural disturbance

- social and environmental pressures
- disturbance related to the ability to learn

Families and their children are assessed and treated on a short– term basis, usually between four weeks and a year.

The staff on the Unit consists of psychiatric nurses, nursery nurses, a special needs teacher, special needs assistants, a child psychiatric consultant, a registrar, an occupational therapist, a play therapist and a music therapist. Social workers, health visitors and psychologists work closely with staff on the Unit.

There are various types of family work at the Croft Children's Unit. The Unit has the facility to admit one or two families (so far these have always been one parent families) from Monday mornings to Thursday evenings. These families generally attend for four to twelve weeks.

Families may also be referred to the Unit for sessional work. This often takes the form of weekly half day programmes, set up specifically to suit the needs of that particular family. In addition, the Unit runs one whole day or half day weekly programme for a group of parents and young children. The group usually runs for six to eighteen weeks and caters for three or four families.

Finally, the Unit runs a 'parents project' which aims to provide support for families with a variety of difficulties who are either expecting a child or looking after a child under the age of eighteen months.

The Unit will cater for the needs of each family in a variety of ways. Initially, the Unit staff may provide 'models' of good child management and help families through feeding and night time routines. However, the emphasis will always be on enabling parents to take control. Play sessions may be set up for families and constructive suggestions will be made to improve relationships in the family during the playing. These sessions will often be videotaped to allow parents to examine the ways in which they have been interacting with their children.

Parents are usually given time to talk about their difficulties with a member of staff on their own and the family may also be offered play therapy or family therapy sessions. Occupational therapy and music therapy could be appropriate either for one, or for more members of the family. Unit staff try to provide a well balanced programme where different types of treatment complement one another.

Although I have been involved in all these different types of family work, in this Chapter I will only talk about individual family music therapy sessions.

Structure of the music therapy sessions

Individual family music therapy sessions usually last about half an hour and I then review the session with the parents for fifteen minutes while the children play with a member of staff in another room. Sometimes we videotape the sessions and use the recordings for the review. If it is a large family and we feel that the parent or parents would not be overwhelmed by working with two members of staff, I often work with a psychiatric nurse from the unit and we will plan and review sessions together. In this case we sometimes choose to take on clear roles such as a challenging role and a conciliatory role, to facilitate the therapeutic process.

Before starting, I explain to the family that we will be making music together and that the adults are going to play with the children. I also explain about the timing and the review of the session and that the sessions will be held at the same time every week for an initial period of four to six weeks.

The activities I propose to the families during the sessions will obviously vary depending on the age of the children and the problems presented. Sometimes the age of the children will range from eighteen months to ten years and it can become quite a challenge to cater for everyone's needs and interests.

Families are often quite desperate by the time we see them on the Unit and I feel it is important for them to perceive music therapy sessions as a time to work and face up to challenges, but overall as enjoyable and fun. If it is not seen in this way, I will lose the commitment of the family and they will probably stop attending. Thus, I try to introduce gradually challenges which I feel the members of the family are ready to deal with in order to make it possible for them to succeed and gain a sense of achievement at each stage.

I generally start by singing a greeting song on the guitar and then encourage children and parents to strum the guitar while I am holding it. After this, I suggest that one child should say the name or point to people who will each strum the guitar once. With older children this idea can be elaborated on by suggesting that a name spoken loudly leads to a loud strum and a name spoken quietly leads to a quiet strum. Alternatively, children can suggest that the person with red socks, or a silver watch, for example, should play next.

Thus, I start the session off in a predictable, non-threatening manner by playing a song on the guitar. Very quickly, however, I involve the whole group, giving both parents and children the control. I will be able to observe how the family members interact, whether they can accept and give directions and whether they can listen to one another.

We then often move on to playing the instruments together, with me leading from the piano. I have a wide range of percussion, string and wind instruments and I may suggest that each person chooses an instrument themselves. However, this choice is usually initially too difficult for the families I work with and will lead to major confrontations and disputes. In addition, the very loud instruments such as the bass drum and the cymbal can be very frightening for young children, or feed into uncontrolled chaos for older children. Many parents will be incapable of hearing their children playing instruments very loudly without perceiving them as 'naughty'. These difficulties will be addressed with the parents and the children but the way the problems are tackled will need to be discussed and planned with the parents. I, therefore, initially frequently select a number of smaller instruments for the group to choose from.

Some families will need encouragement to play freely with the piano and others will need help not to play wildly and chaotically without listening to one another. I can usually do this by varying the way I play the piano, introducing or abandoning familiar structures or songs and changing dynamics and tempi. I try to introduce clear endings by, for example, encouraging the family to put their instruments down and lift their hands up in the air when the piano stops, or by swapping instruments when the piano stops. Sometimes it may be possible to suggest exchanging places when the piano stops and this will then give a parent or a child the 'leading' role from the piano. For some families, however, the chaotic piano playing of a young child will not be accepted by parents.

Playing instruments together can be an easy way for families to be reintroduced to the idea that they can all enjoy an activity together. Each family member is 'equal' in this activity and the usual conflicts regarding control can temporarily be put aside. Later, when the issues of control may be being gradually addressed, I might suggest that we follow different family members musically or that each person has a solo. This will be useful for encouraging listening and giving praise, as each soloist can be rewarded by a round of applause and personal congratulations.

At some stage in the session I usually find it useful to suggest an activity involving movement. This could mean encouraging parents and babies to do 'Row, row, row your boat' type activities, or it could mean dancing, marching, or running around the room. To give another example, parents may lift their toddlers up in the air and pretend they are aeroplanes or jumping frogs.

Children with concentration difficulties will be helped by the variety provided by an activity involving movement. Most children will enjoy interacting physically with their parents and some parents will find it much easier to sing a traditional action song with their child than to play instruments themselves. These are also ideas that can be tried out at home.

I always make sure that sessions have a clear ending. We might, for example, each take it in turns to say goodbye on an instrument, or we might sing songs together chosen by the children. It may also be appropriate to encourage parents to praise children for having overcome a particular difficulty during the session. In general, I think it is important that the last thing we do should be unthreatening and as positive as possible.

After the session is over, the children go into a different room with another member of staff and I review the session with the parent(s). In the review of the very first session I explain to the parent(s) that the purpose of the session is to address some of the difficulties that the family has been experiencing. I stress that the parents are responsible for their children during the session and should praise or direct their children appropriately, even if I am leading the sessions and making suggestions about what we might do in the session.

It usually helps parents to focus on one or two areas of difficulty, such as controlling aggressive behaviour, giving their children more praise, allowing themselves to relax and improvise with their children or dividing attention between several siblings. Sometimes we may decide to explain to the children what we are working on at the beginning of subsequent sessions.

Parents often want to use the review time to talk about their children's problems in other settings, such as school, but I try to help parents focus primarily on what has just occurred and how we might approach the session the following week.

Case studies *

The Jones family

The Jones family, consisting of mother, Tina, Peter, aged four and Lucy aged five months was first referred to the children's Unit because Tina was having difficulties managing Peter's aggressive and disturbed behaviour. Peter's father had left the household when he was only a baby and had no contact with the family. Tina's new boyfriend sexually abused Peter and when Tina found out she broke off the relationship and reported the man to the police.

Initially, the children's Unit arranged a half day weekly programme for six weeks for the Joneses, consisting of play sessions for the three of them, counselling sessions for Tina and, after a couple of weeks, music therapy

---

*   For confidential reasons, names, dates and sometimes genders have been changed in all these cases.

sessions for the three of them. Music therapy was suggested because Tina had expressed an interest in music and because play sessions were very difficult both for Tina and for Peter. Tina felt 'silly' trying to play with toys with her son and Peter was usually too busy being disruptive (for example, shouting and kicking) to take any interest in the toys. It was hoped that he might be motivated to play the musical instruments and that loud playing would provide an opportunity for him to express some of his anger.

I saw the family for two of the planned four sessions owing to sickness and transport problems of the Joneses. During these sessions Peter showed that, although he enjoyed music making and was keen to play the instruments, his concentration was very poor and he had great difficulty listening to adults or accepting directions. In the second session he kicked and punched his mother when she tried to set appropriate limits for him and she had to resort to holding him on her lap until he calmed down. Nevertheless, at times he was warm towards his mother and was able to listen to her on a couple of occasions. He showed no particularly antagonistic behaviour towards his baby sister. Lucy was calm and at ease during the two sessions. She was contented to listen to the music in her bouncy chair and was not frightened by loud noises or by Peter's disturbed behaviour.

Tina clearly enjoyed music and was not shy or embarrassed about using the instruments. She enjoyed singing with both her children, but particularly with Lucy, who obviously loved her mother's singing. I was impressed by the way Tina handled Peter during these two sessions. She stated limits and rules clearly and calmly and used 'count downs' effectively. She was good at remaining calm and not reacting emotionally when Peter was kicking and punching her. In spite of Peter's difficulties she was also good at dividing her time between the two children. It was obvious that although she experienced difficulties at home, there were times when she managed Peter's difficult behaviours very well.

Nevertheless, when reviewing the sessions, Tina seemed unable to focus on any aspects of the sessions other than Peter's disturbed behaviour. She was surprised to hear me say that I thought she was handling Peter very well and seemed to take her own musical abilities and spontaneity for granted. Clearly, Tina greatly lacked confidence and found it difficult to see anything positive either in herself or in Peter. She did not, however, lack warmth and affection for her son as she showed pleasure and pride when I helped her to remember how good Peter had been at some of the musical games we had played during the session. She also needed help to react more strongly to Peter's physical aggression towards her. It appeared that she tolerated the aggression because of her own low self esteem and because she felt guilty and responsible for Peter's sexual abuse.

After the six weeks of sessional work with the Joneses, the children's Unit recommended that Tina would benefit from more intensive work on the Unit and that she should be admitted with Peter and Lucy for four weeks as an in-patient. She started as an in-patient two months later and music therapy sessions continued. The sessional work on the Unit had obviously boosted Tina's confidence to the extent that, when she returned to the Unit, Peter's aggressive behaviour had decreased considerably.

During these next four sessions, I suggested to Tina that we focus particularly on helping her to praise as well as set limits for Peter and on allowing herself to enjoy making music with her children. The family made considerable progress during these sessions.

The clear structures in some of the musical activities (such as turn-taking or anticipating endings of familiar tunes) reassured Peter and allowed him to concentrate better. This gave him a sense of achievement and, because of his mother's praise and encouragement, his confidence grew and his struggles to resist adult direction became less desperate.

Lucy continued to enjoy the sessions and was now able to take a slightly more active part by shaking bells or waving a stick at a drum. Peter was warm and caring towards her and we encouraged him to help her take turns or pass her instruments. This also helped Tina not to focus too much attention on her at the expense of Peter.

Tina's self-confidence and ability to enjoy making music with her children increased considerably during the four sessions. In fact, I often heard her singing to her children spontaneously outside the session and it was also reported to me that she had spent several evenings in the music room with Peter and other children from the Unit, picking out tunes on the piano and the recorder. She had begun to see music as 'one of her things' that she was good at and could have fun with.

The Gabrielli family

The Gabrielli family, consisting of mother, father, Jacob aged seven and Paul aged five, were referred to the Unit because Jacob was showing disruptive behaviour in school and because the mother (Liz) felt she had a poor relationship with Jacob. A series of four weekly individual play therapy sessions were arranged for Jacob and I agreed to see him and Liz for four weekly music therapy sessions. We then decided to extend both play therapy and music therapy sessions for a further four weeks, making a total of eight sessions.

Initially, both Liz and Jacob were shy and reluctant to play the instruments. Jacob would have quickly overcome this unease but was clearly inhibited by his mother's giggling and her embarrassment. Liz's playing was very tentative and she seemed too anxious to keep a rhythmical beat going. In the first two sessions they both played very quietly and were unable to follow my loud piano playing. They did not seem to be used to doing things together and there was little eye contact between them. Although Jacob had a tendency to fiddle with the instruments, he was not disruptive in any way and listened to both his mother's and my directions. Liz spoke in a quiet voice and although at times she was clearly irritated by Jacob's fiddling, she did not raise her voice or change her tone in any way. She did not give Jacob any praise or positive feedback.

When reviewing the first session with me, Liz admitted that she felt uneasy with the instruments but that she felt she would gradually get used to the idea. We agreed that we would use the first few sessions to help Jacob and Liz make more eye contact and communicate more with one another, to encourage both Jacob and Liz to praise and be positive with one another and to see whether we could encourage Jacob to enjoy singing and 'young' activities, rather than behaving like a young adult. I also knew that I would be working on trying to help them both to improvise more spontaneously as I felt that if they could both experience the fun of playing together freely, other difficulties would be easier to address.

By the third session Jacob was thoroughly enjoying the playing. Liz was still tentative but much less anxious. They both enjoyed making up a story and improvising music to accompany themselves. Jacob was no longer worried about appearing to be babyish and, indeed, displayed some babyish behaviours at the end of the session, sucking his thumb and cuddling up to Mum.

In the fifth session Liz became more spontaneous and 'natural' in her playing and also more able to praise Jacob for his achievements. After the session she admitted that, as she had been the eldest of seven children herself, there had never been much time to play or be a child. She was now beginning to enjoy and feel more at ease playing with Jacob. As she became more spontaneous in the sessions, Jacob more often displayed babyish behaviour, seeking physical contact and reassurance from Mum. I encouraged Liz to allow Jacob to do this but to 'normalise' this by saying things like 'Jacob is being a baby now... we all like to be babies sometimes'. At the end of this session Liz also told me that they were beginning to talk about their sessions together at home and remember activities that they had done together. This seemed very positive to me as I felt they were now communicating more, both in and outside the music therapy sessions.

During the last three sessions we worked particularly on helping Liz to use her voice and her face more expressively. For example: Liz would have her back to me and make a happy, sad or cross face at Jacob who had to play corresponding music on several instruments. We also worked on modifying our voices, shouting or whispering, and on using different types of intonation while playing the kazoos. Jacob thoroughly enjoyed these activities and Liz was able to praise his achievements in a sincere way since she was now aware that she had more difficulty being spontaneous than he did.

Although Liz and Jacob's relationship improved tremendously during these sessions, Jacob was still experiencing difficulties at school and at home. Nevertheless, both Liz and Jacob were able to remember their work as an experience they had enjoyed together, and this has helped them to address the other difficulties in a more positive way.

Conclusion

This chapter has shown that music can help recreate a warm, simple interaction between a parent and a child. This may be partly because a mother will remember similar interactions between herself and her own mother. Playing simple musical instruments can help parents to be children again themselves and to rediscover the fun and spontaneity of being a child. This will bring parents closer to their children and they will be able to take part at the same level. The structured, non-verbal nature of many musical activities or improvisations can be very reassuring for families who have become entangled in verbal conflicts, and the delicate issues of control can then be readdressed. Above all, relationships that have become mainly negative can again be seen in a more positive light, as families rediscover the ability to have fun together through music making.

CHAPTER 6

Music Therapy in the Psychodynamic Treatment of Schizophrenia

Hanne Mette Kortegaard
Denmark

Introduction

A psychodynamic understanding of schizophrenia presupposes that each individual has a congenital striving for development. This development is a result of the lifelong process of internalisation, which can include the internalisation of the music therapy relationship. In music therapy improvisation, the mutual sound product – an interpsychic synthesis – may, through its continual internalisation, create the basis for further intrapsychic synthesis. This allows for the growth and increased psychic stability of the schizophrenic patient.

Growth

We each have a congenital striving towards development. This unfolds through the continuing interaction between our emotional and intellectual functions and involves a search for change via creative means of expression, and the intellectual functions of concept and interpretation.

Conceiving the two functions as weights on a balance, striving to maintain equilibrium, we also work to maintain a balance. We may envisage development or growth as a result of an unbalance – a momentary lack of equilibrium – that creates the possibility of new insight and meaning. These functions may also be seen as a mutual defence: the interpretative functions defending us against the chaos of creativity, and creativity defending us against stagnation. Both, however, strive towards equilibrium. This congenital striving for development may be viewed as a striving for unbalance aimed at achieving balance at a higher level.

If a belief in the capacity to return to a state of balance is not established, the striving for equilibrium may result in a paralysis of action. To avoid strong psychic pain from the resulting chaos or unbalance, the normal defence process of achieving equilibrium is accentuated to a degree which prevents development.

A stagnation takes place which is often experienced as a lack of coherence between words and emotions. Given direct access to the creativity within him, in a structured way, the schizophrenic is presented with the possibility of communicating those aspects of his personality without the amplified defence being employed.

Psychodynamic therapy with schizophrenia takes as its point of departure an understanding of fixation having occured at a very early stage of development. The basic defences used are splitting and projective identification (Klein 1946). Maintenance of these defences results in an unintegrated self. The psychotherapy must therefore be directed towards an integration of the self – an intrapsychic synthesis.

Schizophrenia can be understood as an inability to find meaningful symbols for emotions. The schizophrenic experiences himself as unable to put symbols together and think meaningfully.

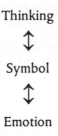

Figure 6.1

The model shown in Figure 6.1 is based on the works of Bion (1954, 1957, 1962a). He believes that the normal process of thought runs from emotion to symbol to thinking and vice versa. When this is not possible the schizophrenic will be unable to compare experiences and emotions and build a meaningful internal world. There will be no basis for intrapsychic integration.

During the projective identification process the schizophrenic does not (re-)internalise the objects projected, but introjects them. This is referred to as schizophrenic identification. A split between the unmodified objects and the ideal conceptions of an object are maintained with accompanying anxiety.

This means that the inner world of the schizophrenic consists of introjected objects which have their own original dynamics unmodified by the external world. They have their own dynamic nature which the schizo-phrenic is unable to identify with or modify.

Internalisation of the therapeutic relationship

The therapeutic relationship not only reproduces earlier relationships, as understood through transference and countertransference, but is also a creator of symbols and constitutes a part of the reality in which the schizophrenic is living.

Through the internalisation of new objects the schizophrenic may be able to gain a stability founded on non-threatening objects. This may allow him or her to 'unpoison' the threatening objects and internalise 'good' objects. This balance may eventually help the schizophrenic to cope with his own 'bad bits', without the latter creating a threat to his or her existence. The schizophrenic is enabled to learn to contain his anxiety.

The model shown in Figure 6.2 is based on the work of Bion (1962b). Beta elements can be understood as not useful and undigestible, alpha elements as useful and mentally digestible. When an infant encounters a beta

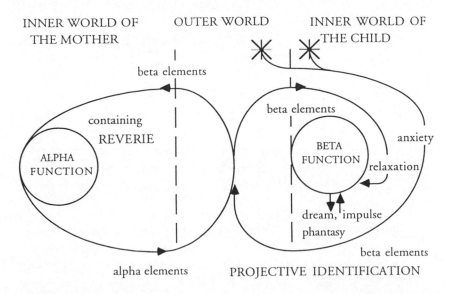

Figure 6.2

element, something he or she cannot make sense of, he or she feels anxiety and projects it onto the mother, perhaps through stressful howling. The mother, in her reverie, changes it, unconsciously, through her healing fantasies, impulses and dreams into digestible bits or alpha elements. The infant can then integrate these into his or her inner world. These will form the basis of the child's own inner reverie function.

Clinical material

When I first met Peter he was 22 years old and had been hospitalised for four years. During this period he had been held in closed units several times. At the time I met him he was in an open unit for younger schizophrenic patients in long term treatment.

It was very difficult to get any information from him regarding his early childhood. He did not know when he was born and could not tell me anything about his family or his childhood.

On first impression he reminded me of a small bird that was unable to fly. He was very polite, answering when asked, but also monotonous. Most answers were 'yes', 'no' or 'I don't know'. I also saw him as a very lonely ship, drifting away without any engine power in the middle of the ocean. Was this ship supposed to meet another ship, or forever drift away?

At the first session Peter came into my room and sat down. I tried to get a conversation started. It was impossible. Suddenly Peter got up and asked 'Shouldn't we just play?' He started to play the piano. I played the marimba.

His music was rigid. He did not respond to my music and did not seem interested in any form of dialogue. After a while I started to play intervals in a steady rhythm (=60) C–E and A–C, over and over again. When I took on and held the rigid, resistant part, he was then able to express himself in a much more dynamic way. His music became more experimental, violent and full of anxiety. From this improvisation I was given quite another view of his inner world which contrasted with the one he had presented earlier on.

We continued playing for about 40 minutes, then Peter suddenly stopped and said that he wanted to go to the toilet. When he came back he said, 'Now we can talk'. He started to tell me about his life.

> 'I have never been born; that was why I'm unable to die. I could never be released. My name is Sten; that means stone. I know nobody – I have no family – I have never had one. I'm raised all over the world – attended all wars – there are no other people in my world. I know that others say it isn't true, but it is. Someone tried to tell me

that I have a mother. The last battle was between the moon and the sun – the sun lost the battle – that's why we now have a cold war – I miss a nice battle.'

Later on I was given more information. Peter was the fourth of five children. His parents divorced when he was seven years old. The marriage had been one long battle. Several times Peter had had to protect his mother and call for help for example; an ambulance. The mother has since lived with different men – many of whom were violent. She is an alcoholic and a drug addict.

When Peter was 16 he started to smoke hashish. In the next two years he isolated himself, only leaving his room when it was dark. During this period he became more paranoid.

After an episode when Peter had had to call for an ambulance because of another battle in the family which left his mother unconscious, Peter had stopped eating. At last his younger sister called for a doctor to get some help.

Peter's life, as I see it, has included a lot of battles in which there was no-one there to protect him. His reaction to this has been to deny his own existence. To protect himself he has been forced to regress to a stage where the fear of destruction battles the fear of contact – fear of non-existence through being made into a stone or of being swallowed.

In the first phase Peter did not respond directly to me in the music. He was still isolated in his own world. After playing we would listen to the tapes. He was unable to tell who had been playing. Peter had put up a defensive wall between his inner world and the outer world. He insisted on the non-existence of the latter.

In the second phase of therapy he started to hear voices telling him to stop drinking and eating. Eventually, he came and told me that the voices had said he was to continue playing music and that then everything would be all right. He seemed to have internalised the music as a part object. This process will be detailed later on in the chapter. He moved his wall of resistance to the psychic space between the outer world (here the music), and my inner world.

In the last phase of music therapy he was aware of our being two people. He could talk about the music after playing. The music became like dialogue and much less chaotic. He was still resistant, but he had opened small doors and accepted me as a living person, as an object in his inner world.

The function of the music

The function of the music in music psychotherapy is to provide a space for the exploration of feelings attached to transference, countertransference and the new symbols created through the therapeutic relationship. Bion (1962a) refers to these functions as containing and maternal reverie.

The early process of object internalisation, the time in the development of the little child during which the use of splitting and projective identification are normal defences, is the time where the child (according to Klein) internalises part objects.

These are often described as the mother's breast or face which are experienced as good or evil. This way of explaining part objects as fragmented body elements is useful, as we are accustomed to thinking in pictures. Music is often understood by translation into pictures. For example, the music sounded 'like a girl – flowers in her hair – dancing in the summer meadow'.

This translation may, in fact, limit our opportunity to understand the quality of music in the therapeutic interaction. Music may be explained through visual symbols but this is not necessary.

The relationships of the schizophrenic which other people are founded on a way of non-thinking, non-understanding, and non-symbolising. The reality of the schizophrenic is not verbalisable to them. This may be a result of the fixation of their development at a preverbal stage.

Therefore, in order to achieve an understanding of the quality of music connected with therapy, I try to understand the objects in the same way as one would approach the non-symbolising infant. Object internalisation will be understood through the framework proposed by Bion (1962a). He says that it is misleading to say that objects are analogous with the static objects of fragmented body elements. Rather, they should be recognised as having a dynamic function within themselves. Part objects deal with nourishing, poisoning, loving and hating.

In viewing part objects as having a dynamic function we can explore the possibility of music as being such an object. This occurs through the internalisation of the adaptative potential of music to participate in the integration and stabilisation of the schizophrenic self. Through the projected material of the two improvising partners the music acquires a nourishing or poisoning function when reinternalised.

This way of working with schizophrenics requires empathy on the part of the therapist. She must continually relate to her manipulating role, in order that the patient may meet a gratifying mixture of gratification and frustration or nourishment and poisoning. This role is described as manipulating because, during the music therapy improvisation, the therapist identifies with the projected elements of the schizophrenic which move from the therapist's inner world to exist in the mutual sound expression, which is often not separated by the schizophrenic into expressions of self/another (see

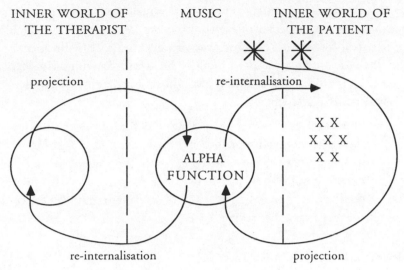

INNER WORLD OF   MUSIC   INNER WORLD OF
THE THERAPIST   THE PATIENT

Figure 6.3

Figure 6.3). The musical intervention of the music therapist may therefore achieve considerable importance regarding the internalising process of the patient.

Music improvisation with its dynamic function allows the music therapist a wide scope of possible interventions. During musical improvisation the therapist is able to relate to the patient's musical expression here and now. The mutual sound product is in dynamic movement. It is transformed before reinternalisation through the two playing partners, the patient and the therapist. The musical expression becomes a symbolisation of the pressing feelings expressed during the improvisation, whether this be an expression of the transference, countertransference or newly created symbols of the therapeutic relationship.

The transformation of feelings symbolised in music not only takes place due to direct reaction of the partners, but also happens in the mutual sound expression. Here the statements of both are at a time meaningfully present: a newly created symbol. The mutual musical expression can therefore be understood as an interpsychic synthesis. This is available for internalisation and establishes the ground for an intrapsychic synthesis.

Free-flowing awareness

Music improvisation offers a free-flowing awareness, in contrast to the focused awareness in verbal dialogue. In verbal dialogue an issue is focused on a common meaning. In music the expression itself is meaningful.

This free-flowing awareness will allow a fusion which encompasses an emotional coming together or interpsychic synthesis; a symbolic symbiosis for better or for worse. This process works both ways. The therapeutic 'get together' also works towards an intrapsychic synthesis within the therapist herself. I wish to emphasise this as a condition for the therapeutic duality.

As Benedetti (1983) says,

> 'the development of the patient and the self-realisation of the therapist are symmetrical phenomena. Only insofar as the psychotherapist by her meeting with her patient is capable of moving towards her own individuation, will the patient be put in position of establishing a world in communion with her psychotherapeutic partner.' (p.42)

Identification of symbols

As stated earlier, psychotherapy must direct itself towards psychic integration in the patient. This integration happens as a result of what goes on in the relationship of the therapist and the patient or the therapeutic duality. Thus, intrapsychic synthesis can be understood as a result of the interpsychic synthesis of the therapist and patient.

This is established between therapist and patient as the therapist is able to move into the world of the schizophrenic. Through identification of the common symbols of the two playing partners, the ability of the therapist to integrate allows for the possibility of internalising in the schizophrenic self, as well as it enriching the world of the therapist.

By identifying with the symbols of the patient and taking them into her own inner world with the understood meaning, the therapist establishes the basis for a counter-identification on the part of the patient. This identification process may be verbally expressed or musically expressed during clinical improvisation through the use of the client's tonal language.

Through a basic acceptance of the patient's symbols, the therapist may understand what the patient's symbols mean and, at the same time, move them out into a dual reality. Interpsychic synthesis can then take place. The patient is given the possibility of internalising newly created symbols and the adaptational function of the therapist. The tonal language identification may occur as the therapist tunes in. This involves imitating the playing of the patient, through intuitively sensing what that patient's way of playing brings forth in the therapist. This imitation may be compared with the mother's imitation of the infant's sounds as confirmation that the sounds are there and that the child is there and may establish contact. Through imitating, the therapist shows to the schizophrenic her basic acceptance of his or her expression, that the language is good enough and also meaningful in the reality of the therapist. Furthermore, the patient's expressions are amplified and the therapist's music complements the musical expression of the schizophrenic. The therapist/the music is charged with a containing function for the projected feelings of the patient.

The mutual sound expression of the client and therapist is a dual reality. Even though the schizophrenic does not realise as much (the presence of the music therapist in the reality), the mutual sound expression is able to be internalised in the self of the schizophrenic. The adaptational function of the therapist may be internalised through an internalisation of the mutual sound expression, or the interpsychic synthesis.

In musical improvisation the music therapist may adapt the projected material without the schizophrenic undergoing the anxiety of having had contact with another person. It is therefore not necessary for them to withdraw from contact. Feelings may be adapted within a symbolic symbiotic duality, not forcing the schizophrenic to abandon her protective feelings of omnipotence or 'I am the king of the world'.

By mirroring the patient's music in her own sound language, the music therapist's integrated self may serve a reverie function in relation to the anxiety which the patient expresses in the music.

By moderating the patient's anxiety and making it her own through giving it her own tonal language, the therapist may 'unpoison' the anxiety. This is done partly by being able to contain it without perishing and partly by a transformation of the musical expression of the anxiety (maternal reverie) which in the interpsychic synthesis in the music may create new symbols for the anxiety; these are then available for internalising as a basis for an intrapsychic synthesis.

The ambiance of the patient is moved out into the dual reality in which the therapist may 'become the defence' or undertake a 'border function' in the patient's near real world. She may then function as a 'psychic skin' protecting the patient's wish for contact from the destructive forces which fear contact. In the mutual sound expression, the sound of the therapist becomes a sort of rhythmical structured sound blanket, holding and soothing.

In accordance with the above, music psychotherapy involves the continuing interaction between the whole selves of two people – therapist and client – within social, ethical and professional conventions. It encompasses verbal, preverbal, conscious, preconscious and unconscious elements. The therapist involves the patient and herself and considers the conduct of both in view of transference, counter-transference and newly created symbols in an attempt to alter positively the symptoms and character of the patient through musical and verbal interventions.

Conclusion

In conclusion, I will give you the opportunity to say goodbye to Peter as I did.

During the session we played together four times. For the first time Peter chose another structure. From not having been able to talk until after the improvisations, he spoke both before and after. For this session he chose other instruments, no longer playing the piano. He started with the zither. I played the glockenspiel. After a while he began to play the marimba. In this improvisation his music became a mixture of his former rigid way of playing and the structure which I normally held during the improvisations. There was a wide variety of themes and dialogues. Peter had taken back the responsibility for structuring his inner world, his own processes.

After the improvisation Peter commented, 'This was good music – farewell', and then walked out.

References

Amtoft, M. m.fl. (1988) 'Internalisering' *Agrippa*, 2.

Balint, M. (1973) *Therapeutiske Aspekte der Regression.* Germany: Rowohlt.

Benedetti, G. (1983) *Skizofreni og psykoterapi.* Odense: Odense Universitetsforlag.

Bion, W. (1954) 'Notes on the theory of schizophrenia', *International Journal of Psychoanalysis,* 35, 113–118.

Bion, W. (1957) 'Differentiation of the psychotic from non-psychotic personalities', *International Journal of Psychoanalysis,* 38, 266–275.

Bion, W. (1962a) 'A theory of thinking', *International Journal of Psychoanalysis,* 43, 306–310.

Bion, W. (1962b) *Learning from Experience.* London: Heinemann.

Buksti, A.S. (1988) 'Intensiv skizofrenibehandling', *Agrippa,* 4.

Cullberg, J. (1987) *Dynamisk psykiatri.* Copenhagen: Reitzel.

Ernst, N. and Ernst, E. (1983) *Symbiosekomplekset.* Copenhagen: Akademisk forlag.

Frohne, I. (1986) *Music Therapy in Social Education and Psykiatri.* Oslo: Oslo Universitets Forlag.

Gilbert, S. (1986) 'Om projektiv identifikation', *Agrippa,* 3.

Goldberg, Frances m.fl. (1988) *Therapeutic factors in two forms of inpatient group psykotherapy: Music therapy and verbal therapy.* New York: New York University Press.

Hansen, E.B. (1986) 'Regression'. Unpublished paper, presented at the Psychotherapy Workshop, Brøndersleu.

Haugsgjerd, S. (1977) *Psykoterapi og miljøterapi ved psykoser.* Copenhagen: Reitzel.

Haugsgjerd, S. (1978) 'Psykoterapi ved psykotiske tilstander I + II', *Agrippa* 1 + 2.

Haugsgjerd, S. (1987) *Grunlaget for en ny psykiatri.* Copenhagen: Reitzel.

Hougaard, Esben (1987) 'Menninger projektet', *Agrippa,* 3.

Karon, Bertram P. (1985) 'Missopfattninger om psykoterapi med schizofrene', *Agrippa,* 3.

Kølbye, Morten (1986) 'En kort gennemgang af Bions Teori'. Unpublished paper, presented at the Psychotherapy Workshop, Brøndersleu.

Klein, M. (1946) 'Notes on some Schizoid Mechanisms'. *The Writings of Melanie Klein.* Vol.3 pp.2–24. London: Hogarth Press.

Langenberg, M. (1982) 'Grensenlosigkeit als Verführung'. *Umschau, 3.*

Mahler, M. (1975) *Barnets psykiske fødsel.* Copenhagen: Reitzel.

Mahler, M.S. (1988) *On human symbiosis and the vicissitudes of individuation.* New York: New York University Press.

Martini, G.D. (1985) 'En præsentation af selv'ets metapsykologi'. *Matrix,* 2.

Nitzschke, B. (1985) 'Frühe Formen des Dialogs'. *Umschau, 3.*

Olsen, E.O. (1986) 'Om Angst'. Unpublished paper, presented at the Psychotherapy Workshop, Brøndersleu.

Priestley, M. (1975) *Music Therapy in Action.* USA: Well-tempered Press.

Priestley, M. (1983) *Analytische Musiktherapie.* Stuttgart: St Ernst Kett.

Rosenbaum, B. (1988) 'Psykotikerens overfring', *Agrippa,* 2.

Rosenberg, R. m.fl. (1985) 'Psykiatri og psykoser', *Stud. med.* 55.

Sandin, B. (1986) *Den zebrastribede puddelkerne.* Denmark: Rosinante.

Storbel, W. (1985) 'Musiktherapi mit skizophrenen Patienten'. *Umschau,* 6.

Tähkä, V. (1983) *Psykoanalytiske psykoterapi.* Denmark: Centrum.

Tillemann, J. (1988) 'Psykoterapi af skizofrene', *Agrippa,* 3.

Varvin, S. (1985) 'Psykose og tenkning', *Agrippa,* 3.

CHAPTER 7

Description of an Experience in Music Therapy Carried Out at the Department of Psychiatry of the University of Genoa

Giuseppe Berruti, Giovanni Del Puente, Roberta Gatti,
Gerardo Manarolo, Caterina Vecchiato*

Italy

Introduction

Music therapy (MT) was introduced into our Department of Psychiatry as a treatment technique for in- and out-patients with psychotic symptoms. It was designed to complement other approaches and therapies, according to each patient's needs. For some of them we considered MT as an attempt to modulate the therapeutic relationship by making it more appropriate to and respectful of the degree of regression presented. For others, mainly in-patients, MT supported their search for greater autonomy and adaptability within the institution. Music therapy was an opportunity to search for a new potential way of being. This was stimulated by attaching a symbolic value to the gestures, rules and actions which guided and characterised the relationship within the music therapy sessions.

The general objective of music therapy is to give all patients an opportunity for communication and socialisation. The treatment also provides the opportunity for a new means of non-verbal communication. This was especially valuable for patients who found conventional psychotherapy difficult. Ultimately, the effectiveness of music therapy could be summarised by stressing two basic components: it stimulates emotions through dramati-

---

* Names are in alphabetical order: each author has contributed equally to this chapter.

sation with emotional reassurance, and it opens up new communication channels. The evocative value of music is used to revive and arouse an emotional world, otherwise unexplored, or little known to the patient himself.

This evocative value also relies on the symbolic functions of music. In order to enable the patients to profit from music therapy effectively, they need to meet specific requirements: willingness to take part in an experience-based group, sufficiently functioning ego-structure, difficulties of isolation and withdrawal, and an interest in musical expression.

The group included a maximum of six people, both men and women. The sessions took place once a week and followed a specific pattern: (a) initial listening to a musical excerpt, (b) a phase of discussion and analysis within the group, (c) a second hearing of the same piece, and (d) a final phase of discussion. At the end of the excerpt, it was anticipated that there would be free verbalising on the part of the group. The group was guided by a psychiatrist trained in music therapy. The session was designed to identify and highlight the ways in which the patients profited from musical excerpts. Special emphasis was laid on emotional overtones, with reference to personal experiences and problems. Both the answers of the individual patients and the emotional development of the group as a whole were considered.

The relational, affective, emotional elements surfacing during the last session directs the music therapist to choose a specific excerpt. He/she also uses his/her own sensitivity and specific culture when examining issues emerging during the session.

The choice of the music and the therapeutic projects are discussed weekly and analysed in a supervision group. During the initial sessions when the group has not yet settled and adjusted, this approach relies on the use of musical excerpts designed to 'probe' the situation: they were not yet related to the dynamics of the individuals and of the group but were used to assess the possible interactions as a result of the musical excerpt. These excerpts are classified on the basis of their prevailing affective tone and validated through a statistical study.

During the sessions, the identification of musical excerpts with special significance requires that the relationship between the musical structure and the content evoked be examined: this serves to identify the most significant and meaningful elements. This analysis led us into the sound/musical symbolism of the individuals, and of the group. The most significant parameters and structures are identified and the listening proposal was then specified and carried out accordingly.

Clinical material

Case study 1

Livia was born 35 years ago in Genoa, with her twin sister, Rita, during the seventh month of pregnancy. They were small and had to be kept in incubators for an extended time, and were fed artificially.

Their mother, a housewife, was affected by a brain tumour and died when the sisters were 10 years old. Livia remembers the onset of the disease and the sudden hemiparesis of her mother. Her mother had asked her for help, but Livia had been unable to call for help as her fear had petrified her.

After the death of her mother, she and her sister spent the following six years in a boarding school. Subsequently, she went back to her family to live with her father, who had meanwhile retired, and her brother. She worked in a plastics factory up to the age of 22 when she had to leave her job to look after her father, who was seriously ill.

During that period she experienced the first important psychopathological event: a depression syndrome for which she was treated as an out-patient. She has never recovered completely, despite the various therapies that followed. On the contrary, she has developed pseudoneurotic symptoms: marked social withdrawal, taedium vitae, severe apathy and an intense experience of incurability and uselessness.

She has been hospitalised several times in psychiatric institutions and has tried to commit suicide as many as six times. During the last hospitalisation she agreed to take part in music therapy sessions. Now discharged from hospital, she lives with a family of acquaintances, consisting of a couple of her own age with two children. Three times a week she goes to the day hospital of the local Health Department and once a week she attends music therapy sessions.

During the sessions, recurrent patterns of interaction within the musical excerpts have arisen. The associations verbalised included stereotypical images, idyllic and naturalistic, but also elements more closely related to personal events. In particular, the excerpts in which the rhythmic element was predominant stimulated images of motion. Sometimes it was the pursuit of a man seen as a possible partner, an escape into her psychoses when faced with everyday difficulties, or escape from a hypothetical pursuer. When the musical proposal was in harmony with pleasurable affects, characterised by peace of mind and well-being, it provided an element capable of modifying her mood. The aesthetic enjoyment stimulated gratifying emotions which urged her to overcome her own withdrawal. The 'beauty' of the music consoled her inner suffering. On the other hand, the musical themes not in harmony with such contents were often rejected or distorted. She detected in these unbearable serenity and well-being. Livia could not, apparently, tolerate seeing her malaise reflected in a 'musical mirror'. She did not, therefore, accept that there was a possibility of working through her suffering: she preferred to deny this suffering by magically merging with a tonifying musical experience.

Music therapy was accepted as it did not ask her to face a 'working-through' process which was currently impracticable for her. She could benefit from the support and holding provided by the setting and the group, while the idealisation stimulated by music strengthened her defences.

Case study 2

Alberto, the third of three brothers and sisters, is 23. His father died when he was nine. At present, he lives with his mother, his maternal grandmother and a brother two years older than himself.

He has been hospitalised twice in a psychiatric clinic following two attempted suicides at short intervals. He has been suffering from a dissociative type of psychosis for several years. The third hospitalisation became necessary due to the complete withdrawal of the patient and a refusal to eat. He discontinued all contact with the Mental Care Services. His drug therapy was based on high doses of anti-cholinergic drugs. These were taken, as the patient admitted, in order to acquire supernatural powers. Television characters became the only accepted interlocutors. The relationships with his relatives had degenerated into violent wrangles.

During his stay in hospital he was asked whether he wanted to join a group of patients following a music therapy programme. After initial mistrust, he accepted. Later on he talked about this experience with satisfaction, since he considered himself as belonging to a group of 'elite' of less 'mad', more sensitive patients. At present, in agreement with his relatives, Alberto continues to take part in the music therapy sessions, although he has been discharged.

During the first session he found it difficult to use the pieces of music he was listening to as evocative and associative. He maintained that he listened to music just for the sake of it but that he was unable to translate what he was hearing into images or emotions. He felt that the only interaction possible with the musical element was to merge with it.

This listening approach was accompanied by a defensive and rationalising process. Alberto, in fact, endeavoured to analyse the excerpts through identifying their structural elements, albeit the more superficial ones. He seemed isolated from the rest of the group, seemingly suffering from mutism. He justified this behaviour by maintaining that he had nothing to say and that he had to learn from the others to be able to express his emotions. As the sessions went on, however, he uttered verbalisations more strictly related to the potential emotional-affective content of the pieces proposed. Though some of his comments were aimed at gratifying the therapist, others seemed genuine. It was as if Alberto had developed an emotional sensitivity of his own in response to the musical excerpts, and was finding a way to express this.

Music, however, played an important role in the patient's daily life. He frequently listened to jazz and rock excerpts, which were an integral part of his cultural background, as well as being symbolic of the myths of his adolescence.

It was possible not to clash with Alberto's preferences while, at the same time, providing a message appropriate to him. He gradually came out of his isolation and overcame his inhibition with respect to the group. He stated that during the sessions he had learnt how to stay with other people and communicate with them. The moment of greatest involvement was when he proposed that the group listen to some pieces of music to which he attached special significance: pieces of jazz music. He expressed associations that conflicted with the possible connotations of the excerpt. These were felt to be delusional. Leaving aside the role played by the interaction between the associations and the music itself, it is worth highlighting the importance of the sessions for providing Alberto with a space sufficiently safe to express and share features of his inner world.

Case study 3

Little is known about Paola's first 11 years of life and it appears that the patient was abandoned in hospital and began living with her adoptive family. Her parents describe her as a docile and very affectionate girl who attended school with good results up to the age of 17. Then she started to show malaise and inner distress and to associate with youngsters addicted to drugs. The following year she fled to England with a friend and stayed in London for approximately two years, leading a life at the limits of the law. Only after a year did she send news of herself to her parents. On her return she was informed that she was an adopted child. Thereafter, her life became more and more chaotic, with increasingly serious asocial behaviour and periods of imprisonment, during which she showed a high degree of aggressiveness. After causing serious injuries to a supervisor, she ended up in a secure hospital.

Back in Genoa, she was repeatedly hospitalised. She was admitted to our Institute after repeated manifestations of self-mutilating behaviour.

From the very first sessions it was clear that Paola was extremely sensitive to musical language. Information on her life history had highlighted a privileged relationship with the sound/music element, even though this was within patterns which were strictly connected to the use of drugs. She accepted our proposal to use music to think and not to abuse herself. The images aroused by the various excerpts allowed her to find adequate representations for her inner world and communicate them. She stated that she received great help from music as it gave her a chance of speaking and expressing herself. As soon as the excerpt was over, she asked to speak as if she immediately needed to vent the emotions she had experienced during the listening. Her emotional participation reached dramatic intensity. During one session the listening caused a fit of discomfort and the patient asked to interrupt the listening. The melancholy melody of the excerpt had aroused in Paola memories related to her tragic childhood and strong emotions. Subsequent to this verbalisation, however, she asked to listen again to the previously interrupted excerpt completely, as if she had gained greater distance from the above-described emotions. The hospitalisation period of Paola had been particularly long (1 year) and the possibility of attending the sessions after being discharged was used by her to keep a connection with this Institution.

We have the impression that, after her discharge, Paola has used the two sessions of music therapy to lessen the pain of the separation experience. It felt like a protraction of leave-taking in the absence of valid working-through means. We believe that this situation has not enabled her to continue to use music therapy as a means of continually reworking the separation experience.

Conclusion

Music therapy has been effectively adopted with psychotic patients. Its use reflects the general trend to integrate different resources and approach modalities in the treatment of psychosis. It aims to identify a means for developing a therapeutic relationship with seriously ill patients, taking into consideration the level of regression exhibited and their need for rehabilitation.

During hospitalisation, patients to a great extent lose their own capacities for adjusting and autonomy. This can be seen as regressive. There is a need to communicate and search for a new personal equilibrium. Music therapy provides a setting for this. Within this context, every act assumes a symbolic value and meaning beyond its concrete existence. It is often through the laying down of rules and direct actions that the therapeutic relationship develops, rather than through verbal means.

Music therapy is a valuable tool for the opening of communication channels, for messages not easily put into words, and for patients who find verbal psychotherapy difficult.

CHAPTER 8

Levels of Interaction in Group Improvisation

Esmé Towse and Claire Flower
United Kingdom

Introduction

This chapter combines ideas from psychoanalytic literature (Bion 1961, Foulkes 1948) with music therapy technique. It is not based on research but on clinical observation. The case material is that of Claire Flower, who worked with a group under the supervision of Esmé Towse.

A problem encountered by many music therapists is that of sharing work with other professionals. As much of our work is done alone on a sessional or part-time basis, we often rely on other professionals for support and supervision, and to liaise between ourselves and ward rounds and case conferences. It is, therefore, imperative that we find a way of understanding and describing patients' behaviour and progress in a language which non-musicians can understand. The authors acknowledge the merit of those music therapists who analyse their musical work in great detail, but wonder how such a specialised knowledge can be applied to the practical situation of working within a multi-disciplinary team.

The role of group work in music therapy is another topic for debate. In the early days of training, there was no reference to groups, other than more formal music groups such as choirs. Our only experience of being in a group was the classes in movement and improvisation. Yet group work seemed so obvious for music therapy. Music, unless produced in extraordinary conditions, such as a sound-proofed room or a desert island, always affects another person or other people. The degree to which we are aware of those others will depend both on our characters and on external reality.

Another area which preoccupies music therapists is the role of the music in our work. This provokes great debate regarding the proportion of verbal and musical content in any interaction. Music in a general sense is crucial to the work to be discussed, although the specific details in the music are not always very important. This point will be made clearer.

Discussion

We would like to illustrate the ways in which we try to analyse groups. Whilst working with groups, we attempt to observe and analyse within the session, but it is never possible to do so to the same degree as in the supervision setting. We will observe the efficacy of the therapist's technique, although it is not intended to criticise that technique or to suggest modifications. That has already been discussed in supervision. This is simply observation and analysis in retrospect as a writer or supervisor.

The group concerned took place in a psychotherapy unit which is very much group orientated. The therapist worked as the only music therapist in the Health District and her post involved only two sessions in this unit. She therefore relied on the other staff to refer into the group. It was made up of six members plus two therapists: a music therapist and a nurse therapist who worked in the unit full-time. It lasted for 24 weeks with a review at the mid point. Initially it was all female. However, one member left at the tenth week as she was discharged from the unit, and was replaced by a man who had specifically requested music therapy on an out-patient basis.

It was the music therapist's first real experience as a group conductor and the first time that the two therapists had worked together. The nurse had experienced working with an art therapist and a drama therapist but not a music therapist. Both therapists, therefore, were having to develop a way of working with the instruments, the group and with each other. This was reflected in the overall progress of the group. At the time, the music therapist was attending the Northern version of the Institute of Group Analysis Certificate Course.

Clinical material

It is useful to work from the general to the specific. We will begin by looking at the overall changes in the group as it developed.

Sessions 1–5

The first sessions were highly structured. The music therapist led the sessions, introducing musical instruments to the group in a variety of exercises. The time was filled with playing and talking. The group looked to the therapists to take the initiative. The group spoke about how they felt generally and about life events.

Sessions 5–7

In sessions 5–7, the leadership of the music therapist was apparent still, but tended to be more relaxed. Musical interplay grew out of initial exercises or comments. The group members became more aware of the here-and-now, showing this through references to the instruments, their own playing and the playing of the others. They still appeared to look to the music therapist for instruction or ideas.

Sessions 8–10

Sessions 8 and 9 were conducted by the co-therapist alone. Although one member of the group made a clear reference to linking an event outside with a musical event in the previous group, it was not taken up. The therapist was clearly anxious. She had brought her own agenda to the group in the form of prepared exercises. In session 9 a change took place. One group member, who was about to leave the group, said that she wanted to look at issues of dependence and independence, thus taking the initiative for the first time. This might have been a reaction to the previous highly structured session. She continued to assert herself in session 10, saying she wanted to play by herself. She had to 'do it alone'. This was followed by silence.

Sessions 11–24

Sessions 11–18 revolved around silence: whether people liked it or not, whether they felt they could do anything about it, and whose job it was to break it. The group began to interact much more freely, allowing the therapists to gradually withdraw leadership. In session 19 the music therapist was sole conductor for the first time. A new dimension appeared in the group. Until that time, the group had looked at what people wanted to do or felt unable to do. Now the therapist suggested that the group might be avoiding things. Angry feelings began to emerge, not about people outside, but about the group itself, the therapists, and the fact that the group was soon to end. The group moved into the ending phase and the process of separation. There was considerable interaction between members and feelings about each other were expressed much more openly.

Overall, the group started out from a position where there were two sets of anxious people: the therapists and the others. In an attempt to alleviate anxiety, the therapists were very active, setting the agenda and taking responsibility for the 'success' of the session. The group responded passively. Around the mid-point of the group, there was a shift towards sharing responsibility. This was influenced by the leaving of a member and the co-therapist's handling of the group. As the group moved into its final stage, it became a working entity, with each person showing the capacity for spontaneity and responsibility.

One of the reasons that the group was able to progress in this manner was that the music therapist was able to analyse the sessions and modify her technique accordingly.

We will now discuss some individual sessions in more detail, as we did in supervision.

Session 2

In session 2 the group were invited to pick a musical instrument and play how they felt. Kate described her playing as 'determined but dithery' and went on to talk about an impending court appearance. Kathy played 'jangly and anxious'. Sheila talked of her anxiety about coming to the centre. Caroline played 'the butterflies in my stomach'. Mary described her playing as 'sad, confused and vulnerable'. There was a long, heavy silence. The music therapist suggested a group improvisation about the atmosphere in the room.

This is a typical music therapy situation in which we seem to concentrate too hard on being 'good' music therapists, mainly attempting to relieve our own anxiety. We use the exercises we have been taught or have thought up to create or follow a theme. This results in our placing too much emphasis on our feelings of responsibility to do something and to make the group do something. There is a danger that we will then fail to observe what is happening in the group. Did the group need to play about their feelings? Clearly each person could verbalise them adequately. If the therapist had been able to sit back and observe the group, she would probably have seen the anxiety just as quickly without going through the exercise. More importantly, she would have been able to wonder what the anxiety might be about.

At one level, there were two stories giving causes for anxiety: Kate's court appearance and Sheila's anxiety about coming to the centre. The therapist could have referred to Kate's situation and perhaps the group would have worked towards giving her support. However, this would have directed the attention inappropriately onto one member and her life outside the group. If the same story were examined as a metaphor, the therapist could have considered the possibility that something was being said about being judged, humiliated perhaps, and forced to do something unpleasant. This could be coupled with Sheila's anxiety about coming to the centre. Is she talking about agoraphobia in a global sense, or could she be saying something about her fear of coming to this particular group? Taking these possibilities together, along with the general feelings of anxiety, the therapist could have made an intervention which could have reached the immediate cause for anxiety in the here-and-now. It seems that the source of the fear was the instruments themselves and the playing of them. In our experience, improvisation groups often remind people of being in places where they will be exposed and judged. School and feelings of inadequacy or unmusicality or being told that one is completely hopeless, are often mentioned in the early stages of improvisation groups. Even when group members have been told by the music therapist that the purpose is not to learn about music, that there is no right or wrong in relation to the instruments, people still relate to the therapist as if they were a hostile and persecutory teacher. It is possible that the whole group shared such a fantasy, and that Kate and Sheila were expressing it for the others. If this were so, the anxiety is clearly about 'having' to play the instruments. The music is crucial, but it is the process of playing, not the product, and not the description of the product as in 'the butterflies in my stomach' that really matters.

The music therapist's next comment moves in the right direction but does not go far enough. She invites the group to play about the atmosphere in the room, focusing on the here-and-now. However, she avoids the real source of the anxiety, namely the instruments, and the possibility that the group see them as threatening, and her as potentially critical and persecutory. Had she been able to play with the various layers of meaning, she could have made a more specific intervention. Following the improvisation about the atmosphere, there was a movement towards playing in pairs. Kate and Kathy played together and Kathy expressed her desire to go to court with Kate to lend her support. Kate chose the metallaphone, often a gentle-sounding instrument, but played strongly. Kathy played the drum. At this point the therapist had several options. She could have pointed out the pairing, reminiscent of Bion's (1961) ideas, or she could have interpreted the choice of instruments. She could have wondered about the strong playing and what it meant for the players and the other members of the group: did it suggest confidence and assertiveness or did it feel aggressive? However, another group member, Caroline, was invited to play and the music therapist suggested that she join with her, reinforcing the pairing. It also led to an interesting reaction. Caroline finished by hitting the tambourine hard, bursting into tears and describing her mother as a 'flibberty-gibbet' who 'did as she wanted to do'. The music therapist was struggling with the issue of providing musical containment by using her skills as a musician rather than confronting the issue of the group being a container. Although she was trying to reduce Caroline's anxiety by offering to play with her, it seems likely that Caroline could not experience this as help but felt herself to be in the position of having to go through with playing for someone else's benefit. The session ended with a group improvisation which Kathy structured with a drum beat. The therapists noted that there was little interaction between people.

Session 13

Now we are going to describe session 13 when the group is joined by Brian. This time the music therapist took a more direct approach and simply asked how people felt about coming to the group. They were able to identify their anxiety about the presence of a new member, a man. They talked about their thoughts about what might happen in the next 12 weeks, Caroline mentioning also the fact of her pregnancy. There was talk of people making contact with their parents. The music therapist suggested making contact in the group through improvising around the theme of conversation.

At the level of objective reality, the group has to deal with accommodating a new member and a male member. It has to go through the process of finding out about him. Playing will take place again in front of someone who is unknown. Brian has got to find his way in a situation where the others are familiar with each other and with the instruments. He says he would like to make contact with his parents. Caroline is in the position of being separated from her mother and is also about to become a mother. At a transference level, the therapists could be the parents and Brian wishes to be recognised and accepted by them. Caroline may be offering herself as an intermediary. Alternatively, the group as a whole could be the desired mother, suggested in the wish to make contact. At an object-relations level, Brian could be asking to be welcomed into the family and nourished by the mother. The music therapist's response was good because it kept all these possibilities open for further development.

Another way of thinking about the situation is that the parents have had a new baby and the rest of the family have to accommodate him. Some interesting playing followed. Kate volunteered to play with Kelly. Mary and

Sheila paired and refused to play, Brian looked for a partner and Kate volunteered. Kate and Kelly's playing used the metallaphone and the tambourine, although Kate said that she really wanted to play the drum but was afraid that Kelly might not like it. Both played loudly but wished they'd played louder. Sheila and Mary disapproved, saying it was too loud. Brian expressed the wish to 'bash the cymbal', which he then did with Kate. Mary, Sheila and Caroline were clearly disgruntled, Sheila said that she'd rather talk than play. They refused to take part in the game, but eventually were persuaded to play in a threesome. The music had little interaction and was noted to have a grudging quality.

A group improvisation followed in which there was interaction. Brian and Kate shared instruments. The music therapist attempted to share the metallaphone with Sheila who immediately stopped playing. Afterwards Sheila and Mary said they felt 'drowned out'. Sheila left early.

The group seemed to be trying to deal with all the issues a new baby brings to a family: curiosity, a wish to protect and love but also rivalry, jealousy, envy and a sense of having been invaded or displaced. Some people wished to play together, others withdrew into angry silence. Contact was pushed away, especially when the music therapist, who had brought the newcomer into the group, tried to make it. Anger and jealousy continued to predominate for the next five sessions.

Session 19

In session 19 (the occasion of the music therapist being the sole conductor) Brian referred early in the group to his feeling that he had done something wrong the previous week. There was a long silence, broken by the therapist's observation that no-one had responded to Brian. Kelly and Sheila said that they had enjoyed the previous week because there had been a lot of talking and not much silence. This was followed by twenty minutes' silence. Kelly broke it saying that she felt anxious and angry. She wanted to 'bash the cymbal' but could not. Kathy and Sheila both agreed, saying that silence was pointless. They would be better off at home. The music therapist seemed to be under attack. She commented that the group seemed to see it as her responsibility to 'get things going'. Some discussion followed. Eventually Brian said that he would like to play and asked the others if they would join him. A group improvisation followed that was energetic and noisy. It seemed disjointed, lacking in rhythmic structure and with a sense of people playing for themselves. There was much laughing and smiling.

The therapist directed her next intervention at an objective reality level. She observed that there seemed to be a difference in the group between them

talking and playing. Some interesting reflection followed. Brian acknowledged feeling less inhibited when playing. Kelly felt she could exercise her
power when playing in a way that she could not when talking. Kathy said
that she felt determined when playing and needed to take this feeling away
with her. Here we have a group where the music therapist has moved
completely away from exercises. She is able to contain her anxiety and
tolerate the silence, even when it feels hostile. Her interventions allow the
group to take responsibility, risks and to play with their thoughts and each
other. Paradoxically, as she moves away from a musical agenda and into an
analytic stance, the group concentrate on the relevance of the instruments.
So, what is the role of the music and the instruments? The music was not
analysed in any depth. The sessions were not recorded, so the supervisor had
no idea of the sounds other than verbal descriptions. But the very existence
of the instruments had an enormous effect on the group. They inevitably
produced feelings.

No-one can be sure what these feelings will be, but we suggest that the
most predominant ones initially are anxiety, apprehension and feelings of
being exposed to scrutiny and criticism. There is, therefore, a fear of
embarrassment and humiliation. The instruments themselves are not bad but
the therapists and the other members of the group are potentially critical
and hostile. As the group develops, the instruments themselves may be
ascribed characteristics. Drums or cymbals may be felt to be frightening and
aggressive; the autoharp may be soothing or nurturing. Sometimes these
thoughts are not voiced but it will be obvious that certain people are
favouring or avoiding certain instruments. Sometimes, thoughts are voiced.
If an instrument is being avoided by one person, it may be played by another
as a deliberate attack, or avoided by the group as a whole, in order to avoid
upsetting someone. If an instrument is favoured, it may have to be shared or
else one person may deprive another.

Session 20

In session 20 the group had really begun to look at the effects of the music.
As the group had been talking about their difficulties in responding with
words, an improvisation was suggested around the theme of 'responses'. It
was described as a very gentle, tentative piece of music with group members
picking up on each other's playing. Kathy stopped playing, very upset. She
said the music reminded her of her father and went on to talk at length about
her relationship with him. He infuriated her because he did not respond to
her but just sat in his chair looking placid, and smiling. Kathy could not
understand how she could be angry with someone so nice but felt that he

did not really see her, somehow. The music had sounded as though there was nothing there. She had got in touch with her longing for contact and acknowledgement. She was asked what she needed from the group and she replied that she wanted to play. At this point the group played loudly and boisterously, although Mary and Sheila did not play. Sheila felt frightened by the loudness, so much so that she seemed to be paralysed. She had wanted to run out of the room but could not. She felt separated from the group and unable to do anything about it. Mary said she would not have been heard, even if she had joined in. This time the music therapist pitched her intervention at the musical level, which, in improvisation groups has to be added to those described by Foulkes (1948). She suggested that it might be possible to play in a way which included everyone. Crucially, she did not suggest how, but the group found a solution. They developed a strong rhythm, giving structure and security to their playing. Caroline added a strong melodic line on the xylophone.

Conclusion

'Everything depends on whether we find the best perspective, the most adequate point of view, in approaching a disturbance. This includes that we concentrate on the right sector, make the right cut out of the whole. Sometimes one sees more under a microscope, another time with the naked eye. If we know the problem already, this is easy enough. But if we don't know, we cannot find out before we find the correct approach, we cannot get the right answers before we ask the right questions... (At times) it is best to stand back and look afresh with the naked eye on the totality of the situation, with a mind keen to observe and as free from prejudice as we can possibly muster.' (Foulkes 1948, p.2)

Throughout this chapter we have been playing with ideas, using a basic structure set out by Foulkes. This process, which makes groups and group work so fascinating, involves improvising in one's head, juggling with ideas and feelings and trying out silent interventions. Groups and improvisation are made for each other.

References

Bion, W.R. (1961) 'Group Dynamics', in *Experiences in Groups.* London: Tavistock Publications, pp. 141–191.

Foulkes, S.H. (1948) *Introduction to Group-Analytic Psychotherapy.* Reprinted 1983, London: Karnac Ltd.

CHAPTER 9

Music Therapy
A Methodological Approach in the Mental Health Field

Gianluigi di Franco
Italy

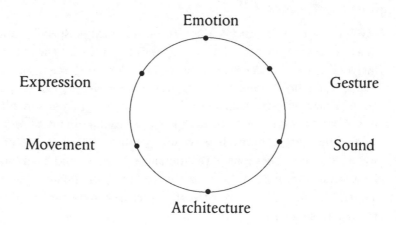

Figure 9.1

Emotion like gesture – gesture like sound – sound like word – architecture like movement – movement like expression – expression like emotion.

Let's start with the term 'music therapy' which is composed of two terms: music and therapy. Music is a sound language, more or less developed as a non-verbal code which is a 'form' of expression and therefore a 'form' of communication which has been expressed by the human being over time. It has acquired different characteristics according to the historical moment, depending on the ethnic context and the emotional state of the one who produces it. Therapy, from the Greek word 'θεράπεία', has the original meaning of 'care', possibly even 'slavery' and 'respect towards parents and gods' – hence the three-dimensional nature of its meaning which comes to be placed within a structure where the care is like the supporter of the superiors. What is inherent in this is the ambivalence between the 'popular' and the 'supernatural' magic. The combination of these two terms forms that word very often used in music therapy contexts and very often misused in 'popular' contexts, perhaps just getting that 'ambivalence' which is contained in the words 'music therapy', that is: (a) music for the therapy, (b) music as a therapy.

The specific point to stress here is the idea that music can be used as a more or less structured language to establish better relations through communication, or with the aim of increasing the ability to communicate of an individual who does not suffer from a definite pathology. At the same time, music may be used in a specific situation where there is an evident pathology in which the communication process is damaged, and one is trying to repair such a fault within a more global therapeutic project to which the individual is entrusted.

I define this premise in order to stress in a very clear way the element of communication which is peculiar to my approach in music therapy. In my opinion, it is always possible to start from the individual with all his bio-affective components, from an axis formed by Expression – Creativity – Communication, within which an expressive capacity is acknowledged in the individual, meaning by this a 'drawing out' of something which results from a necessity, a bio-affective need. Within the same framework the therapist is recognised, and is able to intervene on the level of the basic material, and the expressive aspect, moulding it, articulating it, giving it a 'form'. I call all this an 'elaboration – creative process', always within the above framework, where the individual is endowed with a communication potential. This is the need which gives rise to the possibility of an expression outside this need, which then contains the characteristics peculiar to the individual (elaboration), with the aim of communicating something – an object from the inside to the outside.

I believe that for the most part the realities evaluated as 'pathological' on the level of communication by psychopathology or by the different clinical branches are contained within this framework. There can be a fluent evolution among the three sections of the process, but there can be cruxes, blocks between expression and creativity, or between creativity and communication. What is really important is to understand how the individual, in the journey from his interior ambiance towards the outside, sets himself in this framework. In this regard, sound, in it primordial sense, and music as a more complex language, have a therapeutic potential; but why? Many have offered different answers to the question. I believe that a very important issue to take into account is the phase of pregnancy and therefore the process of birth.

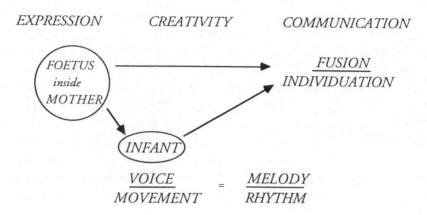

Figure 9.2

A useful concept in this context is that of the relationship between the concept of fusion and that of individualisation. Fusion, in dynamic psychology, is understood as a moment without a space-time definition, characterised by the vanishing or the non-existence of a definite self within an environment 'protected' from a gestalt and affective point of view – by definition preserving the individual from the dangers of the outside environment. Therefore, a dimension of fusion can be seen as a defense mechanism, one of the aspects of a regressive phase, or it can be regarded as the condition in which the embryo evolves during the different phases of pregnancy. At that time the foetus is in an environment of fusion by definition: it is protected by a circular membrane which contains it and feeds it, while through the same membrane it establishes a relation with the mother.

Figure 9.2 shows that, when the foetus is born, it lives for the first time the individualisation as a process which will shape its identity throughout its life. The relationship between the tendency towards fusion and the one towards individualisation will become a 'playing', sometimes a 'dramatic playing', which will determine the effort of balancing these two opposite variables. During birth the very first moment of individualisation is lived as a trauma, a primary trauma where the foetus, now becoming a baby, for the first time does not have any more the 'containment', or 'protection' he had when he was in the maternal womb where communication occurred through filtering membranes. Therefore, at birth, on a communication level, there is the need to express the whole affective sense resulting from this trauma to the external world. Almost always this consciousness is characterised by the use of the voice, which screams to the world its own 'tragedy', without any possibility of being wrong and, at the same time, the first moment of being an individual. The use of movement appears simultaneously or immediately afterwards. If we take into account these two means of expression, voice and movement, we can associate them in music with melody and rhythm. It is not by chance that they appear as fundamental with a 'need' and therefore where incisiveness and immediacy in conveying the emotional information are necessary. There are points here which are useful for us to apply in music therapy.

First, to understand that therapy developed through a sound medium has to include vocal intervention at a vocal level, as the voice is always involved at the first moment of the expressive and, therefore, communicative life of each of us. Obviously, if it is not so, or the cases are very few, we should wonder why. Surely we will find out that there is something wrong which will definitely influence the individual's communication peculiarities. As for the way in which such therapy has to be dynamically defined, it depends on the different problems we have to face. It happens very often that if there is a problem the voice will be the last element to be used as it is the most 'dangerous' expressive channel, which will return us to the original problem. There are many music therapists who have on the one hand a great fluency in communicating through 'instruments' but on the other hand have a great difficulty, a great 'resistance' to expressing themselves through the use of their voices.

In order to focus on the problem of mental health, which copes with the development of relationships and therefore of communication, and to stress particularly the problem of psychosis, I would like to make some points in order to explain better how music, in my opinion, can be set into a process which can become 'therapeutic'. First of all the contract: a psychotic patient, by definition, is not aware of his condition; therefore the therapeutic contract has to pursue strategies which are different from the ones applied to a patient who is aware of his being in a state of malaise and goes to a therapist and asks for help. This is not the case with psychotic patients, both those who are in institutional facilities and those who are not. The issue with them is to move closer to them by offering a series of stimulations on a sound level to understand how they react to sound and then try to define a therapeutic contract in close collaboration with any relatives.

Second, the Group can be considered as a way to face the anguish resulting from 'nothingness', the frustration linked to the task the music therapist is often submitted to. For the reasons mentioned above it is advisable that the patient, after a series of individual sessions, especially if he is particularly 'negative' or 'catatonic', is included in group therapy. Therefore I suggest a music therapy micro-unit composed of patients in a group or even music therapists in a group consisting of:

- a music therapist who acts as a 'container', having the function of 'holding', of 'maternage', who fixes the limits of the 'setting', who contains the phenomena of regression which occur during the sound relation, and who intervenes on a sound level without leaving apart the affective level which comes to be established when using the space of therapy as a space of a transitional playing (see Winnicott 1974).

- a co-therapist who plays the role of a 'replayer', and tries to use the sounds produced by the patients, making the sounds pass through him, and then giving them back either through an imitative process or a real sound dialogue. The choice depends on the degree of the transferencial investment the patients have worked out towards the therapists. Specifically, the co-therapist evaluates:

  ° the position of the bodies in relation to the instruments;

  ° the choice of the instruments and the meaning of such a choice;

  ° the musical production;

  ° the ways of approaching the instruments;

  ° the emotional attitude behind the musical performance;

  ° the interaction between rhythm and melody;

  ° the capacity to listen to themselves and to others;

  ° the capacity to expand and contract the musical phrase.

- an observer who has the function of absorbing, which is defined as a 'sponge' function. He collects the data and follows the dynamic evolution of the group, offering more neutral elements to the micro-unit, which will then work out an homogenous protocol, session by session.

To sum up: three operators are necessary with complementary functions of 'holding', 'replaying' and 'memorising', who can cope with and manage in a better way the communication level peculiar to the psychosis. Clinical examples of this process are given in a paper by di Franco *et al.* (1993).

In my professional experience I have known very few therapists able to manage therapy with a psychotic patient by themselves. It is possible to count them on the fingers of one hand: Buddha, Jesus Christ and maybe Mohammed! A psychotic is expressing a reality of defence from an unbearable suffering; a bomb which bursts out and breaks into a thousand small pieces. Is this what in psychiatry is called a 'psychotic shattering'? I do not know but, as a music therapist who has been working for more than fifteen years with psychotic patients using music therapy, I know that these patients have a communication level very different from the one we define 'logical'.

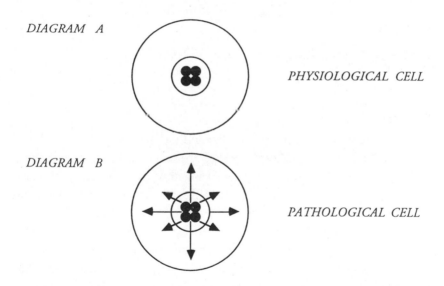

DIAGRAM A

PHYSIOLOGICAL CELL

DIAGRAM B

PATHOLOGICAL CELL

Figure 9.3

Figure 9.3 shows a cellular form which in diagram A has its physiological structure (a membrane, cytoplasm and a nucleus with its sub-nuclei), while in diagram B it has a pathological structure where the sub-nuclei are not contained any more by the nuclear membrane. If we use the structure of the

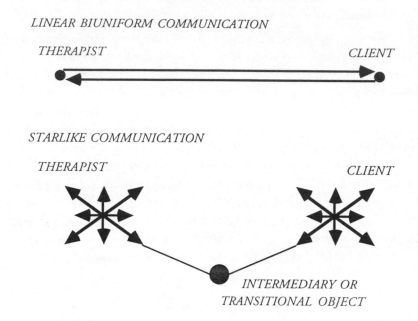

Figure 9.4: Different Communication Levels in the Music Therapy Setting

cells as described above and apply it, metaphorically, to 'psychosis', with regard to its communication aspects, we could say that diagram A stands for the functional, physiological settlement of the individual's affective sphere, while diagram B shows a centrifugal movement of the sub-nuclei due to a break in the membrane because of a biochemical trauma, or to problems occurring during its making. In the former case 'communication' will more easily follow its homogeneous '"logical" straightforwardness'. In the latter case it will be 'shattered' as in the 'psychotic shattering' which reveals itself mainly through the disassociation of ideas as one of its external communication symptoms. I define this second possibility as a 'star-like communication' (see Figure 9.4).

On the level of communication through sound, we can say that through the establishment of a therapeutic relationship with psychotic patients in music therapy, a star-like communication is established. The therapist must necessarily be well trained in breaking down his more structured 'musical' language to get into the meshes of the psychotic disruption in order to reach it, even with just a fragment. This can happen by means of an object-instrument which has been called by Altshuler (1943) and then by Benenzon (1983) 'intermediary object'. I would call it, following Winnicott (1974), 'transitional object', meaning by that a concrete element on which the patient can mediate his desire to communicate. He can transfer his affective energy on it and this device can function as a 'bridge' with the therapist, to establish a better relationship with him. The therapist becomes the 'transitional area' within which the 'music therapy process' can develop in an evolutionary way. Under such circumstances the music therapy process will contemplate the following phases on the part of the music therapist:

(1) Listening

(2) Filtering the listening through himself in order to reach a fragment

(3) Reply through imitation

(4) Reply through a sound dialogue

and the following phases on the side of the patient:

(1) Production

(2) Listening to the imitative reply of the therapist

(3) Listening to the overall response of the therapist.

This process needs an evolution within which the patient can go back to the 'primary trauma', passing through a regressive phase. After that, we have to verify if it is possible, using the sound, to re-establish a more integrated orientation on the level of communication, that is a gradual change to a 'linear bi-uniform communication'. Also, as far as the patient's manual activity, his desire to 'touch', is concerned, I think it is a practical element to use in music therapy, especially with psychotic patients.

Conclusion

I have experimented with this process during the years of my clinical work, from 1978 till 1983, in the psychiatric hospital, Leonardo Bianchi in Naples and during my work as a supervisor of the clinical activities of music therapy micro-units in Mental Health Services in Naples. It is not just as a result of my own experiences that I am convinced of the process I have just described, as a passage from *Analysis of schizophrenia and the psychoanalytical method* by Bion (1979) enlightened me:

> 'A schizophrenic uses language for three aims: as a way of acting, as a form of communication, as a method to think. In circumstances under which another patient would realise you are asking him to

reflect, the schizophrenic patient prefers to act in most cases. For instance: to understand a situation in which there is someone who is playing the piano, he will feel the need of touching and exploring the musical instrument.'

Let us consider again the original concept at the beginning of this chapter. In the mists of time, there was a widespread myth according to which a man called Orpheus had the power to enchant a woman called Euridice and make her fall in love, using the sound of his Cithar. Nowadays we often do not find the easiest way to express things, whereas, because the way through music is the nearest to the truth, we would, therefore, pay a very high price if we had to acknowledge or even more to tell this same truth. Maybe the reason for this is that the world is soaked by false truths, among which we have to find our way, so the human mind elaborates and builds up a series of structures suitable for the defence of this truth. In so doing we run the risk of losing the meaning and the contact, as any loss of contact allows us to avoid the danger of getting in touch with the underlying emotion. However, sound does not offer us any possibility of cheating. When a man finds his own sound inside himself, he cannot but tell it to the world, without ever getting tired of it. This sound is like the cry of joy when you feel very well; it is like the cry of sorrow when you feel very bad; it is like the cry you let out that day, that year when you were born.

References

Altshuler (1943) *Four Year's Experience with Music as a Therapeutic Agent at Eloise Hospital, Michigan Detroit.* Washington, D.C.: The American Psychiatric Association.

Anzieu, D. (1979) *Il Gruppo e L'Inconscio.* Rome: Borla.

Benenzon, R.O. (1983) *Manuale di Musicoterapia.* Rome: Borla.

Bion, W.R. (1979) *Analisi degli Schizophrenia e Metodo Psicoanalitico.* Rome: Armando.

di Franco, G. (1990) *Musicoterapia: Sogno.* Mito: Realta Scientifica Editnews.

di Franco, G., Facchini, D. and Laccetti, F. (1992) 'Musicoterapia per la Psichosi: Un modello per la salute mentale', *Foné,* No 4. Naples: Editnews.

di Franco, G. and de Simone, A. (1983) 'Musicoterapia in una Istituzione Psichiatrica: Evoluzione, Concettualizzazione e Prospettive', in the review *L'Ospedale Psichiatrico.* Naples: Editnews.

Winnicott, D. (1974) *Gioco e Reacta.* Rome: Armando.

CHAPTER 10

Opening Doors
The Effects of Music Therapy with People Who Have Severe Learning Difficulties and Display Challenging Behaviour

Fiona Ritchie
United Kingdom

Introduction

Clients with challenging behaviour are intriguing and amazing. They demonstrate an incredible enthusiasm to survive, a strength of character and a relentless need to be taken seriously. It is unfortunate that the manifestation of this need may be seen as being negative and destructive behaviour: for example, 'attention seeking', 'awkward', 'spiteful' or 'selfish'. Staff deal with such behaviours in many ways: some ignore it, in the hope that it will go away; others divert and distract the attention of the client. They may be verbally abusive, show alternative aggression or physically restrain clients. Within music therapy sessions, alternative strategies are used to deal with such behaviours. Signals from the client are watched for and taken seriously.

Using two short case studies I will illustrate the importance of individual music therapy to clients who have severe learning difficulties and display challenging behaviours and who live in an institutionalised setting. The approach used is eclectic and is informed by humanistic and psychodynamic schools.

Background

The old Victorian hospital was originally built for use as an orphanage. The large grounds are situated in a small rural area, just outside Birmingham. This was home to some 600 clients. However, in line with community policy, many clients have been resettled to their place of origin and it now houses approximately 200 people. Half of the people will be resettled into the community, while the other 100 will move to purpose-built bungalows within the hospital grounds. Buildings now stand empty.

Day services take place in the hospital grounds, and include swimming, art, drama therapy, music therapy, physiotherapy and horticulture.

People who have severe learning difficulties and display challenging behaviour receive few other services, apart from nursing care. The majority have spent most of their time on the ward with little stimulation, apart from (simultaneous) television and radio.

The most important factor to me as a music therapist is to feel empathy towards the client. This is at the core of my work; without it the sessions become superficial. My task is to find out why people do certain things, what it means to them and, through understanding, build a relationship of trust, security and friendship. This, however, takes many years and does not always result in significant changes in clients' external behaviours; however, internally there can be much movement.

John – case study 1

Background

John is 41 years old and lives in an all male ward. He has lived in a variety of wards in the hospital for 34 years.

John was delivered normally. At three months old he developed severe epilepsy which could not be controlled until he was three years old. He still has occasional severe attacks which are brought under control by drugs. As a difficult baby John would be taken to the hospital for respite care. He was admitted to the institution full-time at the age of six, never having received formal schooling.

John has no speech but makes a variety of vocal sounds, the prime one being a loud, raucous scream. He is small in height and of normal weight. He has short dark hair and hazel eyes. He often has cuts and scratches on his face. He spends long periods naked and often pulls his hair out and eats it. As a result, his head is sometimes shaven to prevent him from choking. He eats cigarette ends.

First impressions

When I first met John he was living in a small locked ward. The television set, which was attached to the wall, was the only visible sign of homeliness. The room was depersonalised. John was brought to my attention by his excruciatingly loud, gruff, pitched scream. I turned to the sound and saw him crouched naked in a corner. His head was shaved and his body was covered with scabs which he had scratched until they bled. He seemed like a frightened, pathetic baby clutching himself to keep himself together. He had built a wall of sound to keep people out. I introduced myself to him and he immediately began to scream louder. He cupped his left hand over his left ear and began waving his clenched right hand with his arm outstretched. His right leg jerked and kicked. I backed off, shocked and not sure what to do.

Many people must have encountered John with similar shocked expressions. What effect must this have had on him? Although not quite knowing how I could work with this gentleman, I decided to give him one hour per week individual music therapy.

The first year of therapy

The first year was a difficult time for both of us. For John the music therapy was an alien experience to him. Perhaps it terrified him. The sessions took on a pattern very quickly, to provide security. This pattern lasted for approximately one year.

John would be brought into the music therapy room by me and an assistant. He would be screaming when we went to collect him for the bus and continued screaming until we arrived at the therapy room. I would unstrap him from the wheelchair. He would immediately jump out and undress, struggling to take his clothes off as fast as possible. Sometimes he managed to undress while I escorted him to the music therapy room. He would fling his clothes across the room – still screaming – and sit in the corner, cupping one hand over his ear and stretching out the other arm, clenching his fist and making frenzied movements. His body was positioned to face me, but at first he did not allow eye contact. I felt that his frenzied movements and screaming were directed at me, in an attacking fashion. Perhaps he was scared because I had brought him to an alien environment. What was I going to do to him and what right did I have to take him away from what he knew? I never felt physically threatened by him, but did feel emotionally attacked. I was drained, exhausted and void of feeling at the end of most sessions. It was like being stripped of my own personality, a frightening experience that perhaps John was projecting on to me. He showed me this consistently through externalisation: physically undressing at the start of each session.

If I tried to move towards him, he would stand up and move to the other corner of the room. I felt that it was important for John to have his own time, and freedom to express what he wanted to express. I would not push him into an avenue of my choosing. It was my job to stay with him, to provide a facilitating environment. I hoped he would eventually come to me. Near the end of each session I would count down the final five minutes to prepare for the end. When the session finished, I would encourage him to put his clothes on. He would refuse to do this, grab the clothes from me, scream at me, and fling them across the room. I would try and put on him each item of clothing, but he would have nothing to do with me or the clothes.

I once tried for two and a half hours to get him to put his clothes on and I failed miserably. After telephoning the ward staff for help, a male nurse arrived and in one minute had dressed John.

This pattern continued for a year. I decided to seek help and I went for supervision from a psychoanalytic psychotherapist. She encouraged me to talk more to John. When he screamed I reflected musically the feelings behind the screaming and also verbally told him how it made me feel. I said I was trying to understand his screams: that I wanted to acknowledge his despair, but sometimes it was difficult to know what to do or say.

Slowly the sessions began to change. John's screaming did not last the whole hour. He would scream profusely at first, then tail off into a silence which lasted a few seconds before starting again. The screaming was no longer constant and unchanging; he used it in different ways. His silence increased the impact of his screaming; when he began again the volume would be quieter, which gave him an opportunity to listen to his sounds and alter them if he wished.

Eighteen months into the sessions, John was able to remain quiet for long periods of the time. When he was quiet, I improvised music. I felt he wanted to hear soothing music. He would often crouch in a foetal position and put his hand over his head and watch me while he listened to the music I was playing – quiet, long, serene chords in the base register. They had a dreamlike quality. Perhaps this was exploring another side of John. Often he would move nearer. Once he moved right up to the piano and put his head underneath it, as though listening to the very essence of the sound.

During the later part of the eighteen months, dressing John ceased to be an issue. His doors were beginning to open and he was beginning to trust me. He even initiated this process and occasionally took all his clothes off at the beginning and immediately put them back on.

Our relationship began to develop rapidly and I felt that we were becoming much closer. I would go to collect him on the ward; he would immediately stand up and pull me towards the door. This was important for the ward staff to see. They knew he was enjoying the sessions and wanted to leave the ward. At this point I also liaised with his keyworker and explained why I was doing music therapy with John. I showed a video of a session and explained what I was doing. They keyworker made jokes about it, but did have one positive thing to say: John was listening to the music. It had gained his attention, which the keyworker felt was unusual.

Each time I collected John I would acknowledge the staff. It was important to build a relationship with them to minimise feelings of envy, mistrust and overprotectiveness that they might have had towards my work with John. In time the staff began to prepare John for my arrival. They did not subject him to ridicule as often when I was there, and acknowledged that he recognised me and was capable of building relationships.

Two and a half years

John was responding positively to the sessions but still received no other service. I decided to work with him twice a week. During this period there was one session which was, I feel, the turning point in our relationship.

John had managed to abscond from the ward into a fenced off part of the garden. He had climbed up the fence, without any clothes on, and had fallen over the other side onto hard ground. When I went to collect him I was not told about the incident, but I immediately saw that John was in a lot of pain. His back was bruised and he was limping. He was very distressed and screamed more than he had done for several months. He took my hand and pulled me towards the door: his actions showed me he wanted to go. We struggled to the bus. Sitting seemed painful for him. We got out of the bus and he immediately took his clothes off in the middle of the car park. My first reaction was to get him inside. It was cold and I did not want people staring at him.

Eventually, with help, I got him indoors and took him to the toilet. When he went into the toilet he was faced with a full-length mirror. He began to scream irritably. He scratched the sores on his body and they bled profusely. He then tried to cover the mirror by taking boxes from the floor and stacking them against the mirror. I was astonished. This was a shocking experience for John. He was in a vulnerable state and seeing himself naked in a mirror was too much for him to cope with. The frantic actions of trying to cover the mirror, trying to make things safe, failed: he still saw himself. He again aggressively scratched his body, making himself bleed further. He smeared the blood on the mirror. It was at this point he seemed to plead with me to help him to contain his anguish.

I felt powerless. What can you say to someone who has just realised what they look like and how other people view them? I sat close to him and held his hand. He showed no resistance. I tried to talk to him, saying that it must be a shocking experience, but that people really did care about him. Feeble words for such a distraught man, but I hoped that my being there and feeling the pain with him would be enough to help him keep himself together.

After this harrowing session, our relationship changed. He would move close to me and sit by me, listening intently without screaming. Perhaps he realised that, if he wanted to change and to enjoy people's companionship, he would have to open a few more doors. Only he could do this for himself. He also had to be prepared for the consequences once the doors were open. He showed vulnerability which before he had kept locked away. Screaming had been his defence. A rather more painful existence might confront John as he began to care about himself and others around him.

John became exceptionally sensitive. He would sit very close to me, watching me play. My music took on a different quality: rather than harsh, atonal, rhythmic sounds which were quite disjointed, the music was melodic with harmonic progressions which lingered before they resolved. Perhaps a more positive side of John was showing. Maybe he was starting to feel good about himself and this was reflected in my clinical improvisations.

I began to introduce John to other people within the hospital. I was concerned that after three and a half years the dependency for both of us was becoming too great. I wanted John to build relationships with other people. At first he was not ready to take this on board.

I introduced him to the swimming teacher and helped them to become acquainted with each other. During the first four sessions I was careful not to become involved, but sat at the edge of the pool watching, to give him reassurance. The first session was interesting: I felt proud watching John as he walked round the pool. He seemed to be enjoying himself and was able to accept other people around him. I was also feeling frustrated. It had taken me three years to form a relationship with him, but he was allowing somebody else to do it in a matter of minutes. Of course, it showed how confident he felt at being able to cope with new people. He now goes swimming regularly. I also integrated him into other hospital day services and helped him join an individual art session.

Ending

Soon after this introduction of John to other people and services, my job changed. I could have continued working with John but after much thought decided not to. I had worked intensively with him for four years. He had made other friends and I felt it was time that we both let go. I slowly stopped the sessions while making sure that there were other services for him to join. He now goes to art, swimming, a multi-sensory area and is included in small excursions outside the hospital. I still see him occasionally and he looks well and contented. When I see him with other people I do feel jealous – the little baby with whom I used to work has now grown up and is capable of building other relationships. He is an independent person.

Having worked so closely with John and seen the opportunities that opened up for him, I decided to analyse in greater detail the processes of music therapy with clients who have similar difficulties. I began a research project to formalise the changes people show during music therapy sessions.

Jane – case study 2

Background

Jane is 33 years old. She lives in a mixed sex, single storey ward which houses people with severe learning and physical disabilities. She has lived in the hospital for 24 years. She was admitted at the age of nine because she was becoming too difficult to manage at home. There is little recorded concerning her early years of life.

She is 4ft 3in in height with short blond hair and blue eyes. She has Downs Syndrome and has severe challenging behaviour. Jane has no speech but continually makes 'raspberry' sounds. She avoids contact with people and if peers or staff go towards her she will viciously scratch and spit, making people wary of getting too close to her. Her spitting must have taken many years to perfect – she has an excellent aim, nearly always making a direct hit on your face. She is viewed as having a stubborn nature and will smear faeces on the wall on the ward if she becomes distressed.

When I first began to work with her she was receiving no day service and spent the majority of her time crouching in a corner or running up and down the ward. Jane presented a threat to her peers with physical disability. She has pulled people out of their wheelchairs, broken people's arms and one gentleman had his head split open in a ferocious assault by her.

First impressions

During the first visit the television and radio were on loudly. This was not uncommon, but here there was a difference; despite the noise, I felt a deadness of sound. Clients sat motionless and lifeless around the television, of which they took no notice.

Jane had been pointed out to me when I first started working at the hospital; 'one to be avoided' I think the expression was. I went to look for her. I walked into the dining area, a sparsely decorated room with tables, chairs, curtains hanging off the rail and one picture, which was so high up it could not be seen. This room was regarded as Jane's room, she spent most of her time here. Anything ornamental had been ripped, flung or broken by Jane, hence the sparseness.

My eyes caught sight of a small figure crouched in the corner of the room. She was the only person there. I stayed where I was and introduced myself. She could have been an attractive lady but had rather a haggled appearance; her clothes were ripped and did not sit properly on her, her blond hair was straggly and looked as if it had never been combed; she had scratches on her face and arms. Jane looked at me with piercing blue eyes and crinkled up her face. Still squatting she thrashed her head and upper body from side to side in a violent manner. I then understood why her hair looked as it did. Suddenly she stood up. This tiny lady ran towards me. I stood still, not quite knowing what this meant and put my hand out to greet her. This was obviously the wrong interpretation, she grabbed my arm and began to dig her nails into my skin. As she dug them in, she scraped them along my arm onto my hand. With a pained expression, I bent down to try and release her hand. With lightening speed she gripped onto the top of my blouse and pulled me down, trying to rip it.

Strangely, I did not yell out for assistance. I was so taken aback, I was speechless. A nurse saw what was happening and came to help me; she prized Jane's hands off me and pulled her away from me. She shouted at her and said to me, 'This is Jane!'. As I left, rather shaken, I turned round to see Jane crouched in a corner, with a smile lighting up her face. She had achieved what she had set out to do.

I made arrangements for music therapy sessions to be available twice weekly for half an hour. A psychology assistant, Ruth, had observed Jane in her home environment, using the Julie Wilkinson challenging behaviour scale (1989), to give a taxonomy of her behaviours. Ruth was also at hand during the first few sessions in case of emergencies.

Music therapy sessions

I collected Jane from the ward for the first session. A member of staff put her coat on and sat her in a wheelchair. Although she was fully mobile, she would not walk out of the ward. She always went by wheelchair and expected to be taken and brought back in this fashion. If anything different was offered, Jane would scratch and spit at you before going back to the dining room. I hoped that when we knew each other better she would walk with me.

During the first few sessions a pattern developed. Immediately inside the music room Jane would jump out of the wheelchair and run across the room. She would sit on the carpet, in a lotus position, by the window. She would face the piano, suitably distanced from it and the rest of the instruments. Jane started the sessions like this every time. (Out of the 38 sessions we have had so far, she has only deviated from this pattern twice.)

At this time Jane showed no interest in playing any of the percussion instruments and I felt no desire to hand them to her. I was very wary of her. Instead, I placed them on the floor near to her, trying not to make her feel pressured but, at the same time, trying to show her they were there if she wanted them. I sat at a distance from her and showed her different instruments, watching her facial and body gestures for any clues as to how she was feeling. What I got was an almost continual 'blowing' sound. Her usual trick was to blow 'raspberries' loudly, and then spit in your face. If I sat anywhere near her she would do this, aiming rather expertly for my glasses. If I sat near the piano and did not look at her, she would not spit. However, as soon as I lifted my head she would be watching and immediately spit and blow raspberries. This felt like a 'peek-a-boo' game with a different meaning. I constantly talked to Jane about my feelings about this behaviour. I stated that I did not enjoy this game and I felt she was using it to keep me away from her. Perhaps she had felt unheard and 'spat on' in her life?

For the half hour Jane would remain in the same position: isolated, blocking off my presence and taking no notice of her environment. The main movements were her spitting, blowing raspberries and thrashing her head and upper body from side to side.

My clinical improvisations were quiet but did not have a calming feel to them. They were highly charged and full of emotion, with many changing harmonic structures. I tried not to look at Jane until I felt that she could cope with the directness eye contact gives. I felt eye contact was too frightening for her and should not be pushed. Many things can be shown in eyes – perhaps she was not ready for this emotional communication.

During one early session, as I played the piano in a highly charged manner, I felt a deep sadness overwhelm me. I looked up and found Jane silently crying. I felt she knew I was looking at her but she lowered her head and clasped her hands over her eyes. I continued to play because I felt I had to support her musically. She was not ready for me to get physically close to her and if I had stopped this would have destroyed the closeness we both felt. The session ended without a word but with a much deeper feeling between us. Jane lifted her head and looked at me with tear-stained eyes; she did not spit at me.

Jane and I have had 39 sessions together. I am amazed at the speed things have happened, and the trust Jane now has in me. I am used to waiting longer. As soon as she sees me on the ward, she runs towards me, takes my hand and drags me to the wheelchair. Staff on the ward feel she knows when I am due to collect her and that she is waiting for me. They commented that she is always desperate to go out with me – even when she is ill.

She still has her 'space' in the music room but now spontaneously stands up and explores it. She will direct me by taking my hand and guiding me to her wheelchair if she wants to go, or other instruments in the room. She has played instruments – mainly the lyre, which she strums with great precision and delicacy. This is a completely different side of Jane from the one I see on the ward. We have, however, had some very difficult sessions. At times she has been aggressive towards me and Ruth, the psychology assistant, who sometimes videoed sessions. However, I do feel I can understand why she has been aggressive for the majority of times.

One such instance was in the early stages of therapy. I was beginning to sit nearer to her and to play different instruments. I was also making more eye contact with her. Looking back on the situation, I feel I was demanding too much of her. She seemed to be opening up to me quickly and I did not take as much time as I should have. I sat closer and closer to her and rolled the drum beater towards her. When I did this the second time she jumped up and began to scratch my neck. She was manically laughing and she then burst into tears. She was changeable and quite out of control. After prising her off me, I sat a long distance away from her as I felt she would have done it again had I stayed there. After this I gave her more space and allowed her to direct the session. Perhaps she felt I was not listening to her and was too interested in external results, rather than giving her the time she needed.

I also used to have Ruth video every sixth session for my research purposes. At the beginning Jane did not seem to mind. I explained why Ruth was there and what I was going to do with the video. Gradually, as our relationship was developing and Jane was beginning to show more intimate and deep feelings, she seemed more uneasy about Ruth being in the room. I wish I had picked up Jane's signals earlier. Instead, I waited until she could not take any more. The last time Ruth videoed, Jane was distressed. She kept looking at me and Ruth, she tried to scratch me; I said I did not understand why she seemed upset. She then very plainly showed me.

She ran towards Ruth, jumped on her and began to pull her towards the floor. Ruth put the camera down and tried to release Jane. Jane started to laugh and cry manically. I held her hand tight and told Ruth to leave and to take the camera. I no longer video her sessions and have no intention of doing this again. My research had been intruding into my work and I was not aware that this had been happening. Jane was telling me our sessions were private and that they had to remain so in order to keep her trust. I was to keep the sessions confidential and closed to outside people. I was moved by this session, angry at my stupidity, and sad for Ruth. Worst of all, I was convinced that Jane would not trust me for some time; I had done irreparable damage to our relationship. However, Jane quickly forgave me and we are now stronger for having understood each other – I learn many things from my clients!

It is still early days for Jane and me. I wonder how she will structure and guide the sessions. I do know that her aggressive outbursts have diminished. She has virtually stopped spitting and blowing 'raspberry' sounds. She is deeply affected by my music and in turn I am deeply affected by her presence.

Discussion

I have tried to show the benefits of a humanistic and psychodynamic approach to music therapy for people with severe learning difficulties who display challenging behaviour. By valuing the client's actions and non-verbal communications through interpreting them, musically or verbally, I believe that this client group can be given the chance to change their institutionalised way of living and become more spontaneous and free thinking people.

I often ask myself what is special about music therapy. Is it the clinical improvisation, the therapist, or the building of a relationship that makes it unique? Without any of these, I believe music therapy could not work.

My main aim is the building of a relationship between client and therapist, through the music and the interpretation of its meaning. How can you understand a moment of spontaneous music-making between client and therapist which you begin and end together, where you give each other eye contact, a smile, or there is a thought-provoking silence. We feel that it has meaning for both of us, but words and intellectualising are not enough. The feelings which one is left with are all important.

It is hoped that future research will develop a framework within which to examine this approach to music therapy.

Conclusion

There has been much change in the hospital. The new philosophy of community care resulted in the expanding of day services and the closing down of wards either to be resettled in the community or in purpose built bungalows within the hospital grounds.

Good things have resulted from these changes, but there is still far to go. The lack of understanding about people's emotional responses and needs is still a difficult thing for staff to acknowledge and deal with. It is much easier for them to focus on concrete activities, such as teaching programmes for life-skills. These are important goals, but they must be seen as part of a much wider view which looks at the client in many different ways. Behavioural, humanistic and psychodynamic approaches can work together towards similar goals. Respect for different views is a good starting point. Our clients can only benefit from this integration.

References

Ritchie, F. (1991) 'Behind Closed Doors', *British Journal of Music Therapy*, 5, 4–9.

Rothschild, H. (1967) *The Psychodynamic Meaning of Music*. Jerusalem: Pinchas Noy University Hospital.

Stokes, J. and Sinason, V. (1992) 'Secondary Mental Handicap as a Defence', in Waitman, A. and Conboy-Hill, S. (eds) *Psychotherapy and Mental Handicap*. London: Sage.

Wilkinson, J. (1989) Challenging behaviour scale. *Mental Handicap Research*, 2, 1, 87–104.

Yalom, I.D. (1980) *Existential Psychotherapy*. New York: Basic Books.

I would like to thank Shirley Lawrence and Ruth for all their patience, and the *British Journal of Music Therapy* for allowing me to re-use my case study.

CHAPTER 11

Individual Therapy with a Man Who Has an Eating Disorder

Ann Sloboda
United Kingdom

Introduction

This chapter describes individual music therapy with Brian. He received therapy while he was a patient at an acute psychiatric unit that specialised in eating disorders. Before detailing the case, currently held ideas regarding eating disorders will be reviewed.

Eating disorders

Anyone who has been on a diet will recall that at times food takes on a greater meaning than merely satisfying physical hunger. It becomes associated with a goal of self-improvement, achievable only through determination and self-discipline. Food can be associated with guilt and failure if the dieter succumbs to too many 'forbidden' foods, and with success and elation if the target weight is reached.

For people with eating disorders, food has acquired such massive emotional connotations that it becomes the focus of their lives. The term 'eating disorders' is an umbrella term used to cover the syndromes of anorexia and bulimia nervosa. Anorexia in its broadest sense can describe people who persistently refuse to take in food. Bulimia describes those who eat, often compulsively, but then purge themselves of food, usually by vomiting. However, many people with eating disorders suffer from both syndromes. They share an investment in not eating, and fear of food and what it can do to them.

From a variety of social and family backgrounds, sufferers seem to share an underlying lack of self-esteem and feelings of unworthiness. Orbach (1986) feels that low self-esteem is too mild a term to describe the strength of negative feelings experienced by these people. She uses the term 'self-hate' to describe their deep dissatisfaction with their own internal life, which seems to be at the root of the need to control and change themselves in such a concrete way. Linked with the desire to control their appetite and get thinner is the desire for a new self without needs and wants; a self over which they have control.

The development of eating behaviour has a clear connection with family dynamics. Food and feeding are central issues in early relationships with parents and can involve anger, negotiations and power struggles from the early months. Refusing to eat (either openly, or covertly, by vomiting in secret) is experienced as a way of defying or breaking free of parental control.

The systematic process of dieting and getting thinner can initially give people a feeling of being successful and in control. Self-esteem can be gained by what Orbach (1986) calls: 'practising the self-denial of dieting and living out the life of a person with no needs'. The pursuit of slimness is of the utmost importance, not only as slimness *per se*, but in the context of what 'fat' and 'thin' symbolise for the person with an eating disorder. In their work with anorexics and compulsive eaters, both Orbach (1986) and Woodman (1981) found that 'fat' was associated with failure, greed, need, indulgence, loss of control and depression. 'Thin' represented control, success, efficiency, independence, self-sufficiency and self-discipline.

Much of the literature about these conditions (Orbach 1986, Woodman 1981, Crisp 1980, Bruch 1978) mentions only women. Little has been written about male sufferers, although a comparative study of male and female anorexics (Margo 1987) concluded that the general picture of the illness in males is similar to that in females. While some physical symptoms of anorexia, in particular the loss of menstruation, are exclusive to the female sufferers, the psychological issues underlying eating disorders are shared by both sexes.

Therapeutic setting

By the time people are admitted for treatment to a psychiatric unit, they are often caught in a vicious circle, relentlessly pursuing thinness as their only measure of success. Although many are at a dangerously low weight, all are terrified of putting on any weight, as getting fatter means 'failure'. Elaborate daily routines are required in order to avoid digesting food. These involve deception and secrecy, for example, finding secret places to vomit after meals; avoiding social situations where people eat together; lying to family and friends about one's food intake, and so on. It is easy to see how people with eating disorders become cut off from other people and increasingly isolated in their secret world.

All the patients I work with feel their eating disorder to be their most important skill. Their control over food and ability to keep their weight low is experienced as something uniquely their own. Brian often said: 'It's the only thing I'm good at'. A young woman with anorexia remarked: 'I failed at school, but succeeded with anorexia. It's my profession.' Another said: 'If I let go of my eating disorder, what will I have left?' The belief that the eating disorder is protecting them (albeit precariously) from experiencing life as a meaningless void made sufferers understandably reluctant to give it up. On admission they all want to 'get better' (i.e., feel better), but none wants to get fatter.

Nursing staff in the unit are involved in negotiating eating programmes with patients and therefore confront them about eating on a daily basis. As a music therapist I am able to work with people in a more indirect way. One aim of music therapy with this client group is to help each person understand the function their eating disorder has in their lives, and what purpose it serves.

Little has yet been written on the subject of music therapy with people with eating disorders. The only two papers I have encountered are by Nolan (1989), concerning group techniques with bulimic patients, and Heal and O'Hara (1993), focusing on individual work with a client with Downs Syndrome and an eating disorder. Nolan views the ability of music to elicit extra-musical associations as the most significant contribution of music to therapy with this client group. He sees this as: 'a bridging process between musical expression and the conscious expression of feelings'. This certainly seems relevant to my own patients, as they had great difficulty in recognising and expressing their feelings. Their eating disorder seemed to function as a visible symptom of painful feelings but a defence against experiencing them.

People were very willing to discuss their conditions and eating behaviours. However, they did this in an intellectualised way, which, although informative for staff, only served to distance patients themselves from experiencing their feelings. The experience of improvising musically was a much more spontaneous and immediate one. It did, for many, elicit associations and images, and people grew able to link the quality of their own improvisations with aspects of their internal world and everyday relationships. In individual music therapy I improvised with patients and discussed the quality of their music with them. I aimed to support them in experiencing and gaining a greater understanding of their own feelings. The account of the work with Brian will illustrate his growing awareness of his own emotions and the function of his eating disorder in both expressing and numbing his emotions. The music Brian played was central to the therapy, which vividly communicated both his emotional state and his ability to relate to another person.

Clinical material

Brian is a 36-year-old man, married with one child. Since the death of his father in 1988 he and his elder brother have run the family business. His mother is still alive. He had suffered from anorexia and bulimia since the age of eighteen, and had been admitted to several hospitals for in-patient treatment during his twenties. He described his treatment in these units as punitive, claiming that he had put on weight in order to get out of hospital and then lost it as soon as he was discharged.

Brian had been slightly overweight as a child. He described his family as close, and his mother as overprotective. In his teens he began to want to lose weight. He felt that his mother gave him too much to eat, but was reluctant to defy her openly. His solution to this conflict was to eat everything she gave him, and secretly vomit later. This pattern continued into his marriage and through his twenties and thirties. When he felt distressed or anxious, he would binge-eat to comfort himself. (These binges often included alcohol.) The comfort was short-lived, to be replaced by disgust and fear of getting fat. Brian would then induce vomiting, after which he felt at first relieved, then guilty and miserable.

He was caught in a vicious circle:

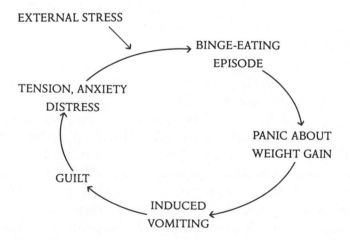

On admission to the unit Brian had reached crisis point and was bingeing and vomiting several times a day. He attributed this crisis to the recent death of his mother-in-law, of whom he had been very fond. Her death brought back memories of the death of his father, for whom, he said, he 'had not grieved properly'. His wife had threatened to leave him if he did not seek treatment, and he agreed to be admitted as an in-patient.

Brian was referred to individual music therapy shortly after his admission and had weekly sessions for nearly eleven months. His music therapy treatment spanned his initial three month period as an in-patient, his transition to day patient, and finally out-patient status. Apart from holiday breaks Brian attended regularly and never cancelled a session. He had a total of 40 music therapy sessions in all.

My first meeting with Brian was at his initial assessment, in which he presented as diffident, well-mannered and anxious to please. He spent much of this session talking about his previous hospital treatment; hoping that he would have a better experience this time, but also fearing that he was beyond help. He said he valued the time away from his family whilst in hospital. He spoke of his frequent bingeing and vomiting, which had been secret, but became, as the frequency increased, impossible to keep from his family. He said he felt unable to cope; ashamed and disgusted with himself.

After twenty minutes, I encouraged him to experiment with the musical instruments, and to play a duet with me, assuring him that I would give him support on the piano. (He had no previous musical experience.) Brian said that he was very nervous, but selected a glockenspiel and began playing. In contrast, he then chose a large drum which he played softly but rapidly and continuously. The improvisations were both very short, as even a slight pause in my piano playing would cause Brian to stop, thinking I had finished. He said that he only felt able to play when I was supporting him on the piano.

Brian was willing to come for regular therapy, although he said that he had found the session 'nerve-wracking'. We discussed the idea that the way he played the instruments and related to me in future sessions could be used to look at his own feelings, and relationships with others.

In my assessment report to the unit team I suggested that individual music therapy work with Brian would focus on:

- building trust and self-confidence
- exploring family relationships
- acknowledging and expressing negative feelings
- developing self-awareness and self-acceptance.

Stage 1: early sessions – the external bully

Although Brian found it difficult to improvise freely in the early sessions, he was able to do so when I suggested clear themes on which we might improvise. These themes emerged from our discussions at the start of each session. In the first few weeks Brian spoke at length about his difficulty in asserting himself with his family. At my suggestion, he chose instruments to represent different family members, and improvised on each instrument in a way that aimed to illustrate the character of each person.

An example of this is Brian's third session, which he began by talking anxiously about his family. Interestingly, his worries focused on his mother and brother (rather than his wife and children). He feared what he imagined to be their fury and contempt. Having described his brother Denis as 'overpowering', Brian chose the largest drum to represent him. He played in a rapid, repetitive manner; pounding the drum aggressively in a way that allowed for little, if any, dialogue with the piano. When I commented on this, Brian admitted that he had not left any space in his playing to listen to the piano. He considered this an accurate portrayal of his brother, whom he experienced as a domineering bully, who did not listen and who criticised him continually.

To represent his mother he chose a wooden gato drum, which he played equally rapidly in a repetitive circular movement. He felt that this music resembled his mother, who, he said 'kept going on and on, saying the same thing'. In discussion, Brian spoke of his dissatisfaction with his own passive role in family interactions, especially with his mother and brother. He said he felt weak, ineffectual and under their control. According to Brian, the only times when he felt in control of anything were the times when he was making himself vomit.

In the sessions that followed, all of Brian's improvisations had similar qualities. These included:

- a frantic, agitated beating action, producing fast quavers
- very few, if any, rests or pauses to indicate phrasing
- a lack of clear rhythm or structure
- a lack of awareness and interaction with the piano (or whatever instrument I played)
- an inability to slow down, or indicate that he was going to stop playing. (He would usually stop playing suddenly, without warning.)

Brian linked these qualities with the external figures of his mother and brother, often choosing them as themes for improvisation. However, when we improvised freely without a theme, the same tense and aggressive characteristics were present. I began to suspect that they were also attributes of Brian's inner world.

Stage 2: the internal bully

After three months in hospital Brian had achieved his target weight. He became a day patient; spending evenings and weekends at home. In sessions he was very anxious, and spoke of his fear of 'gaps' in his day that he used to fill with bingeing and vomiting. He felt overwhelmed by feelings of fear and despair that he could no longer mask by his eating behaviour. He feared a relapse. I found myself affected by Brian's anxiety, and in some sessions behaved more directively than I had intended to. In sessions 14 and 15 I encouraged him to play slow music, with 'gaps' or rests in. (I hoped this might help him both to relax and to experience some of the feelings he feared so much.) However, at this stage, he found this impossible and, whatever I played on the piano, his playing was as fast and frantic as ever.

Despite his fears, Brian did not resume his vomiting behaviours, and began to reduce his days at the hospital, returning to work for at first two, then three days a week. He continued to feel unhappy and insecure, even though he appeared to be progressing well. He still felt demoralised by his brother's criticism, but began to examine his own inability to stand up to it.

In session 25, (shortly after the summer break), we discussed his sadistic treatment of his own body; how he starved it, crammed it and purged it. Brian acknowledged that he was constantly criticising himself and expecting criticism from others. A persistent bullying voice thundered inside his head. The resulting tension often seemed unbearable, and Brian longed to relieve this by bingeing and vomiting. He played a long improvisation depicting this feeling of tension, in which he played two drums simultaneuosly.

This improvisation lasted ten minutes in all, and seemed longer to me. Rather than deciding when to finish, Brian seemed to drum relentlessly until exhausted. It was the first improvisation that Brian had allowed me to record. In early sessions, he had only played for twenty or thirty seconds at a time, and had been too self-conscious to tolerate being recorded. I felt that this session showed some significant developments in Brian's music. He was now fully involved in much longer improvisations that vividly conveyed some of his feelings. He began to realise how much pressure he continually put on himself.

Stage 3: challenging the bully – beginning to use another voice

In the weeks that followed, we discussed the need for Brian to allow expression to other feelings, and not allow them to be squashed by his internal bully. He spoke of a sad, vulnerable part of himself that was longing to speak and be heard. In session 27 he played an improvisation (on metallophone and drum) that he subsequently titled: 'Listen to me, let me speak'.

According to Brian, the metallophone represented his 'sad' voice which wanted to be heard, but was often overwhelmed by the drums that represented his own critical voice. I pointed out to Brian that although he had only allowed limited space to his sad voice, his metallophone playing had melodic qualities and phrasing that made it easier to support on the piano. The 'sad' voice seemed to offer possibilities for dialogue and relationship.

Outside the sessions, it appeared that Brian was daring to risk showing more vulnerability in his family relationships. He said that he was communicating more of his feelings to his wife, and that they were getting on much better together. He spoke with regret of the way that his eating disorder had cut him off from his wife and children for so many years. In October (after eight months of therapy), Brian told me that his wife was expecting their third child. His feelings were ambivalent; a mixture of pleasure and worry about the extra responsibility involved.

By November, Brian was back at work full-time, apart from the time spent attending the unit for music therapy and weekly sessions with his key nurse. Judging by external standards, he was now coping with 'normal' life, although he still felt very insecure about his weight and food intake, and still doubted his self-worth. Therapy work on improving his self-acceptance could have continued for years, but this was not possible in an acute unit. (It was fortunate that Brian had been able to attend as an out-patient for as long as he did.)

In session 36 we agreed to finish therapy after four more sessions. In a ten minute improvisation entitled simply: 'How I feel'. Brian played the metallophone throughout, in a way that resembled the 'sad' voice mentioned above. This time, however, his playing had a relaxed, reflective quality to it. He was able to maintain a steady pulse of three beats to the bar, in a much slower tempo than he had been able to manage some months earlier. His characteristic frantic drumming did not occur in this piece. I was struck by the way in which he was now able to interact with me on the piano, using imitative phrases that gave a sense of genuine dialogue.

Conclusion

In our final session, I asked Brian for some feedback on his period of music therapy and on what he felt he had gained from it. He said: 'I learned that I had different feelings; I could be sad, or happy, or angry. I used to feel as if I was on a treadmill of the same desperate feelings all the time'. Significantly, he said that it was his experience of playing music that had convinced him of the variety and validity of his emotional experiences.

For a client who struggled to make sense of his emotional world, music therapy provided an alternative way of exploring it.

References

Abraham, S. and Llewellyn-Jones, D. (1987) *Eating Disorders: The Facts*. Oxford: Oxford University Press.

Bruch, H. (1978) *The Golden Cage: The Enigma of Anorexia Nervosa*. London: Open Books Publishing Ltd.

Crisp, A.H. (1980) *Anorexia Nervosa: Let Me Be*. London: Academic Press

Heal, M. and O'Hara, J. (1993) 'The music therapy of a mentally handicapped anorexic adult', *British Journal of Medical Psychology*, March, 33–41.

Margo, J.L. (1987) 'Anorexia nervosa in males, a comparison with female patients', *British Journal of Psychiatry*, 151, 80–83.

Nolan, P. (1989) 'Music therapy improvisation techniques with bulimic patients', in E.K. Baker and L.M. Hornyak (eds) *The Handbook of Techniques in the Treatment of Eating Disorders*. New York. Guilford Publications.

Orbach, S. (1986) *Hunger Strike*. London: Faber.

Woodman, M. (1981) *The Owl was a Baker's Daughter: Obesity, Anorexia Nervosa and the Repressed Feminine*. Toronto: Inner City Books.

CHAPTER 12

Music
A Mega Vitamin for the Brain

Denise Erdonmez
Australia

Most music therapists do not think of the brain as an integral part of the music therapy experience. They work from an intuitive base, determining the aims of a session according to the emotional and social needs of the client. This chapter looks at the specific effect of music on neurological activity.

In working with adult clients suffering from illnesses associated with brain dysfunction, it is important to know something of which areas of the brain are affected and how this impacts on our choice of music therapy method. Consider the following four clinical examples:

> A patient with Parkinson's Disease (PD) stands in a frozen stance unable to initiate a step forward. The music therapist starts to sing a song with a strong rhythm. The client's frozen stance is unlocked and she takes a faltering step forward, then gets into the rhythm of walking.

> A patient with Alzheimer's Disease is very confused, does not know her name, nor can she answer simple questions. A familiar song is sung and she sings the lyrics and melodic line accurately.

> A client following a left hemisphere cerebro-vascular accident (CVA or 'stroke') is rendered aphasic and dyslexic. He is unable to read books or magazines, yet he retains the ability to sight read music in complex keys fluently.

A client in a relaxed state listens to flute music, which she associates with a trip she had taken to France. She recalls walking along the river and says she can recall the smell of the river and the trees along the bank.

In each of the examples above, the response to music is due to brain mechanisms involved in the perception and processing of music information.

In our music therapy clinical work, our observations of response are essential – we note the quality of the client's response, we note any social interaction as a result of the response and we may connect the response to aspects of the music stimuli. Rarely do we stop to consider that with each experience of music the client's brain is stimulated. All emotional responses to music originate in the brain – each response to music, be it singing, playing or moving, originates in the brain. Why, then, is it not common for music therapists to discuss their work in terms of brain processes? Perhaps it is because our training hasn't incorporated sufficient knowledge of brain processes. Perhaps it is because music therapists tend to be wary of this type of research, sometimes on the basis that the findings of that research may intrude or negatively influence the intuitive and interactive nature of the music therapy process. It is imperative to bridge the gap by advocating research findings that have direct relevance to the way we proceed in music therapy clinical practice.

There are hundreds of structures and systems operating within the brain and only a few, which relate to music therapy clinical practice with adult clients, will be mentioned.

My interest in music and the brain has evolved over 20 years of clinical work, in psychiatry and in working with older adults who have disease affecting the central nervous system – for example Parkinson's Disease (PD) and Huntington's Disease, with those following cerebro-vascular accidents (CVA) and also with those suffering dementia. My most recent work has been with adult clients who do not have physical disease, but who are motivated towards a greater integration of self through Guided Imagery and Music (Bonny 1978a and 1978b).

Parkinson's Disease

In the first clinical example above, the client was a woman with Parkinson's Disease. It is common for people with Parkinson's Disease to experience a 'freeze' in initiating movement. Parkinson's Disease affects the basal ganglia, a group of structures connecting various centres of the brain – the hub of activity of the brain. Particularly affected are the areas of the substantia nigra and putamen and these are necessary for relaying stimuli that relate to the initiation of movement. The transmission of impulses includes mechanisms that both stimulate the movement and those that inhibit the movement. The symptoms of Parkinson's Disease include tremor, rigidity, bradykinesia (loss of spontaneous movement) and loss of posture. These symptoms occur because the cells in the substantia nigra die off. These cells are essential for changing amino acids into dopamine, a neurotransmitter necessary for relaying impulses. Thus levels of dopamine are severely decreased. The synthetic drug L-Dopa has been used quite successfully with some patients to replace dopamine, but it is not successful for all people with PD.

Problems with movement arise when a movement has to be initiated, as, for example, in starting to walk. Patients do better when they are given an external cue to start the movement. This is where music comes in. Music as an auditory cue activates neural pathways to enable the person to initiate walking. One theory is that any external cue will activate the process – it may be a visual cue. However, my experience is that a music cue, in the form of a well-known song with a strong rhythm does the trick remarkably well. Often by singing a song or providing rhythmic chanting, the person is able to take that first step and then establish the body sway that is essential for maintaining the rhythm of the walking. Why would the rhythm be important? We know that rhythm is represented diffusely within the brain that is, – different areas of the brain are activated by rhythm – thus impairment to one section of the brain will not totally eclipse response to rhythm. We also know that rhythm provides a structure and order, both essential elements to motivate movement. What is important when cueing a patient with Parkinson's Disease is that the music therapist doesn't engage in verbal discussion, but gets straight to the singing with a good strong beat. The music here overrides the block in transmission of impulses.

A further benefit of rhythmic music is as a motivator for exercise. A study was carried out by Veronica Cosgriff and others at the PD Society residential care programme in Nottingham, in 1986. Music was introduced at a two week holiday programme for 11 people with Parkinson's Disease (Cosgriff 1988). The prime aim of the music session was to assist exercising, particularly weight transference, rocking (to assist body sway) and rotation. Cosgriff found that the tempo of the music needed to be modified according to the task.

Over the two week period the range of creative movement of the guests improved with the addition of music. The characteristic tremor was decreased. The guests commented on their ability to persevere with tasks when live music was performed (guitar and flute music were performed live). Music of an essentially rhythmic nature stimulated movement; however, repetition of the same music was less effective than if the music stimulus was changed at regular intervals. Inappropriate music aggravated some problems; for example, arhythmic music resulted in walking difficulties. Thus variety in the music was important as long as the music was rhythmical in structure.

Music is also used in the treatment of people with Parkinson's Disease for expression of emotion and to assist speech. Jennie Selman reports of her work with a patient with Parkinson's Disease in which singing and improvisation assisted in his expression of feelings. Selman (1988) notes that the patient's responses were inconsistent. This is to be expected with a disease of deteriorating character; nevertheless, the patient showed clear signs of increased musicality despite his deteriorating neurological state.

Alzheimer's Disease and other types of Dementia

In my second clinical example of the confused woman able to sing the melody and lyrics of songs, we again turn to brain structures to understand the power of music to override the symptoms of severe disease.

The key symptoms of Alzheimer's Disease include advancing memory loss and confusion, difficulty in learning new tasks, personality changes, impaired language and advancing loss of mobility, to mention a few. The progression of the disease is remorseless, affecting not only the patient but all members of the family. The immense strain on families as care-givers is ably expressed in the title of Mace and Rabins' book *The 36-Hour Day* (Mace and Rabins 1981).

The benefits of music therapy meeting the social and emotional needs of people with Alzheimer's Disease are well described in the music therapy literature (see Bright 1988), and in keeping with my topic I wish to address the issues of memory and memory loss and why it is that music will activate memories in long term storage while other stimuli, particularly verbal stimuli, fail.

It is important to note that memory recall changes as a result of ageing. Some authors have suggested that in ageing people it is not a matter of loss of memory, rather a difficulty in accessing the information (Butler and Lewis 1982, Jorm 1987). As we age we selectively remember information, rather than lose it. We also selectively forget information which has less relevance for us.

An analogy to human memory systems may be drawn with the hard disk of a computer. When the memory is exceeded, the hard disk needs an up-grade of memory capacity. This can't happen with human beings. If we consider the huge amount of information carried by the brain's memory capacity over 60 or 70 years of life experience, it is easy to see why certain bits of information get relegated to deeper levels of 'storage'; thus they are harder to recall. Little wonder that there needs to be a hierarchy of memory storage.

Damage to the brain as a result of Alzheimer's Disease is due, in part, to the loss of acetylcholine, a neurotransmitter, which results in many impaired cognitive functions. Long term memory can be remarkably well retained, indeed memory for events from early adulthood can become the focus of the person's sense of the present; for example, it is common for older women with Alzheimer's Disease to become distressed because they believe that they must go home to meet the children after school, or that 'my husband will be waiting'. Clearly, the retained selected memory relates to life experience, not to specific factual information, for example telephone numbers. It is this observation which gives us some clues about memory retention in people with dementia.

It used to be that music therapists followed a Reality Orientation approach in working with clients with dementia (Riegler 1980). Every opportunity to bring clients into the 'real' present was emphasised. In music therapy a case was made, appropriately enough, that music provided the structure to reinforce reality. In recent years, however, the concept of Validation (Feil 1982) has come to be more practised and accepted. In Validation theory, it is the experience of the person at that moment which needs to be validated. In the case of the older woman needing to meet the children, a Validation approach is to ask about the children, to validate the experience of the client as the client experiences it, instead of how we believe the client should experience it. This is where music fits in. The client is unable to respond with her name, doesn't know what day it is (is that really important?) but joins in singing 'Two little girls in blue', with the melody and the lyrics correctly rendered. This is recall of material in long term memory storage. It is recall of information originally laid down by rote learning, and it is these skills, this material, which is well preserved. On the other hand, we need to be aware that short term memory storage is severely impaired in people with Alzheimer's Disease or other dementia conditions.

How is it that one type of memory is affected more that the other? Many structures of the brain are involved in preserving memory (Wittrock 1977). Long term memory is housed, in part, within the limbic system (see Figure 12.1). The hippocampus and amygdala are the two important structures here. The hippocampus is important for simple recall, but the amygdala is essential in mediating the rearrangement of memory images and material into long term memory storage (Restak 1984). The amygdala stores those memories

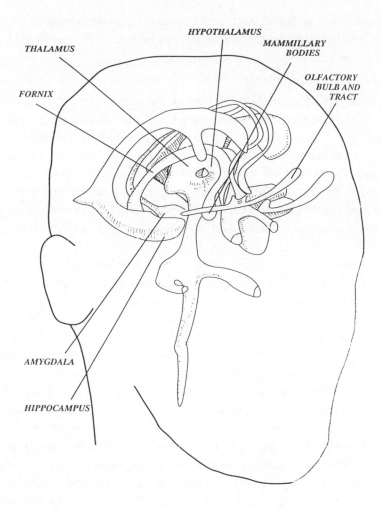

THALAMUS

HYPOTHALAMUS

MAMMILLARY
BODIES

OLFACTORY
BULB AND
TRACT

FORNIX

AMYGDALA

HIPPOCAMPUS

Figure 12.1: Diagram of the connections of the Limbic System

which have an emotional component. Emotions related to past memories, however, are more difficult to access than the images of those past events. Thus it is easier for patients/clients to describe the event and more difficult to describe how they felt at the time (Restak 1984). We remember best memories that are associated with positive feeling, whereas negative feelings tend to be more difficult to access. Thus times of crisis and conflict are difficult to recall and describe. The ramifications for music therapy are obvious. Frequently, we use songs to evoke reminiscence for our clients. We need to know that describing the event is easier than describing feelings, so that our questions to prompt discussion can be modified accordingly.

Cerebro-vascular accidents

The third clinical example mentioned at the start of this paper relates to damage as a result of a left hemisphere CVA. The relevant brain system in discussing CVAs is that of hemispheric specialisation (sometimes also referred to as hemispheric lateralisation or cerebral dominance). Research in this area was at its forte in the 1960s and 1970s, reaching a plateau in 1977–78. The popular right brain theory evolved from these years. The 'New Age' movement has tended to claim the right hemisphere for its own, and this is a simplistic view at best as to how life styles may be improved or altered.

The early research in hemispheric specialisation asserted features of the left and right hemispheres of the brain. In people who are right handed, the left hemisphere was described as the dominant hemisphere processing information that is linear, sequential, logical, analytical, verbal, differentiating, objective and factual. The right hemisphere (in right-handed people) was thought of as the non-dominant hemisphere, processing stimuli that are global, wholistic, pre-verbal or non-verbal, expressive, gestural, metaphoric, subjective, diffuse and empathic. Later research, however, (reviewed in Geschwind and Galaburda 1985) made a case for bilateral representation of language functions in people who are right handed, 'ranging at one extreme from almost total left hemisphere dominance, through varying degrees of left superiority, to equal dominance, or, at the other extreme, moderate right-sided dominance' (p.430). In the case of left handed people, 60 per cent show left hemisphere dominance and 40 per cent right hemisphere dominance (Geschwind and Galaburda 1985).

Research in the 1960s and 1970s focussed on localising areas of each hemisphere responsible for certain tasks. Penfield, a Canadian neurologist, undertook extensive studies of conscious subjects by stimulating different parts of the cerebral cortex with electrodes (Penfield and Perot 1963). It should be pointed out that stimulation of the brain surface does not cause pain, since the brain does not have pain receptors as such. In the study Penfield found that when the temporal lobe of both left and right hemispheres was stimulated, subjects heard music. Some heard songs, some heard music, some heard hymns, and others heard sounds like whistling. These auditory responses were heard more often in the right temporal lobe than the left. Thus the temporal lobe of the right hemisphere was thought to house music memory.

Further studies attempted to locate specific areas of the brain responsible for certain music tasks. Gordon and Bogen (1974) studied the differences in processing music information between left and right hemispheres by inject-ing sodium amytal into each of the carotid arteries in turn, thus anaesthe-tising one hemisphere and isolating the unaffected one. When the left hemisphere was anaesthetised speech and language abilities were severely disrupted but subjects were able to sing. When the right hemisphere was anaesthetised the subjects' singing ability was markedly impaired and, interestingly, their speech became monotone. The study therefore suggested that while speech centres are located in the left hemisphere of the brain, the intonation and expressivity involved in speech clearly required right hemi-sphere involvement. These findings still hold true today.

Bever and Chiarello (1974) conducted studies using a two group sample – musicians and non-musicians. Their findings showed that musically trained people had a right ear/left hemisphere bias for responding to the task, whereas non-musicians showed a left ear/right hemisphere preference for processing the task. The difference in hemisphere involvement occurred because the musicians were listening analytically, whereas the non-musicians were listening for the gestalt or patterns in the music.

Gates and Bradshaw (1977), in a critical overview of research in hemi-spheric specialisation and music, drew the conclusions that there must be inter-hemispheric specialisation activity in processing musical stimuli, and that the nature of the task is the important variable. They conclude that because of the complexity of music behaviours, involving perception, memory recall, associations triggered by memories and extra-musical re-sponse such as imagery and emotion felt through the body, music must be represented in both hemispheres, each operating according to its own specialisation, but in tandem, as determined by the nature of the test task.

How does this research relate to music therapy? First, we know that people who have suffered a left hemisphere CVA will most commonly show evidence of aphasia – loss of expressive speech. These patients, of course, are still capable of singing, in that they can keep pitch and can faithfully reproduce the rhythm and melodic contour of the song. They may even approximate some of the lyrics. Thus the singing of songs allows an avenue of expression denied them through the usual verbal means.

The most important issue for us in music therapy, however, is that musically trained clients utilise different areas of the brain when experienc-ing music, compared to clients who are non-musicians.

In a recent study of Prior, Kinsella and Giese (1990), two groups of people were studied – 13 with left CVA damage and 13 with right CVA damage. Musical tasks included perception of rhythm, pitch variation in familiar and unfamiliar songs and production of a well-known song. People suffering left CVA effects showed impairment on the rhythmic tasks that were perceptual in nature. They also did less well on the singing tasks, although this result was not statistically significant. By far the most interesting result was that patients who had premorbid music ability did better in each group. The authors make the point that in undertaking studies related to music perception, premorbid musicality levels need to be addressed. One such scale is put forward by Grison (1977).

1. Showed no interest in music; did not care to listen to it or sing.

2. Occasionally sang familiar melodies such as nursery rhymes and regional songs; sometimes listened to music on the radio.

3. Enjoyed singing and had a repertory which was maintained and augmented; was a critical listener of music on the radio; bought records and listened to them frequently.

4. Played an instrument but was not trained in theory or sight reading.

5. Played an instrument; fair sight reading ability and general musical knowledge.

6. Was an excellent musician on both the practical and theoretical level.

In music therapy practice, an initial assessment of a client following a CVA needs to take into account pre-morbid levels of musicality. If we know that our client is in group 5 or 6, then we can expect the client to be able to grasp musical tasks of greater complexity and plan our music therapy aims accordingly. Conversely, damage to specific areas of the brain needs to be assessed in clients who have been competent musicians. Botez and Wertheim (1959) outline a series of tests for dysfunctions of musicality in musicians following brain impairment – these dysfunctions are grouped under the term 'amusia'.

At the start of the paper I quoted the case of a man following a massive left CVA with severe impairment to the frontal, parietal and temporal lobe (see Erdonmez 1991, for the full case study). The CVA rendered the client aphasic and dyslexic. He was unable to read prose in either books, magazines or daily papers. On the Grison scale of pre-morbid musicality he was rated 6. He had been a pianist and organist and had completed the highest levels of music examinations. As a result of the CVA his right hand was paralysed, but he began to rehabilitate his piano performance skills using the left hand only. The most remarkable aspect of his rehabilitation was that, despite being dyslexic for the written word, this client was able to read music notation at sight fluently. Over the years I have been working with him, his performance skills have improved dramatically. After the CVA he could play only in simple keys of C and G major. After two years of therapy, his repertoire included Beethoven Sonatas and Bach Inventions, which he played with his left hand (the treble line), with me providing the bass line with my left hand (a two left-handed duet). Presently he is playing the Preludes of Scriabin, in complex keys.

This client has been a long-term client, which raises a further interesting factor in our music therapy practice. Frequently, music therapists work with clients over several years. Our contributions to the client's development may be more substantial than we think, if we consider that we are feeding neural pathways with the music experience.

Guided imagery and music

The fourth clinical example given at the commencement of the paper related to an adult client with no physical illness but undergoing a Guided Imagery and Music experience.

GIM is a method by which people experience images and deep emotion in a relaxed state, while listening to specifically designed tapes of classical music. The experiences of the client are relayed to the therapist (or guide), who supports and encourages the imagery process (Bonny 1989, Bonny and Savary 1990).

Imagery occurs for the client in very many different forms. Sometimes the imagery is visual, sometimes kinesthetic, sometimes auditory, sometimes olfactory. Images may be logical and rational, for example scenes by the beach, walking through forests, climbing hills, swimming in rock pools. Often the imagery can appear non-rational as it becomes symbolic of other issues, for example following a yellow light, floating on the back of a bird, ploughing through the earth to plant a seed. When the imagery is kinesthetic it is felt in the body, for example a heavy chest, the chest opening out, fire alight in the body, iron bars in the feet. Each of these images may suggest an issue to the therapist who may help in deepening the focus on the image for further clarification.

Imagery can become transpersonal, when the body of the person is transformed into some other form, for example the client lying on the back of an albatross becomes the albatross, or a light shining within the body starts to radiate energy.

Aspects of the neuropsychology of GIM

Goldberg (1989) notes that GIM brings together the perception of music, the production of sensory imagery and emotion. Sometimes the emotion can be felt without imagery occuring and sometimes imagery can be experienced without felt emotion, which raises the question 'what happens first, the imagery or the affect?'

The limbic system in the mid-brain governs the interpretation and experience of emotion (see Figure 12.1). Through the olfactory bulb and olfactory tract, sensations of smell are relayed to the temporal lobe as the olfactory nerve synapses with the medial surface of the temporal lobe.

The thalamus is responsible for the relay of sensory information and integration of this information. All sensory fibre tracts (including auditory, visual, kinaesthetic and gustatory, but excluding the olfactory sense), synapse in the thalamus. Hence, several sensory modalities can be evoked at the one time.

From the thalamus, nerve impulses are relayed to the cerebral cortex (motor cortex) and to the hypothalamus. The hypothalamus is responsible for the functioning of the autonomic nervous system – the sympathetic and parasympathetic nervous systems, which govern body temperature, the experience of emotion (pleasure and pain) and the release of hormones through the pituitary gland.

The hippocampus houses short term memory and prepares the neural processing of information for long term memory storage. The amygdala houses old memories.

In Guided Imagery and Music we see how the limbic system functions to integrate the auditory experience of the music, which is processed through the thalamus and links in with the processing of all other sensory modalities, except that of the olfactory sense. The thalamus sends the sensory information to the hypothalamus, where emotions are relayed. Emotions may activate the autonomic nervous system and give rise to sensations such as chills up the spine, or other 'peak' experiences. The final step is the relaying of information to the hippocampus and amygdala to make new connections for memories and to match the image with old memories.

Through GIM the limbic system of the brain is activated, integrated and synchronised. We can only wonder at the fascinating process GIM provides where we hear music, experience imagery and feel emotion aroused by both the music and imagery in association with memories.

Music therapy methods and neuropsychological process

In recent years psychologists have introduced a framework to describe tasks as top-down/bottom-up processes (Gardner 1982). As mentioned before, the complexity of the music task for the client will determine processing strategies and brain activation. Tasks which involve a wholistic approach to music (basic perceptual, responsive tasks) can be termed top-down tasks, in that they work from a global perspective. Improvisation is one method we use in music therapy that involves a top-down strategy, so does Guided Imagery and Music and so do other music therapy methods where there are no directives or instructions, and where the 'gestalt' of the experience is of paramount importance.

Consider a group improvisation session where there are no directions, no instructions, and where clients are free to explore not only the music sound, but the musical and non-musical interrelationship with others in the group. There are no analytical processes here, but there is an enriched 'gestalt' experience.

In specific music tasks, such as asking clients to sing the melody of songs, sequencing music material and rehabilitation of piano skills in a client post-CVA, the strategies we use are more analytical and demanding. These may be termed bottom-up tasks, in that they work from the specifics to the whole. We require our clients to build up, as it were, from one skill to another. As we set our aims for a music therapy session (or series of sessions) we need to be more aware of the hierarchical nature of skills. If we take our client's pre-morbid level of musicality into account, we might more accurately gauge the higher potential of some clients.

I believe that we, as music therapists, can add to the knowledge of brain functions in that we work with a highly creative art form, which activates many areas of the brain. We need to work alongside psychologists and neuropsychologists in order that we are better informed about the effect of music on brain functions, and so we can better inform other professionals about our clients' non-verbal functioning level.

Given that many of our music therapy approaches rely on perception, memory, emotion felt, associations and physical response, we can say that music therapy activates many key areas of the brain. Music feeds the brain, like a vitamin. Given that music feeds all aspects of the person, it obviously is a mega vitamin!

References

Bever, T.G. and Chiarello, R.J. (1974) 'Cerebral dominance in musicians and non-musicians', *Science*, 185, 137–139.

Bonny, H. (1978a) *Facilitating GIM Sessions.* Baltimore, MD: ICM Books.

Bonny, H. (1978b) *The Role of Taped Music Programs in the GIM Process.* Baltimore, MD: ICM Books.

Bonny, H. (1989) 'Sound as Symbol: Guided Imagery and Music in Clinical Practice', *Music Therapy Perspectives* Vol. 6, 7–11.

Bonny, H. and Savary, L. (1990) *Music and Your Mind: Listening with a New Consciousness.* New York: Station Hill Press.

Botez, M.T. and Wertheim, N. (1959) 'Expressive Aphasia and Amusia', *Brain*, 82, 186–202.

Bright, R. (1988) *Music Therapy and the Dementias: Improving the Quality of Life.* St Louis: MMB.

Butler, R.N. and Lewis, M.I. (1982) *Ageing and Mental Health* (3rd Ed). St Louis: Mosby.

Cosgriff, V. (1988) 'Intensive Music Therapy in a Two-week Residential Programme for People with Parkinson's Disease', *Bulletin, Australian Music Therapy Association*, Vol.11, No.4, Dec., 2–11.

Critchley, M. and Hensen, R.A. (1977) *Music and the Brain: Studies in the Neurology of Music.* London: Heinemann Medical Books.

Erdonmez, D. (1991) 'Rehabilitation of Piano Performance Skills Following a Left Cerebro-Vascular Accident', in K. Bruscia (ed) *Case Studies in Music Therapy.* Philadelphia, PA: Barcelona.

Feil, N. (1982) *Validation: the Feil Method.* Ohio: E. Feil Prod.

Gardner, H. (1982) 'Artistry following Damage to the Human Brain', in Ellis A. (ed) *Normality and Pathology in Cognitive Functions.* London and New York: Academic Press.

Gates, A. and Bradshaw, J.L. (1977) 'The role of the cerebral hemispheres in music'. *Brain and Language*, 4, 403–431.

Geschwind, N. and Galaburda, A. (1985) 'Cerebral lateralisation – 1: biological mechanisms, associations and pathology'. *Archives of Neurology*, Vol.42, May, 428–459.

Goldberg, F. (1989) *Toward a Theory of Guided Imagery and Music.* Baltimore, MD: Institute for Music and Imagery.

Gordon, H.W. and Bogen, J.E. (1974) 'Hemispheric Lateralisation of Singing after Intracarotid Sodium Amylobarbitone', *Neurol. Neurosurg. and Psych.*, 37, 727–738.

Grison, B. (1977) cited in Benton, A.L. 'The Amusias', in M. Critchley and R.A. Henson (eds) *Music and the Brain: Studies in the Neurology of Music.* London: Heinemann Medical Books.

Jorm, A.F. (1987) *Understanding Senile Dementia.* Sydney: Croom Helm.

Mace, N. and Rabins, P. (1981) *The 36-Hour Day.* Baltimore, MD: Johns Hopkins University Press.

Penfield, W. and Perot, P. (1963) 'The brain's record of auditory and visual experience', *Brain,* Vol.86, part 4, 596–696.

Prior, M., Kinsella, G. and Giese, J. (1990) 'Assessment of musical processing in brain damaged patients: Implications for laterality of music', *Journal of Clinical and Experimental Neuropsychology,* 12, 2, 301–312.

Restak, R. (1984) *The Brain.* New York: Bantam Books.

Riegler, J. (1980) 'Comparison of a reality orientation program for geriatric patients with and without music', *Journal of Music Therapy,* 17, (1), 26–33.

Selman, J. (1988) 'Music therapy with Parkinson's Disease', *British Journal of Music Therapy,* Vol.2, No.1, 5–10.

Wittrock, M.C. (1977) (ed) *The Human Brain.* Englewood Cliffs, NJ: Prentice-Hall.

CHAPTER 13

Music Therapy's Role in the Diagnosis of Psycho-Geriatric Patients in The Hague

Josée Raijmaekers
The Netherlands

Introduction

The increasing average age and number of old-aged people in the steadily more complex and changing Dutch society has resulted in an increase in psycho-social and psychiatric problems amongst the elderly. The music therapists at the Rosenburg Psychiatric Centre in the Hague have, since 1985, been involved in the diagnosis of these clients and in giving advice for the improvement of their care.

This chapter offers a description of the specifically music therapy orientated observation programme which was designed for this purpose. The programme is especially geared to observe the emotional, cognitive and interactive functioning of the elderly. Characteristic of this programme is, amongst other things, the way in which a great variety of data is compiled and processed within a short space of time. In this respect an essential element is the clearly defined way in which the tasks are divided between the two music therapists involved. Attention is also given to the multi-disciplinary framework within which all this takes place, music therapy's specific contribution, what is subsequently done with the information, and the shortcomings and benefits of this way of working.

Psycho-geriatrics

Psycho-geriatrics deals with disorders which become most apparent after the age of 65 years. Disorders which often occur are:

- amnestic syndrome (consisting of disorders in cognition)
- paranoia and aggression
- all kinds of neurotic syndromes
- depression.

Although many of these syndromes occur in all populations, some important distinctions are to be pointed out on how they appear in elderly people:

- First, in elderly people there is a decrease of ability in all functions, resulting in a diminished overall effort.

- Second, there are many changes in environment: for instance retirement, the loss of close relatives and good friends, moving house, loss of social roles, and so forth.

- Third, the loss of good health.

- Fourth, the problems of the elderly are influenced by their longer life history in comparison with adults and children. Time will play a different role, as the elderly person has more history in his or her memory and less time left.

Inherent in this phase of life is parting and mourning. Often the question of the meaning of life is raised in the face of approaching death. In the literature, particularly that to do with dementia, much is written about functional disorders in cognition: disorders relating to orientation, language, actions, recognition and memory. The way a person with cognitive disorders adapts to or reacts to all kinds of situations, for instance an unknown situation such as a music session, can reveal a great deal about an individual's psychodynamics. Defence mechanisms such as regression, denial, rationalisation and projection often present themselves. For example, denial of the decease of a beloved member of the family may be easier than emotionally coping with it, or to accuse others of theft hides the own dysfunction of memory if one cannot find something again.

A question which plays an important role in this is, 'How did the client cope with losses in the past, especially emotionally?' Emotional aspects of old age are seldom mentioned in the literature. However, in my opinion the subjective experience of the client remains one of the most important aspects of the clinical picture.

Slaets (1991), clinical psychogeriatrician and Head of the Psycho-geriatric Observation Department, teaches us about the neurology of the brain – that cognitive disorders are placed in the cortex. For emotions, the limbic system is an important neurological circuit. Subjective experience is found in the foremost part of the brain beneath the cortex. However, integration in behaviour and the resulting behaviour itself are cortical functions.

A dementing client might show, because of his or her cortical dysfunction, deviant behaviour. In this behaviour, nevertheless, emotions might be incorrectly or insufficiently integrated. In other words, the external behaviour can give misleading information about inner experience. Some people have serious cognitive dysfunctions and, at the same time, an intact emotional life. This is the case with people who have brain damage, for whom adequate expression of their emotional life is not possible any more. It also applies to people with a functional psychiatric disorder, such as depression, in whom the cognitive functions seem to be disturbed, but not structurally.

Music enters through the ears and brainstem. It may influence the limbic system directly, even before entering the cortex. It may immediately touch the brain structures that are closely involved in emotional experience. Associative listening to music and playing musical instruments in a simple way – as is usual in music therapy – requires different neurological processes from the use of language. In this context I would like to point out that in dementia linguistic dysfunction frequently occurs. It is well-known that aphasia patients often talk better when they do so to melody.

The music therapy programme

The growing demand for music therapy with the elderly and, more specifically, the request of Dr. Slaets for a contribution to the observation and diagnosis of his clients led to the development of an observation programme. In this programme we are most interested in the client's emotional, cognitive and interactional world. Generally speaking, it is concerned with whether clients will be able to reach and find ways of expressing feelings of their own within the constantly changing situations of music therapy. In other words, does someone still have at his or her disposal a musical language of his own and how does this 'musical vocabulary' sound; is it still functional towards others and to what degree? Some of the problems we were and are confronted with include:

- Creating and testing playing and listening situations which appeal to the client's abilities of expression, communication, association and integration.

- Searching the most basic and unequivocal procedures (both in music and in the instruction) by which the client's emotional world is stimulated directly.

- Creating functional methods of collecting and reporting information.

All this had led to music therapy focusing on three fields of observation: emotion, cognition and communication. This has been worked out in six elements which, according to the involvement and capacity of the clients, are presented in changing order and duration. The elements are divided over two music therapy sessions with an interval of one week: the first session involves active music therapy, the second listening. The programme is shown in Figure 13.1.

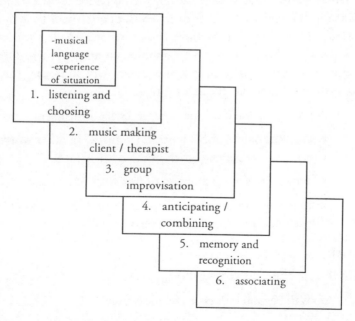

Figure 13.1

In presenting the programme, two music therapists are involved. The role of the instructing and supporting therapist is, besides instructing, to meet directly the client's reactions, both the positive and the negative and to keep them involved with the programme. The second therapist's role is to collect more objective information on registration forms which have been developed by us to this end.

The observation programme
1. LISTENING AND CHOOSING

The therapist introduces the musical instruments (cymbals, small harp, xylophone, drums and timpanetti, commonly called 'hat boxes') and asks the participants for their preferences. Meanwhile, the second therapist observes how the participants react to this, as yet, unknown situation: do they have an overall picture of the complexity of the instruments involved; is one able to choose between several instruments and, if so, how does this person arrive at this particular choice?

2. MUSIC-MAKING CLIENT/THERAPIST

The therapist invites each participant individually to explore the instrument preferred and play it. He supports them by playing a similar instrument. If no definite choice has been made, the therapist will make a choice, based on his impressions up until then. (One can also, incidently, start from the instrument which arouses the least aversion). Meanwhile, the second therapist observes:

- o in what way the participant explores the instrument
- o what is the nature of his musical language; in other words, which musical parameters does the participant use
- o which feelings are connected to this musical language
- o is there any contact with the therapist (in this question the subjective experience of that therapist will play a role).

3. GROUP IMPROVISATION

In this situation the second therapist observes:

- o does the group influence the individual:
  - (i) as to his musical language: does the participant use more or less musical parameters or, just as many as in the one-to-one contact with the therapist?
  - (ii) as to contact in playing: is there any at all and, if so, with whom and when and how?
- o and the emotional experience

The observer can also check and compare phenomena which occurred before.

4. ANTICIPATING AND COMBINING

The therapist invites the participants to imagine which instruments will sound well together. The observer decides whether a participant can still use his more abstract abilities.

In the daily hospital routine it is now one week later and we start with:

5. MEMORY AND RECOGNITION

Do the participants recognise us when we enter; or do they only show memory when we speak of music or even after the therapist brings out some instruments and plays them? Or don't they remember anything at all of the week before? Meanwhile, the therapist has the opportunity to create an atmosphere of trust in order to arrive at an explanation of the programme of this session.

6. ASSOCIATING

(Associative listening is the evocation by music/a musical excerpt of a subjective, affective reaction).

Five musical excerpts, each representing a set of values are played:

- old age
- action
- religion
- childhood
- warmth

On the basis of this form, the therapist asks the participants to choose the word which best expresses the emotion heard and felt in the music. Before the participants listen to an excerpt, the therapist carefully examines what the words mean to them. The tape is then stopped after each excerpt and the participants make their choice.

Finally, comes the associating to a free improvisation. The improvisation Niek (the other therapist) and I play has an A–B–A structure. A is played on a small harp, piano; B on drum and cymbals, forte and with crescendi and diminuendi. Niek calls for everybody's fantasy (or, as the lady from the video recording understands: 'So, what does it make you think of?'). In this process of associative listening, the cognitive element is highly mixed with the emotional.

1	• OLD AGE • ACTION • RELIGION
2	• TOGETHER • ALONE • JOY
3	• RELIGION • ACTION • CHILDHOOD
4	• CHILDHOOD • RELIGION • OLD AGE
5	• ALONE • ACTION • WARMTH

Group Improvisation on Big Drum

can (not) manage to play for long/short time

does (not) finish

does (not) avoid contact

imitation/dialogue/repetition

pulse/rhythm/dynamics

skin surface used: edge/small/large

emotional involvement

joins in the group pulse: yes/no/sometimes

participates in musical interactions: yes/no/sometimes

takes up musical challenges: yes/no/avoids

assessment of music making: yes/no

Figure 13.3

Data collection

Figure 13.3 shows a fragment of data collection. Information is gathered simply by underlining the appropriate words. A group mostly consists of two or three people. A form is filled in for each of them and notes are made of any special events which might occur. After a session the first therapist adds to this his subjective findings. Both objective material and subjective information are valued.

Use of information

What is done with the information gathered in the two 45 minute sessions? The information is arranged under a number of relevant categories:

General information, not obtained specifically by music therapy, about life history, but also about the present and about future expectations.

Information obtained by music therapy:

- the ability to understand instructions
- memory
- choosing, exploring, combining
- musical language
- musical contact and interaction
- reaction to both simple and more complex situations
- social functioning
- assessment of music making
- multiple choice and free associating.

After all this arranging of relevant items, final remarks are added. This information is then taken to a meeting of the multi-disciplinary team. This meeting is attended by a representative of the nursing staff, the psychogeriatrician, the occupational therapist, the psychologist, the psycho-motor therapist and even the dietician (she observes, when it is appropriate (when a client still lives on his or her own) whether someone can or cannot any longer cook a meal), and, of course, one of us.

All information is brought together and, by discussing it we try to reach valid statements about diagnosis. The music therapy information will partly confirm what others have observed. This in particular concerns the world of the subjective experience of the client and how this subjective experience relates to his or her cognitive and communicative parts, where music therapy can offer new or more detailed information.

References

Bakker, T. (1987) 'Psychogeriatrie. Model voor een dynamische systeem-analyse', *Metamedica* 66.

Gabriels, J., Niewenhuijzen, N. van and Raijmaekers, J. (1986) 'Muziektherapie met psycho-geriatrische patienten', in R. Adriaans, F. Schalkwijk and L. Stijlen, (eds) *Methoden van Muziektherapie.* Nijkerk: Uitgeverij Lemma.

Nieuwenhuijzen, N. van, (1991) De trommel: een aanval van soldaten. Het opzetten van een muziektherapeutisch observatieprogramme ten bate van psychogeriatrische patienten. Lezing te Enschede ter gelegenheid van een symposium over muziektherapie bij de ouder wordende mens.

Slaets, J. (1991) Hersenverwerking en de totstandkoming van complex gedrag en beleving. Lezing te Enschede ter gelegenheid van een symposium over muziektherapie bij de ouder wordende mens.

Part II

Research

Literature Review

Applied Research

CHAPTER 14

Music Therapy Research to Meet the Demands of Health and Educational Services

Research and Literature Analysis

Tony Wigram

United Kingdom

Any discussion on research in music therapy must first consider some of the motivations behind research, and then look at the current initiatives that are taking place in the field. It is also important to look at the different research methods that are being used, and pay some attention to where the future need for research lies. This chapter will attempt to consider some research practices in Europe, with reference to some of the studies currently underway. One can learn much from the past, and this chapter also looks at the literature, particularly that of the last five years. The author has attempted to break down the distribution in leading English language journals of the areas of work and the classification of research and other articles from the substantial body of literature, particularly that of the United States and, to a lesser extent, that of Great Britain and Europe.

There is a considerable amount of material now on music therapy, and it is accumulating in a wide variety of clinical areas. In Great Britain, the development of research programmes at the City University has encouraged many people, and the conferences, both in music therapy and art therapy, have proven very inspirational to people in the field. In Europe, the conferences that were held in 1983 in Paris and 1985 in Genova also provided a focus for finding out much about the different styles of music therapy; and the most recent conference in Holland in 1989 attracted presenters from all over the world.

Five research conferences have taken place at the City University on music therapy. The first, in 1983, on research aspects in music therapy, demonstrated immediately the debate that was going on in the profession and with other professionals about effective methods of research in our field. It began to question the traditional controlled methods of research using objective measures that have been the predominant direction of American music therapy research and which have considerable limitations for individual case design and psychotherapeutically based work. The second conference, in 1986, entitled 'Presentations in Music Therapy Research' continued the theme both of finding alternative methods of research, and of indicating the need for some additional research into the musical process and client-centred research.

In the third conference, techniques of research were explored. These included video sampling and self-evaluation (Hoskins 1987), which advocates the development of New Paradigm models of research (Reason and Rowan, 1981) as a developing and useful methodology for psychotherapeutically based research. The conference also included a piece of research exploring the value of parental involvement in therapy sessions with autistic children which involved a more traditional research design looking at outcome (Warwick and Muller 1987).

One of the recommendations from the fourth day conference on music therapy at the City University (in 1988) was the setting up of a research group by the professional association in England, which resulted in a small group of people, currently involved in research, meeting together at infrequent intervals to discuss the problems and difficulties they experienced, and to battle against some of the isolation that people engaged in research feel. Another useful outcome of this initiative was the development of the Music Therapy Research Register in England, which was published in 1991 (APMT 1991).

The fifth conference at City University (1991) included papers which integrated a psychodynamic approach into the area of research. Penny Rogers presented her music therapy work with clients who had been sexually abused. Margaret Heal described a psychoanalytically-informed project in 'The Development of Symbolic Function in a Woman with Downs Syndrome'. Steve Dunachie's work was based on musical analysis and compared the improvisations of adults with learning disabilities with those of children with normal intelligence. As yet these papers are unpublished.

In the last three years, research conferences at the City University have involved other art therapists, including dance, drama and art, and an arts therapies research group was also established by Helen Payne, who has recently edited a book on arts therapies research (Payne 1993).

I have been involved in the music therapy research group and the arts therapies research group, and have found meetings and discussions both stimulating and challenging. Although I have undertaken conventional evaluation of both group and individual sessions in my clinical setting, my research interests were largely inspired by the initiatives at the City University of Leslie Bunt and Sarah Hoskins, as well as my awareness of the vulnerability of music therapy to challenges regarding its efficacy and value. However, I freely admit that at first I was intimidated and quite put off by the prospect of research, as I expect many of my colleagues are. According to the Oxford Dictionary, research is 'careful search or enquiry; an endeavour to discover facts by scientific study of a subject, course or critical investigation' (Concise Oxford Dictionary 1949). Perhaps, then, it is the word 'science' or 'scientific' that rests uneasily with music therapists, who balance themselves between the world of science and the world of art. Scientific, in the dictionary, is described as 'according to rules laid down in science, protesting soundness of conclusions, systematic or accurate'.

At a recent seminar of the Arts Therapies Research Group, therapists from different arts therapies considered some of the reasons why they were researching, some of the questions that had occurred to them, and some of the fears they suffer from. Some of the comments on motivation were interesting:

- To be able to explore issues of research in a situation that isn't intimidating, where people will be open about what they think they are doing.

- To be practical, scientific, realistic within an artistic medium.

- To establish a dialogue between art form, therapy and academic enquiry.

- To discuss the ways that therapists work that can be acceptable to be researched, and can be written up and valued in the literature without having to be tagged it with a PhD to be made authentic.

- To validate, find out and perhaps invalidate aspects of arts therapies.

- To set up a process which asks the right questions, and uses the most appropriate research design and methodology.

Some of the fears expressed were equally revealing, and perhaps provide evidence as to why research in the arts therapies has been slow in starting:

- Fear that the research will stay vague and stuck in dualism: artistic–academic.

- Fear of losing the 'butterfly' element in clinical practice (intuition), if it is rescarched.

- Fear of undertaking the research in the wrong way.

- Fear of being considered an expert.

- Fear of finding out that what is important to the researcher might not be valued by the administrators.

- Fear that it will be disconnected and dry.

In the spring of 1986, three therapists working in a children's hospital in Miami published a paper in the NAMT *Journal of Music Therapy* called 'Where's the Research' (Siegal, Cartwright and Katz 1986). Their study was undertaken to try to find out whether the music therapists working in the South East region of the USA were participating in, or were interested in research. Of 310 music therapists surveyed, only 141 responded, a response rate of 45 per cent. It is worth reporting one part of the conclusions of this paper:

> Twenty-five per cent of the respondents not currently involved in research indicated the following reasons for not conducting research: no time available outside of work hours, lack of funds, and absence of research in their job descriptions. Twelve per cent reportedly had no interest in pursuing research, and nine per cent felt they were not sufficiently trained. Other reasons advanced were that facilities did not allow research, no time was available during working hours, the respondent was new at the facility, and facility populations were unstable. (Siegal *et al.* 1986)

It is a sad but rather familiar story, and yet the encouraging facts are that, despite such limitations in resources, time and additional skills, a substantial variety of research is underway and in Britain this is often done by music therapists working in the clinical field, rather than through university initiated work, whereas in the USA research is almost exclusively centred in the universities programmes.

My background in research originated from rather amateurish, and certainly unscientific, attempts to evaluate the effectiveness of my work with children and adults with learning difficulties. Conscious of my need to acquire research skills, I recently finished a qualifying degree in psychology at London University, where I undertook courses in Research Design, Research Methodology and Statistical Analysis. Here, I was introduced to the joys of scientific evaluation through controlled trials, becoming quickly used to manipulating independent variables, measuring dependent variables, controlling for order effects, and ensuring that all the laboratory studies I did had reliability, validity and were capable of replication. I also learnt how to choose subjects of a broad population sample, match subjects and ensure that all aspects of a study were tight and sound. Also, I got used to conceiving a hypothesis, and then testing it out objectively through the means of controlled trials. Statistical analysis of results took me to even greater heights of scientific excitement, as I struggled with parametric and non-parametric tests, analysis of variants, means, standard deviations and correlation tests. It was a very good discipline, and, for the type of research that I was simultaneously involved with, these methods and designs were quite applicable.

Looking at some of the research that has been going on in England and Europe, one can see evidence of a variety of different research modalities, the majority of which are still concerned with the outcome of therapy. Bunt's (1987) study in the early 1980s looked at links between childhood development and processes in music therapy with handicapped children. He used questionnaires to assess the role of music therapy, but also looked at behavioural changes in children, using time-based measures for video analysis, evaluating the difference between when the children had music therapy and when they didn't, as well as comparing music therapy against other play activities. This type of within-subjects design was also employed by Odell-Miller, (1993) who compared the effects of music therapy with reminiscence therapy in a group of elderly mentally ill people. The results showed that music therapy was most beneficial when held on a regular weekly basis. Observational methods were used to evaluate significant events in the patient's behaviour. Similarly, Oldfield (1990) looked at the difference between music therapy and play activity in clients with severe learning difficulties, analysing videotapes to see what changes occurred. Although the methods of measuring and evaluating may differ, the main emphasis has been on outcome research in England. A study by Sutton (1993), looking at the parallel development of music and language in speech and language disordered children is at present under way, and Pavlicevic's (1989) studies in Scotland, looking at the effects of music therapy in enhancing rehabilitation of chronic schizophrenics, involved comparing a matched group of 21 patients who attended individual music therapy sessions with 20 patients who were seen for ten weekly sessions. Her results showed significant improvement, both in their musical interaction rating scores, and in formal psychiatric measures, and adds tremendously valuable weight to the body of evidence that music therapy has a measurable influence and effect.

Video analysis seems to be one of the most common techniques of evaluating what is happening in the music therapy session, and was used by many of these studies, as well as the study by Lawes and Woodcock (1993) on the effect of music therapy sessions with clients who have self-injurious behaviour. The study by Ritchie, currently under way, will evaluate change and progress in clients without comparing it with another condition. Van Colle (1992) is looking at the behaviour of both the therapist and the child through observation of music therapy sessions with two groups of four severely and multiply-handicapped cerebral palsy children.

The musical material in improvisational music therapy has grown up in parallel to outcome research, as demonstrated by Dunachie's (1992) study on the comparative improvisations of mentally handicapped adults and pre-school children, and Lee's (1992) study on both the analysis of the structure of music, and the 'critical moments' in improvisation, such as moments of high emotion, moments of depression, silence and so forth. Other styles of analysis have included careful investigation into mother–infant interaction in comparison with music therapy interactions (Heal 1993).

Some substantial research is also taking place investigating the physiological effect of sound and music on certain physical and psychological conditions. Vibroacoustic therapy has emerged as an adjunct form of music therapy involving the passive treatment of clients with a combination of relaxing music and a pulsed low frequency tone. Studies have investigated the effect of this treatment on clients with cerebral palsy, anxiety, self-injurious behaviour and also the normal population (Skille, Wigram and Weeks 1989, Wigram 1991, Wigram 1993).

In The Netherlands, research is generated from both the training institutes and a research committee of the Dutch Association. The music therapy laboratory in Niemegen is undertaking research both on site and in psychiatric hospitals nearby, and is looking at the value of music therapy on different neurotic problems, such as compulsive personality disorder, anorexia nervosa, depression and contact disturbances, and aphasia.

Included in a wide diversity of studies is a study currently under way at the Academic Hospital in Amsterdam on the influence of music on the respiration of babies. This study may find correlations with the existing work in the United States (Maranto 1991). In studies on premature babies, music has been shown to promote weight gain, reduce movement, reduce irritability and crying behaviours, increase feeding behaviours, stimulate development, increase blood oxygen levels, reduce stress-related behaviours, and subsequently decrease the length of hospitalisation.

In Germany, the work at the medical faculty of the University of Witten/Herdecke has involved the methodological approach of ethology or clinical anthropology, as described by Aldridge and Pietroni (1987). The process of research is built up from the early observations that are made of what is happening in the therapy, where questions can be raised from the observations that are made, which stimulate the next stage of research. A single case design as a result of individual music therapy sessions is the predominant modality of work here (Aldridge 1990). In subsequent papers, Aldridge and Brandt (1991) have looked at music therapy and inflammatory bowel disease. Working on the basis that the inflammatory bowel disease could have an immunological basis, and that chronic stress has been shown to alter the immune system (Baker 1987, Patterson 1988, Stein et al. 1985) and thereby recovery, the research focussed on the value of the music therapy as stimulating positive emotions, enhancing coping responses and enabling recovery. This was a very interesting piece of research, as it involved comparing the behaviour of patients with inflammatory bowel disease and elements of their musical improvisation. For example, a lack of gut motility is evident in a lack of rhythmic flexibility, and an unresponsiveness to tempo changes and lack of rhythmical phrasing. The fact that they are increasingly introverted and restricted in their relationships, as well as often being quite rigid, is reflected in their music: quiet playing, involving no personal contact within the playing, a difficulty in contacting them in the musical relationship, and repetitive playing, returning to the same tempo and rhythmic pattern and being unresponsive to tempo changes.

Aldridge's techniques have often involved correlating the evidence of a pathology with the way a client improvises. Another study (Aldridge 1991) to investigate this looked at the correlations between speech patterns of type A behaviour clients, such as increased voice volume, fast speech rate, short response latency, emphatic voice and so forth, and the same communicative features in improvised music. At a recent conference in London, I was reminded of the idea, not in any way new, that one of the values of music therapy – indeed of many complementary medical applications – is at the pre-disease stage, where people who build up stress-related disorders can benefit before the disorder becomes an acute or chronic disease or illness.

The journals of music therapy provide one with an insight into where research is going on, and also the contributions made from various clinical fields. While not wanting to devote a lot of time to reviewing the literature, this paper would be incomplete without some evaluation of the content of journals, particularly over the last five years. In America, some regular reviews have looked in the past at the content of the *Journal of Music Therapy*, published by The National Association for Music Therapy (Jellison 1973, Madsen 1978, Gilbert 1979, James 1985, Decuir 1987, Gfeller 1987, Codding 1987). Wheeler (1988) undertook an analysis of literature from music therapy journals that included the *Journal of Music Therapy*, *Music Therapy*, *Music Therapy Perspectives* and the *Arts in Psychotherapy* (Wheeler 1988). Wheeler's study was based on the model used by Decuir in 1987, with the addition of the author's name.

Codding's (1987) analysis looked at 158 articles published in the *Journal of Music Therapy* between 1977 and 1985, and produced some interesting results. In particular, she found the research mode of enquiry was predominantly experimental, and that statistical designs are more prevalent than are behavioural designs in experimental research. Also, and perhaps surprisingly for me, she found that more studies had been conducted in clinical than in university settings.

Gfeller's (1987) study entitled 'Music Therapy Theory and Practice as reflected in Research Literature' noted themes in music therapy practice in America, including:

1. The prominence of behavioural and psycho-analytic theories as influencing clinical practice.

2. The value of music to enhance self-esteem, to socialise and to energise through rhythm.

3. Lack of studies with elderly and physically handicapped compared with the number of people working in these fields.

4. Low incidence of articles on work in adult psychiatry.

5. Low incidence of articles concerning music's influence on physiological change, but with increasing interest in this area (in fact only 9% of the total 243 articles referred to the physiological influence of music). Eleven per cent of the articles indicated practice or effect of music therapy was linked to psycho-analytic theory, and 20 per cent linked to behavioural theory. Data based studies make up one half of the surveyed articles and are much more prevalent in the field of learning difficulty and non-handicapped than in the psychiatric population.

This chapter now looks at the period between 1987 and 1991, and using the model first employed by Decuir (1986) and latterly by Wheeler (1988), the analysis concentrates on the type of articles written, a breakdown of the areas in which research is taking place, and in studying two of the journals, where the initiative for the research originated from. While not intending to provide as comprehensive an analysis as Wheeler developed from Decuir's original model, this analysis will give some indication of the situation over the last five years, and include a survey of articles in the *Journal of Music Therapy* (NAMT), *Music Therapy* (AAMT), *The Arts in Psychotherapy*, *Music Therapy Perspectives* (NAMT) and the *Journal of British Music Therapy* (BSMT/APMT).

Decuir's (1987) study gave a detailed breakdown, including the title of the articles and the general mode (clinical, research, general), broken down into fourteen clinical areas, four theoretical areas and one area to do with

Table 14.1: Decuir's Breakdown of Clinical and General Areas of Articles – *Journal of Music Therapy* 1964–1986

Title	No. of Papers
Clinical	
Special Education and Childhood Exceptionality	28
Childhood and Adolescent Psychiatry	14
Mental Retardation and Developmental Disability	45
Speech and Communication Disorders	11
Adult Psychiatry	19
Alcohol and LSD	6
Community Mental Health and Day Treatment	12
Gerontology	11
Group Psychotherapy	16
Behavioural Approaches	44
General Medicine	11
Auditory Impairment and Vocational Rehabilitation	9
Visual Impairment and Physical Impairment	10
Music Therapy and Autism	8
	246
Theoretical	
Psychology of Music/Influence of Music on Behaviour	51
Philosophy, Music and Psychoanalysis	10
About Music Therapy	40
Evaluation in Music Therapy	9
	110
Training	
Education and Training of Music Therapists	33
	33

education and training. He concluded that the 'research in music therapy is sparse in all of the traditional clinical areas, with the possible exception of mental retardation'. Table 14.1 shows the variety of areas in which Decuir was categorising articles in the JMT.

Table 14.2: Synthesis of Decuir's Review of JMT Articles 1964–1986:
Results in percentages

Topic	Investigation area				
	Clinical	Research	General on Musical Elements	Research Outcome	Behavioural
1. Special Education/ Learning Disability	12	24	8	31	56
2. Autism/Child Psychiatry	22	2	0	9	32
3. Sensory/Physical Impairment	6	10	2	23	57
4. Adult Psychiatry	35	7	10	21	15
5. General Medicine	1	4	0	45	35
6. Elderly	5	3	0	54	0
7. Training and General	18	50	80	8	25
Total	**21%**	**63**	**15**	**18**	**32%**

Table 14.2 condenses these nineteen separate categories into seven, and gives an indication in percentages of the distribution of papers in clinical, research and general areas. It shows a predominance of research papers overall, and particular in the area of training and general papers. I have also tried to identify those papers where the research or topic was predominantly looking at the musical elements in music therapy, as compared with those papers where behavioural or outcome research was undertaken. The total percentages over all categories give an indication of almost twice as many papers on behavioural work/outcome research. The Table also indicates a predominance of papers in the area of training and education of music therapists and theoretical/philosophical papers compared with the clinical areas.

Following Decuir's model, I reviewed articles in the five of the journals of music therapy, categorising them into seven areas. Again, the results of

Table 14.3: Percentages in Clinical Areas of Total Number of Articles Published in American and British Journals 1987–1991

Topic	Journal					
Area	JMT	MT	AP	MTP	JBMT	Total %
1. Special Education Learning Disability	17	6	3	15	25	15
2. Autism/Child Psychiatry	4	3	7	5	7	5
3. Sensory Handicap	11	3	7	10	5	8
4. Adult Psychiatry	6	30	18	8	12	12
5. Elderly	9	0	0	5	5	5
6. General Medicine	21	30	39	31	10	26
7. Training and General Research	31	27	25	24	36	29

Table 14.4 Percentage of Clinical, Research and General Published in the Field of Special Education and Developmental Disability – 1987–1991

	Clinical	Research	General
JMT	53	9	0
MT	8	100	0
AP	6	0	0
MTP	37	22	5
JBMT	41	6	4

Table 14.5: Percentage of Clinical, Research and General Papers Published in the Field of Autism and Child Psychiatry – 1987–1991

	Clinical	Research	General
JMT	7	4	0
MT	8	0	0
AP	12	0	0
MTP	9	11	3
JBMT	18	0	0

Table 14.6: Percentage of Clinical, Research and General Papers
Published in the Field of Sensory and Physical Disability

	Clinical	Research	General
JMT	13	13	0
MT	8	0	0
AP	12	0	0
MTP	9	11	10
JBMT	6	0	8

Table 14.7: Percentage of Clinical, Research and General Papers
Published in the Field of Adult Psychiatry – 1987–1991

	Clinical	Research	General
JMT	13	4	0
MT	38	0	0
AP	29	0	0
MTP	16	0	5
JBMT	12	14	17

Table 14.8: Percentage of Clinical, Research and General Papers
Published in the Field of General Medicine – 1987–1991

	Clinical	Research	General
JMT	7	29	8
MT	38	0	4
AP	41	0	40
MTP	25	22	33
JBMT	23	14	8

Table 14.9: Percentage of Clinical, Research and General Papers
Published in the Field of Gerontology – 1987–1991

	Clinical	Research	General
JMT	7	9	0
MT	0	0	0
AP	0	0	0
MTP	3	11	5
JBMT	6	0	0

Table 14.10: Percentage of Clinical, Research and General Papers
Published in the Field of Training of Music Therapists,
and General Papers – 1987–1991

	Clinical	Research	General
JMT	0	31	92
MT	0	0	56
AP	0	100	60
MTP	0	22	38
JBMT	0	6	58

articles written in these journals over the last five years show a dearth of papers in the clinical fields, apart from the increasing applications of music therapy in general medicine. All five journals have a high percentage of articles in the training and general research field.

Tables 14.4–14.10 give a further breakdown of the material in these five journals, identifying within the various fields of clinical practice, training and theory, how the articles can be divided into clinical, research or general papers. From these tables, one can see the emphasis each journal has in specific clinical areas, and the percentage in each case in overall proportion to the content of the total number of articles in each journal.

Finally, a breakdown of the papers into clinical, research and general articles overall is presented in Table 14.11. This shows a predominance of research papers in the *Journal of Music Therapy*, with a fairly even balance between clinical and general papers and the other four journals, which contain only a limited number of research studies.

To some extent the analysis of the literature speaks for itself. We are suffering from a lack of research in the clinical field, and even where some studies have been done they are in quite selective areas. There is a growing enthusiasm and motivation for research in many areas, and it is common to find in the clinical field that music therapists are evaluative in their approach

Table 14.11: Categories of Articles in Percentages – 1987–1991

Journal	Mode of Article		
	Clinical	Research	General
JMT	21	62	17
MT	41	3	56
AP	61	3	36
MTP	40	11	49
JBMT	47	19	33

to their work. This is vital for the future development of services in such a new and to a certain extent 'unproven' scientific field. With the development of such information services as the Documentary Information and Communication System, the ability to access the material in the literature and locate collaborators in a specific field will become easy, and a great aid to research. There are already existing databases which have been compiled on music therapy, although these are mainly centered in the USA. The arguments between those who favour qualitative research and those who are more based in quantitative analysis should be reconciled, as research calls for a variety of approaches, and perhaps more particularly a blend of process and outcome studies.

References

Aldridge, D. (1990) 'The development of a research strategy for music therapists in a hospital setting', *The Arts in Psychotherapy*, 17, 231-237.

Aldridge, D. (1991) 'Physiological change, communication and the playing of improvised music: some proposals for research', *The Arts in Psychotherapy*, 18, 59-64.

Aldridge, D. and Brandt, G. (1991) *The Arts in Psychotherapy*, 18, 113-121.

Aldridge, D. and Pietroni, P.C. (1987) 'Research trials in general practice: towards a focus on clinical practice', *Family Practice*, 4, 311-315.

Baker, G.H. (1987). 'Invited review: psychological factors and immunity', *Journal of Psychosomatic Research*, 31, 1-10.

Bunt, L.G.K. (1987) Music Therapy for the child with a handicap: Evaluation of the effects of intervention. Ph.D Thesis (unpublished) City University, London.

Chesney, J. (1987) 'Is psychotherapy research possible?', in 'Starting Research in Music Therapy', proceedings of the third music therapy day conference, City University, London.

Codding, P. (1987) 'A content analysis of the *Journal of Music Therapy*', *Journal of Music Therapy*, 24, 195–202

The Concise Oxford Dictionary (1949) Revised E. Macintosh. Oxford: Clarendon Press.

Decuir, A. (1987) 'Readings for music therapy students: An analysis of clinical literature from the *Journal of Music Therapy*', in C.D. Maranto and K.E. Bruscia (eds), *Perspectives in Music Therapy Education and Training* (pp. 57–70). Philadelphia: Temple University.

Dunachie, S. (1991) 'A comparison of children's use of musical improvisation and adults' with learning difficulties'. Paper presented at the fifth Music Therapy Research Conference, City University, London.

Dunachie, S. (1992) 'Improvisation in Children and Adults'. Paper presented at the European Conference: *Music Therapy in Health and Education in the European Community*, King's College Cambridge. London: BSMT Publications.

Gfeller, K. (1987) 'Music therapy theory and practice as reflected in research literature', *Journal of Music Therapy*, 24, 178–194.

Gilbert, J.P. (1979) 'Published research in music therapy, 1973–1978: Content, focus and implications for future research', *Journal of Music Therapy*, 16, 102–110.

Heal, M. (1991) 'The development of symbolic function in a young woman with Downs Syndrome'. Paper presented at the fifth Music Therapy Research Conference, City University, London.

Heal, M. (1993) 'A comparison of mother/infant interaction and the client/therapist relationship in music therapy session'. Paper presented November 1991 at CIBA Workshop Seminar: Evaluation of Music as a Therapeutic Intervention. In A. Wigram, R. West and B. Saperston (eds) *Music and the Healing Process: A Handbook of Music Therapy*. Chichester: Carden Publication.

Heron, J. (1981) Experimental Research Methodology, in Reason, P. and Rowan, J. (eds) *Human Enquiry: A source-book of New Paradine Research*. Chichester: Wiley.

Hoskins, S. (1987) Productive and counter-productive issues for therapist and researcher in 'Starting research in Music Therapy'. Proceedings of the third music therapy day conference, City University, London, New Paradigm Research Methodology.

James, M.R. (1985) 'Sources of articles published in the Journal of Music Therapy: The first twenty years, 1964–1983', *Journal of Music Therapy*, 22, 87–94.

Jellison, J. (1973) 'The frequency and generaly mode of inquiry of research in music therapy, 1952–1972', *Council for Research in Music Therapy*, 35, 1–8.

Lawes, C. and Woodcock, J. (1993) 'Music Therapy in people with severe learning difficulties who exhibit self-injurious behaviour', in A. Wigram, R. West, and B. Saperston, B. (eds) *Music and the Healing Process: A Handbook of Music Therapy*. Chichester: Carden Publications.

Lee, C.A. (1992) 'The analysis of therapeutic improvisatory music with young people living with the virus HIV and Aids'. Unpublished Ph.D thesis, City University, London.

Madsen, C.K. (1978) 'Research on research: An evaluation of research presentations', *Journal of Music Therapy*, 15, 67–73.

Maranto, C.D. (1991) *Application of Music in Medicine*. Washington, D.C.: NAMT Publications.

Music Therapy Research Register (1991) Great Britain: APMT Publications.

Odell-Miller, H. (1993) 'An investigation into the effects of music therapy with elderly mentally ill people', in A. Wigram, R. West and B. Saperston (eds) *Music Therapy and the Healing Process: A Handbook of Music Therapy*. Chichester: Carden Publications.

Oldfield, A. (1990) 'The effects of music therapy on a group of profoundly mentally handicapped adults', *Journal of Mental Deficiency Research*, 34, 107-125.

Patterson, J.M. (1988) 'Families experiencing stress', *Family Systems Medicine*, 6, 202-237.

Pavlicevic, M. and Trevartten, C. (1989) 'A musical assessment of psychiatric states in adults', *Psychopathology*, 22, 325–334.

Payne, II. (1993) (ed) *Handbook of Inquiry in the Arts Therapies: One River, Many Currents.* London: Jessica Kingsley Publishers.

Reason, P. and Rowan, J. (1981) (eds) *Human Enquiry: A Source Book of New Paradigm Research.* Chichester: Wiley.

Rogers, P. (1991) 'Working with clients who have been sexually abused'. Paper presented at the fifth Music Therapy Conference, City University, London.

Siegal, L.S., Cartwright, J.S. and Katz, E. (1986) 'Where's the Research?', *Journal of Music Therapy*, 23 (1), 38–45.

Skill, O., Wigram, A. and Weeks, L. (1989) Vibroacoustic therapy: the therapeutic effect of low frequency sound on specific physical disorders and disabilities', *Journal of British Music Therapy*, 3, 2, 6–10

Stein, M., Keller, S. and Schleifer, S. (1985) 'Stress and neuroimmodulation: The role of depression and neuroendocrine function', *Journal of Immunology*, 135, 827-833.

Sutton, J. (1993) 'The Guitar Doesn't Know this Song: An Investigation of Parallel Development in Speech/Language and Music Therapy', in M. Heal and A. Wigram (eds) *Music Therapy in Health and Education.* London: Jessica Kingsley Publishers.

Van Colle, S. (1992) 'Music therapy process with cerebral palsied children: connections with psychoanalytic models, particularly those of Winnicott and Bowlby'. Unpublished Ph.D thesis.

Warwick, A. and Muller, P. (1987) The linking of two disciplines in research: Psychology and Music Therapy, in 'Starting Research in Music Therapy', proceedings of the third music therapy day conference. City University, London.

Wheeler, B.L. (1988) 'An analysis of literature from selected music therapy journals', *Music Therapy Perspectives*, 5, 94–101.

Wigram, A. (1991) 'Die Wirking Von Tiefen Tonen und musik auf Den Muskel-Tonus Und Die Blutzirkulation'. *Zeitchrift Des Osterreichiscren Berufsverbands der Musiktherapeuten*, 2, 3–12.

Wigram, A. (1993) 'The feeling of sound: The effect of music and low frequency sound in reducing anxiety and challenging behaviour in clients with learning difficulties', in H. Payne (ed) *Handbook of Inquiry in the Arts Therapies: One River, Many Currents.* London: Jessica Kingsley Publishers.

CHAPTER 15

Applications of Music in Medicine

Cheryl Dileo Maranto
United States of America

The interrelationships between music and medicine are broad and varied. For purposes of this paper, the term 'music and medicine' refers to the use of music therapy in the treatment and prevention of physical illness and disease. During the past 15 years, these applications of music therapy have been given considerable emphasis in the United States, as evidenced by the growing number of published research and clinical articles on the topic. The purpose of this paper is to provide an overview of this research in the various medical areas where music therapy has been applied and to describe commonly used music therapy techniques.

Classifications of music and medicine

Because the area of music and medicine is diverse, containing many practices and uses of music, there is a need to define and classify the strategies used in treatment. This differentiates the practice of music therapy as a discipline from the quasi-therapeutic uses of music by non-music therapists (an example being the use of background music in medical waiting rooms). Implicit in the definition of music therapy are the following criteria: (a) a trained music therapist, (b) a patient assessment procedure, (c) a goal-oriented music therapy treatment process, and (d) appropriate evaluation procedures.

In addition, it is assumed that both music and the therapeutic relationship with the patient are necessary components of the therapeutic process, with either assuming a different level of importance at various stages of treatment depending upon the needs of the patient (Maranto 1991, 1992, 1993).

Music therapy may also relate to the medical treatment of the patient in a variety of ways: (a) supportive to medical treatment (e.g. the use of music listening during kidney dialysis); (b) as an equal partner to medical treatment (e.g. the use of singing in conjunction with medication as a treatment for respiratory disorders); or (c) as a primary intervention for a medical condition (e.g. the use of music listening to directly suppress pain) (Maranto 1991, 1992, 1993).

The relationship between mind and body

Applications of music in medicine may adhere to a variety of theoretical orientations in medicine, particularly with regard to the relationship (or lack thereof) between the mind and the body. Some of the most current thinking in the United States is based upon Engel's biopsychosocial model of illness (1977) which emphasizes the integral relationship and interconnectedness between the mind and the body and the influence that each has upon the other. Thus, psychosocial phenomena can contribute to biomedical illness and, conversely, biomedical illness is associated with changes in psychosocial phenomena. For example, it has been demonstrated that traumatic life events, such as the death of a spouse may contribute to immunosuppression and ultimately to cancer in the surviving spouse. Conversely, an illness such as myocardial infarction may inevitably cause psychosocial events such as depression and disturbances in family interactions. It should be noted that the field of medicine has acknowledged the existence and causation of psychosomatic illness in the past; however, these new theories may account for illness far beyond what was previously viewed as psychosomatic.

If one accepts this theory of the mind/body relationship, a host of questions follow, including:

1. What psychosocial phenomena (including personality traits) predispose an individual to disease?

2. Which psychosocial phenomena influence the course of the disease and longevity of the patient?

3. How does the mind actually communicate with the body in neurological and biochemical terms?

4. What type of treatment, besides medical, can help prevent and treat disease?

The amount of research which currently seeks to address these questions is growing. For example, psychosocial phenomena such as stress, depression, feelings of helplessness, inability to express feelings, the meaning of the illness, expectations, and so forth, are considered contributing factors to both disease and the ultimate course of diseases. In addition, a number of researchers are identifying specific biochemical messengers in the body which serve as the form of communication between the brain and the body. These chemicals (neuropeptides) once thought to be produced only in the brain, are also produced outside the brain, in various parts of the body; furthermore, receptors for these substances have been found throughout the body. New discoveries have linked these biochemical messengers to various bodily systems, most importantly the immune system. The relatively new area of psychoneuroimmunology seeks to confirm the suspected intimate relationship between psychological events, the nervous system and immune system.

Various non-medical treatments have been proposed and studied which are influential in preventing disease and achieving health. These include: biofeedback, hypnosis, meditation, psychotherapy, exercise, diet, and imagery. Music is widely used as an adjunct to a number of these procedures. However, the effectiveness of music therapy as a treatment modality in and of itself continues to grow in importance.

Music and medicine

Standley (1986, 1989) has conducted two meta-analyses of experimental research in music and medicine. Results of these analyses (although results vary with each individual study) reveal that subjects who receive music as part of the medical treatment generally score about one standard deviation above the mean on dependent measures as compared to control subjects (N.B., subjects who receive music achieve more satisfactory results than controls).

Examples of these biomedical dependent variables are as follows: pain, need for pain medication, perceived length of labour, blood pressure, pulse rate, exhalation ability, muscle tension, respiration rate, stress hormone levels, EMG levels, headache intensity, centimeters of dilation, infant apgar scores, grasp strength, nausea and vomiting intensity and length, intracranial pressure, and length of hospitalization. Psychosocial dependent measures were: anxiety, perceived mood, attitudes, perceived childbirth experience, perceived contentment, responses to hospitalization, distraction from medical procedure, sleep satisfaction, choice of anesthesia, helplessness and pleasure (Maranto 1992). It is obvious that the variety of dependent measures studied reflect the diverse applications of music in medicine, including childbirth, surgery, rehabilitation, neonatal intensive care, and so forth.

Treatment goals in music and medicine are equally varied, depending on the condition of the patient, medical procedures used and individual needs. Examples of these include: reduction of autonomic responsivity (heart rate, blood pressure, electromyography, etc.); facilitation of deep, rhythmic breathing, pain suppression, decrease of stress hormone levels, reduction of preoperative anxiety, distraction during medical procedures, reduction of depression associated with procedures and/or illness, facilitation of decision-making regarding treatment, facilitation of support among patients and families, and enhancement of immune functioning (Maranto 1993).

Goals in music and medicine in general may be summarized according to the following:

1. Elimination of stress and anxiety

2. Elimination of pain

3. Elimination of depression, helplessness, etc.

4. Enhancement of immune functioning.

Medical procedures or illness almost always elicit feelings of stress, loss of control, and fear of the unknown. These feelings manifest themselves in increased autonomic responsivity or stress reactions which may interact in a negative way with the medical procedure or illness. Reduction of these factors may enhance the success of the medical procedure as well as the overall health of the patient.

Pain is a common by-product of illness and medical intervention. The experiences and reactions to pain, while variable from individual to individual and highly subjective in nature, are also responsible for increased autonomic activity. Reduction of and distraction from pain may influence the course of recovery and influence the quality of life for the individual.

Feelings associated with illness and medical procedures typically include depression, helplessness, isolation, withdrawal, loss of control, and so forth. Recent research has noted the relationship between patients' feelings and attitudes and the onset of and course of an illness. Reduction in these negative feelings may have direct physiological benefits for the patient.

Optimal immune system functioning is necessary to prevent illness and to recover from illness. Recent research in music therapy has demonstrated that even relatively short periods of music listening may significantly increase at least one measure of immune functioning present in saliva (Maranto 1993). These preliminary results hold much promise for the future of music and medicine and much research attention needs to be devoted to this particular area of study.

Although the majority of music therapists in the world would have no doubt of the power of music to facilitate health and healing, a sceptical, pragmatic health professional may ask 'What are the benefits of music as opposed to other methods of intervention?' Music therapists would respond in the following manner. First, music appears to have the ability to affect individuals on both biomedical and psychosocial levels simultaneously. Thus music appears to be a particularly efficient and immediate treatment modality for the treatment of medical illness. Second, music, as opposed to most other medical interventions is non-invasive and painless. Third, the use of music has few contraindications and few if any side-effects. Fourth, music is easily accessible to patients both in treatment and in home care. It allows the patient to assume some level of responsibility and participation in his own treatment. And lastly, music is cost-effective when compared with the sky-rocketing costs of other types of medical intervention (Maranto 1992, 1993).

In music and medicine, as in music therapy, the full range of experiences are made available to the patient. These include: passive/receptive methods, improvisational methods, and performing possibilities (Maranto 1992, 1993). Obviously, the physical condition of patients (particularly those with severe or terminal illness) is a major consideration in the selection of music experiences. In addition, the practical application of music as an adjunct to medical treatment must be considered in light of the physical and situational restraints of that treatment. For these reasons, much (but not all) of the research in music and medicine in the United States has examined passive/receptive methods. It is the task of further research to investigate the influence of improvisational and performing media on health.

Various factors appear to be considerations in selecting music for passive/receptive methods. These include the following: (a) familiarity with the music, (b) preference for the music, (c) history and associations with the music, and (d) characteristics/elements of the music. It is noted that these factors will vary depending on the passive/receptive method used and the therapeutic goal.

Several research studies have emphasized the importance of using music that is familiar to the patient in music listening procedures. It is speculated that unfamiliar music may cause an 'orienting response' due to its novelty that may undermine the desired therapeutic goals, particularly if the goal is relaxation.

Similarly, several studies have pointed to the need to use the patient's preferred music or preferred music styles in music listening procedures. Anecdotal evidence again demonstrates that music that is disliked by the patient will yield results, particularly in stress reduction, that are counterproductive.

The music therapist must carefully assess the patient's history and extramusical associations to the music to determine which of these will contribute to the therapeutic goal. As music therapists are aware, relatively benign pieces of music, by the therapist's standards can cause abreactive reactions if negative images and associations are elicited.

The music therapist must examine the particular elements of the music, i.e., rhythm, tempo, harmony, tension, timbre and so forth, to determine if these are consistent with the particular therapeutic goal. When the therapeutic goal is to effect physiological responses, these elements may be key determinants of the desired response (Maranto 1993).

Principles of music and medicine

The following principles of music and medicine are presented as a rationale and guideline for the therapeutic use of music in medicine. This list is derived from the research literature as well as clinical practice (Maranto 1993).

1. Music elicits physiological responses. A considerable amount of early research has studied the influence of music on various physiological parameters, including heart rate, blood pressure, electromyography, skin resistance, skin temperature, muscular responses and so forth. What we know at this point is that music does influence bodily processes and functioning. However, the direction of the response cannot always be predicted. There appear to be many individual, confounding variables related to physiological responses to music. Because music is such a complex stimulus, and physiological reactions are equally complex, it is impossible at this time to establish a consistent one-to-one relationship with predictive power.

2. Music elicits psychological responses. The ability of music to influence mood and affective responses in individuals is perhaps a core theory in music therapy practice. As with physiological responses, however, the discipline of music therapy has not yet reached a paradigmatic stage. Again, many individual variables need to be considered as well as the context of the therapeutic relationship and the specific music therapy methods used.

3. Music evokes imagery and associations. The ability of music to elicit extra-musical associations is widely known and accepted. Again,

these are highly individualistic, depending upon the culture, previous musical experiences and history of the individual. When these factors are taken into consideration, more accurate predictions for these effects can be ascertained.

4. Music elicits cognitive responses. Cognitive responses to music are unique to the individual, for it is the individual alone who can assign cognitive meaning to the musical experience. Cognitive responses to music may be key determinants in the effectiveness of therapeutic interventions, particularly in music and medicine. It is suspected that cognition plays a mediating role with regard to the individual's interpretation of the meaning of the music which is subsequently conveyed to bodily processes. Another aspect of this phenomenon is the differential responses to music (on all levels) that result from musical training. As individuals become trained musicians, responses to music may be more or less intense.

5. Music may cause physiological and/or psychological entrainment. Entrainment is a process in physics whereby two objects vibrating at similar frequencies will tend to cause mutual sympathetic resonance. In the area of music and medicine, for example, music has the potential to 'entrain' heart rate via its pulse, or to 'entrain' breathing through its rhythm. Preliminary studies in this area have showed fascinating results. The phenomenon of 'iso-moodic' responses to music are well known in clinical practice. By matching the music to the client's existing mood, changes in the client's mood can be altered through subsequent changes in the mood of the music.

6. Physiological, psychological, and cognitive responses to music are unique for each individual. This principle has been emphasized previously. As non-music therapists attempt to develop audio-tapes geared towards the amelioration of specific problems, for example stress, one is constantly reminded of the fact that music used in music and medicine must be individually tailored to the individual through careful selection, composition, or improvisation to meet his or her unique goals, characteristics and history.

7. Music elicits psychological, cognitive, and physiological responses
    simultaneously; these may or may not be interrelated. An
    interesting phenomenon in some of the research on music and
    stress is the lack of concordance among various types of responses
    to music. For example, when listening to sedative music, it is not
    uncommon for subjects to report they are relaxed, while
    physiological measures may reveal an increase in autonomic
    reactivity. There can be much speculation on the cause of this
    phenomenon relying on various psychological theories; however,
    there is no overriding explanation at this point.

8. Elements of music, as well as the music gestalt, must be taken into
    consideration. As stated above, specific elements of the music, i.e.,
    rhythm, tempo, texture, harmony, tension, timbre and so forth,
    must be examined as they relate to the desired response. For
    example, the pulse of the music may be examined as it relates to
    the entrainment of heart rate. In addition, the influence of music
    as a gestalt will likely elicit a greater response from the client than
    an isolated metronome pulse.

9. Music may have an enhancing or diminishing effect when combined
    with other methods of treatment. It is a common assumption that,
    if a non-music therapy technique is effective, for example
    biofeedback, it will be more effective with music. While this is the
    case in many instances, there are some situations where music may
    have a diminishing effect particularly when cognitive shifts in
    attention are demanded of the individual. An example of this is
    when music is used in combination with imagery that is directed
    by the therapist.

Specific applications of music in medicine

This section provides a summary of clinical and experimental research in the
various areas of medical practice. The reader should be advised that the
amount of research upon which this summary was drawn varies from area
to area. Thus, some results have been replicated more than others. However,
it is hoped that this summary may provide ideas and an impetus for additional
research. Summaries are presented in tabular form.

Table 15.1: Music in Surgery

Music listening has been shown to:

- significantly reduce stress hormone levels
- decrease anxiety
- diminish side effects of anesthesia and amount needed
- reduce pulse rate; stabilize blood pressure
- reduce postoperative pain and need for pain medication
- increase speed of recovery
- increase verbalizations about surgery
- in research with large groups of patients, significantly better outcomes in psychological, physiological, and behavioural parameters were revealed.

Table 15.2: Music in Neonatal Intensive Care Units

Music listening has been shown to:

- promote weight gain and reduce movement
- reduce irritability, crying and stress behaviours
- increase feeding behaviours
- stimulate development
- increase blood oxygen levels
- decrease length of hospitalization.

Table 15.3: Music in Pediatric Medical Care

Passive and active music experiences have been shown to:

- decrease anxiety
- increase verbalizations related to illness
- reduce stress symptoms
- assist families with issues related to the child's illness.

Table 15.4: Music in Physical Rehabilitation

Passive and active music experiences have been shown to:

- structure rhythmic movement
- improve motor functioning
- reinforce desired movements
- decrease muscle tension
- improve motivation for therapy
- enhance acupuncture efficacy.

Table 15.5: Music in Respiratory Care

Passive and active music experiences have been shown to:

- entrain respiration
- improve respiration and vital capacity
- reduce anxiety associated with medical procedures (bronchoscopy).

Table 15.6: Music in Burn Care

Passive and active music experiences have been shown to:

- reduce pain
- reduce heart rate during debridement
- elicit joint mobility
- augment respiratory exercises
- reduce psychological trauma.

Table 15.7: Music in Pain Management

Passive and active music experiences have been shown to:

- influence psychological and physiological aspects
- enhance self-regulatory procedures
- enhance relaxation
- decrease verbalizations about pain
- increase pain tolerance and threshold
- decrease pain medication needed.

Table 15.8: Music in Stress Reduction

Passive music experiences have been shown to:

- decrease muscle tension
- decrease psychological anxiety
- decrease blood pressure
- decrease corticosteroid levels
- decrease finger temperature
- affect circadian amplitude
- decrease overt signs of anxiety.

Table 15.9: Music in the General Hospital or Intensive Care Unit

Passive music experiences have been shown to:

- decrease anxiety
- decrease pain
- improve comfort
- provide an element of control for the patient
- provide a diversion
- elevate mood.

Table 15.10: Music in Labour and Delivery

Passive and active music experiences may:

- decrease fear and anxiety
- compress time during labour
- serve as a distractor/focal point (Lamaze method)
- regulate breathing
- enhance Lamaze procedures
- increase euphoria of birth
- reduce pain
- promote wellness of infant
- decrease length of labour
- influence dilation time.

Table 15.11: Music in Oncology/Terminal Illness

Passive and active music experiences may:

- decrease pain
- provide distraction from illness
- increase verbalizations related to illness
- reduce anxiety
- provide measure of control/reduce helplessness
- help patient deal with issues of illness and dying
- assist families with issues related to the patient.

Special techniques used in music and medicine

There are a number of techniques that are used in music and medicine. It should be noted that these techniques may also be relevant to other areas of music therapy practice, for example psychiatry. A brief definition, possible uses, and considerations for use are provided for each technique. It is noted that the list of techniques used in music and medicine includes a number of others not discussed here and this list should not be considered comprehensive.

Music listening

In this common technique, the patient listens to music free-field or through headphones. The music stimulus may be live music, tapes, records, or CDs. This technique may also be combined with vibroacoustics.

The purpose of the music listening experience is usually to reduce pain, anxiety, and so forth. Considerations for its use include the following: (a) music must be carefully selected to meet the therapeutic goals, (b) music must also be carefully selected according to the unique needs and aspects of the individual, (c) consideration must be given to the timing of onset of the music. For example, if music listening is used during a painful medical procedure, the music listening should be timed to begin before the onset of the pain, (d) attention should be given to the duration of the listening experience so that habituation does not occur, and (e) the patient should be given control over the music and volume.

Music Vibroacoustic Therapy

In this technique, music and/or low frequencies are applied directly to the body. Often, there is simultaneous music listening. It is used for a variety of therapeutic goals, including improved circulation, relaxation, pain reduction, and so forth. When specific low frequencies (30–120 Hz.) are added to the music, the vibrational effect is enhanced. Considerations for its use include the specific medical condition, as some may be contraindicated, and the resonance areas in the body targeted for intervention. In addition, other elements of the music should be considered as they relate to vibration (e.g., intensity and rhythm).

Toning

Toning is a technique wherein improvised and sustained vocalizations or singing on various pitches are used to improve respiration and enhance relaxation. It is also used to regulate breathing, control pain, and enhance focus and concentration.

Entrainment

As stated previously, entrainment is achieved by matching music to the physiological and/or psychological aspects of the patient. The music is then gradually changed in the direction of the therapeutic goal with corresponding effects noted in the physiological/psychological domains. It is used to directly elicit therapeutic change particularly in pain management or relaxation. In considering its use, music must be selected or improvised to match precisely the existing condition of the patient. The patient may be an active participant in selecting, designing or improvising the music and should ultimately determine if it is suitable. In addition, the music must be structured to progress to the desired therapeutic state.

Music-Elicited Imagery

This technique involves listening to music in a very relaxed state in order to elicit spontaneous imagery related to therapeutic goals. It is used to elicit imagery more directly than with verbal stimuli, to intensify a desired response to music, to enhance focus and concentration, and to enhance positive affective responses to music. Considerations include: the ability of the patient to image and the selection of the music to match the desired therapeutic goal. A relaxation induction is generally given by the therapist prior to the onset of the music and an imagery focus is suggested at the beginning of the music. The length of the music is generally limited to avoid the client's loss of focus. Generally, the images are discussed following the music-listening period in the light of their relevance to the client. Usually, there is no interaction between the client and the therapist during the music listening.

Music and Directed Imagery

In this technique, music and specific suggestions for imagery are given to the patient who is in a very relaxed state. The directed images are relevant to the therapeutic goal, for example enhancement of immune functioning, and may involve the imaging of specific bodily processes. The assumption is that the imagery will have a direct impact on the functioning of the body (immune system). This technique is used often with individuals who have limited capacity in directing their own images or who need the structure of directed imagery.

Careful consideration must be given to the music which must support the imagery and not detract from it by causing a sensory overload or cognitive shift. The therapist must also use care to pace the directed imagery in a way that is consistent with the client's own production of the images.

Guided Imagery and Music

The Bonny Method of Guided Imagery and Music involves a process wherein a person in a relaxed state listens to carefully selected music. During this process, spontaneous images are reported to the therapist who provides suggestion for focusing and deepening the experience. The images are discussed following the music-listening process. In this method, the therapist and music work in tandem to achieve the desired goal. It is used to explore the psychological issues related to illness as well as the causes of illness. It helps the patient achieve creative ways to deal with the illness and in some cases may directly affect the course of the illness via the remission of symptoms. This process requires a patient who is sufficiently motivated to undertake this type of therapy and a therapist who has had special training and experience with the method.

Music and Verbal Relaxation methods

This technique involves combining music with traditional verbal relaxation methods, such as progressive muscle relaxation, autogenic training and/or suggestion. Music is used to enhance the effectiveness of the other techniques in helping the client focus attention, to provide direct cues and support for relaxation, as well its direct solicitation, to structure the relaxation process, to assist in generalizing the response to other areas outside the therapy setting, and to prevent habituation to verbal directions.

The success of the music may to some degree depend on the success of the method it supports as well as the clinical population for whom it is used (highly anxious patients may derive greater benefits than low-anxious). The session should be long enough to elicit the desired effect and avoid sensory overload to the patient or cause cognitive shifts between the music and verbal instructions. Thus, music should match the verbal directions as closely as possible. In addition, the music should be designed to entrain the desired response.

Music and biofeedback

In this technique music is used as an adjunct to traditional biofeedback procedures of various types; for example, EMG, skin-temperature, EEG, and so forth. Music is used to provide a cue for relaxation as well as to elicit and structure relaxation directly. In addition, when music is used as the feedback mechanism it will assist in reinforcing relaxation. Music can also be useful in helping the patient generalize the relaxation response to other settings.

The delivery of music and biofeedback is a consideration in that they may be delivered either simultaneously or sequentially. There are advantages and disadvantages to both of these approaches. However, music should not mask other types of auditory feedback if used. Music should be selected to elicit entrainment, and again should avoid cognitive shifts and sensory overload.

Future directions in music and medicine

Current research in music and medicine supports the belief that there is much more to discover about the influence of music on health. Of particular significance is the research involving music and immune response which, in the future, will shed some important light on the ability of music to enhance the body's self-healing potential directly. There are still many questions to be answered in this area which holds much promise for our professional futures.

Future research should also consider moment-to-moment interactions with the music and the effect of this on physiological processes. As the equipment develops for continuously monitoring physiological responses in a sophisticated way, it will be possible to assess more accurately the elements of the music that have the greatest effect on physiological change.

Additional research is needed on comparisons of music interventions with other types of intervention, including medical. If music therapy is to gain greater acceptance in the health-care field, we will need to ascertain that music is as effective, if not more effective than other treatment methods.

To achieve this, we will need to work collaboratively with medical personnel who can provide their expertise with regard to the selection of dependent variables, equipment, and so forth.

Obviously, this has implications for the training of music therapists who have interest in working in the area of music and medicine. Specialized training and experience in a number of additional areas will be required.

Lastly, because of the specialized nature of music and medicine and the need for collegial support and sharing of information, international exchange in this area will continue to be critical. International information and communication systems, such as the DICS established by the Hogeschool Nijmegen in Holland will undoubtedly facilitate the progress that needs to be made in music and medicine.

References

Engel, G.L. (1977) 'The need for a new medical model: A challenge for biomedicine', *Science*, 196, 129.

Maranto, C.D. (1991) (ed) *Applications of Music in Medicine*. Washington, D.C.: The National Association for Music Therapy, Inc.

Maranto, C.D. (1991) 'A classification model for music in medicine', in C.D. Maranto (ed), *Applications of Music in Medicine* pp.1–6. Washington, D.C.: National Association for Music Therapy, Inc.

Maranto, C.D. (1992) 'A comprehensive definition of music therapy with an integrative model for music medicine', in R. Spintge and R. Droh (eds) *Music Medicine*. St Louis: MMB.

Maranto, C.D. (1993) 'Music therapy and stress management', in R. Woolfolk and P. Lehrer (eds) *Principles and Practices of Stress Management*. New York: Guilford Press.

Standley, J.M. (1986) 'Music research in medical/dental treatment: Meta-analysis and clinical applications', *Journal of Music Therapy*, 23, 56–122.

Standley, J.M. (1992) 'Meta-analysis of research in music and medical treatment: Effect size as a basis for comparisons across multiple dependent and independent variables', in R. Spintge and R. Droh (eds) *Music Medicine*. St Louis: MMB.

Selected Bibliography

Music and Surgery

Bonny, H.L. and McCarron, N. (1984) 'Music as an adjunct to anesthesia in operative procedures', *Journal of the American Association of Nurse Anesthesiologists*. 55–57.

Cherry, H., and Pallin, I. (1948) 'Music as a supplement in nitrous oxide anesthesia', *Anesthesiology*, 9, 391–99.

Chetta, H.D. (1981) 'The effect of music and desensitization on preoperative anxiety in children', *Journal of Music Therapy*, 18, 74–87.

Crago, B. (1980) Reducing the stress of hospitalization for open heart surgery. Unpublished dissertation, University of Massachusetts.

Kamin, A., Kamin, H., Spintge, R. and Droh, R. (1982) 'Endocrine effect of anxiolytic music and psychological counselling before surgery', in R. Droh and R. Spintge (eds) *Angst, Schmerz, Muzik in der Anasthesie*, pp.163–166. Basel: Editiones Roche.

Locsin, R. (1981) 'The effect of music on the pain of selected post-operative patients', *Journal of Advanced Nursing*, 8, 6, 19–25.

Locsin, R. (1988) Effects of preferred music and guided imagery music on the pain of selected post-operative patients. Doctoral dissertation, College of Nursing University of the Phillipines.

Padfield, A. (1976) Letter: Music as sedation for local anesthesia, *Anesthesia*, 31, 300–301.

Sanderson, S. (1986) The effect of music on reducing preoperative anxiety and postoperative anxiety and pain in the recovery room. Unpublished master's thesis, The Florida State University.

Shapiro, A.G.H. and Cohen, H. (1983) 'Auxiliary pain relief during suction curettage', in R. Droh and R. Spintge (eds) *Angst, schmerz, Muzik in der Anasthesie*, pp.89–93. Basel: Editiones Roche.

Siegel, S.L. (1983) The use of music as treatment in pain perception with post-surgical patients in a pediatric hospital. Unpublished master's thesis, University of Miami.

Spintge, R. (1982) 'Psychophysiological surgery preparation with and without anxoolytic music', in R. Droh and R. Spintge (eds) *Angst, Schmerz, Muzik in der Anasthesie*. pp.77–88. Basel: Editiones Roche.

Spintge, R. and Droh, R. (1982) 'The pre-operative condition of 1910 patients exposed to anxiolytic music and Rohypnol (Flurazepam) before receiving an epidural anesthetic', in R. Droh and R. Spintge (eds) *Angst, Schmerz, Muzik in der Anasthesie*. pp.193–196. Basel: Editiones Roche.

Spintge, R. and Droh, R. (1988) 'Ergonomic approach to treatment of patient's perioperative stress', *Canadian Journal of Anaesthesia*, 35, S104–S106.

Tanioka, F., Takazawa, T., Kamata, S., Kudo, M., Matsukia, A. and Oyama, T. (1985) 'Hormonal effects of anxiolytic music in patients during surgical operations under epidural anesthesia', in R. Droh and R. Spintge (eds) *Angst, Schmerz, Muzik in der Anasthesie*, pp.285–190. Basel: Editiones Roche.

Music in Neonatal Care

Caine, J. (1989) The effects of music on the selected stress behaviors, weight, caloric and formula intake and length of hospital stay of premature and low birth weight neonates in a newborn intensive care unit. Unpublished Master's thesis, The Florida State University.

Chapman, J.S. (1978) 'The relationship between auditory stimulation and gross motor activity of short-gestation infants', *Research in Nursing and Health*, 1, 29–36.

Falb, M. (1982) The use of operant procedures to condition vasoconstriction in profoundly mentally retarded (PMR) infants. Unpublished Master's Thesis, The Florida State University.

Katz, V. (1971) 'Auditory stimulation and developmental behavior of the premature infant', *Nursing Research*, 20, 196–201.

Larson, K.L., Ayllon, T. and Barrett, D.H. (1987) 'A behavioral feeding program for failure to thrive infants', *Behavior Research and Therapy*, 25, 39–47.

Lininger, L. (1987) The effects of instrumental and vocal lullabies on the crying behavior of newborn infants. Unpublished master's thesis, Southern Methodist University.

Owens, L.D. (1979) 'The effects of music on the weight loss, crying, and physical movement of newborns', *Journal of Music Therapy*, 16, 83–90.

Paden, L.Y. (1974) 'The effects of variations of auditory stimulation (music) and interspersed stimulus procedures on visual attending behavior in infants', *Monographs of the Society for Research in Child Development*, 39, 29–41.

Music in Pediatric Care

Chetta, H.D. (1981) 'The effect of music and desensitization on preoperative anxiety in children', *Journal of Music Therapy*, 18, 74–87.

Fagen, T.S. (1982) 'Music therapy in the treatment of anxiety and fear in terminal pediatric patients', *Music Therapy*, 2, 13–23.

Froelich, M.A.R. (1984) 'A comparison of the effect of music therapy and medical play therapy on the verbalization behavior of pediatric patients', *Journal of Music Therapy*, 21, 2–15.

Marley, L.S. (1984) 'The use of music with hospitalized infants and toddlers: A descriptive study', *Journal of Music Therapy*, 21, 126–132.

McDonnell, L. (1979) 'Paraverbal therapy in pediatric cases with emotional complications', *American Journal of Orthopsychiatry*, 49, 44–52.

McDonnell, L. (1983) 'Music therapy: Meeting the psychosocial needs of hospitalized children', *Children's Health Care*, 12, 29–33.

McDonnell, L. (1984) 'Music therapy with trauma patients and their families on a pediatric service', *Music Therapy*, 4, 55–66.

Robinson, D. (1962) 'Music therapy in a general hospital', *Bulletin of the National Association for Music Therapy*, 11, 13–18.

Scheifflin, C. (1988) A case study: Stevens-Johnson syndrome. Paper presented at the annual conference, Southeastern conference of the National Association for Music Therapy, Inc., April, Tallahassee.

Music in Respiratory Care

Ammon, K. (1963) 'The effects of music on children in respiratory distress', *ANA Clinical Sessions*, p.127–34.

Behrens, G.A. (1982) The use of music activities to improve the capacity, inhalation, and exhalation capabilities of handicapped children's respiration. Unpublished master's thesis, Kent State University.

Haas, F., Distenfeld, S. and Axen, K. (1986) Effects of perceived musical rhythm on respiratory pattern', *Journal of the American Physiological Society*, 1185–91.

Marks, M.B. (1974) 'The 1974 Bela Schick Memorial Lecture: Musical wind instruments in rehabilitation of asthmatic children', *Annals of Allergy*, 33, 313–9.

Metzler, R., and Berman, T. (1991) 'The effect of sedative music on the anxiety of bronchoscopy patients', in C.D. Maranto (ed) *Applications of Music in Medicine*. Washington, D.C.: National Association for Music Therapy.

Music in Burn Care

Barker, L. (1991) 'The use of music and relaxation techniques to reduce pain of burn patients during daily debridement', in C. Maranto (ed) *Applications of Music in Medicine*. Washington, D.C.: National Association for Music Therapy, Inc.

Christenberry, E. (1979) 'The use of music therapy with burn patients', *Journal of Music Therapy*, 16, 138–148

Schneider, F. (1982) Assessment and evaluation of audio-analgesic effects on the pain experience of acutely children during dressing changes. Unpublished dissertation, University of Cincinnati.

Music and Pain

Bob, S.R. (1962) 'Audioanalgesia in podiatric practice: A preliminary study', *Journal of the American Podiatry Association*, 52, 503–504.

Brown, C.F., Chen, A.C. and Dworkin, S.F. (1989) 'Music in the control of human pain', *Music Therapy*, 8, 47–60.

Budzynski, T., Stoyva, J. and Adler, C. (1971) 'Feedback-induced muscle relaxation: Application to tension headache', *Journal of Behavior Therapy and Experimental Psychiatry*, 1, 205–211.

Camp, W., Ward, W.D. and Chapman, L.F. (1962) 'Pain threshold and discrimination of pain intensity during brief exposure to intense noise', *Science*, 135, 788–789.

Carlin, S. Ward, W.D., Gershon, A. and Ingraham, R. (1962) 'Sound stimulation and its effect on dental sensation threshold', *Science*, 138, 1258–1259.

Epstein, L., Hersen, M. and Hemphill, D. (1974) 'Music feedback in the treatment of tension headache: An experimental case study', *Journal of Behavior Therapy and Experimental Psychiatry*, 5, 59–63.

Fowler-Kerry, S. and Lander, J.R. (1987) 'Management of injection pain in children', *Pain*, 30, 169–175.

Godley, C.S. (1987) 'The use of music therapy in pain clinics', *Music Therapy Perspectives*, 4, 24–27.

Goloff, M.S. (1981) 'The responses of hospitalized medical patients to music', *Music Therapy*, 1, 51–56.

Herth, K. (1978) 'The therapeutic use of music', *Supervisor Nurse*, 9, 22–23.

Howitt, J.W. (1967) 'An evaluation of audio-analgesic effects', *Journal of Dentistry for Children*, 34, 406–411.

Jellison, J.A. (1975) 'The effect of music on autonomic stress responses and verbal reports', in C.K. Madsen, R.D. Greer, and C.H. Madsen, Jr. (eds) *Research in Music Behavior*, pp.206–219. Teachers College Press, Columbia University.

Lavine, R., Buschbaum, M. and Poncy, M. (1976) 'Auditory Analgesia: Somato-sensory evoked response and subjective pain rating', *Psychophysiology*, 13, 140–148.

Maslar, P.M. (1986) 'The effect of music on the reduction of pain: A review of the literature', *The Arts in Psychotherapy*, 13, 215–219.

Melzack, R., Weisz, A.Z. and Sprague, L.T. (1963) 'Strategems for controlling pain: Contributions of auditory stimulation and suggestion', *Experimental Neurology*, 8, 239–247.

Moore, W.M., McClure, J.C. and Hill, I.D. (1964) 'Effect of white sound on pain threshold', *British Journal of Anaesthesia*, 36, 268–271.

Rider, M. (1985) 'Entrainment mechanisms are involved in pain reduction, muscle relaxation, and music-medicated imagery', *Journal of Music Therapy*, 22, 183–192.

Robson, J.G. and Davenport, H.T. (1962) 'The effects of white sound and music upon the superficial pain threshold', *Canadian Anaesthetists' Society Journal*, 9, 105–108.

Wolfe, D.E. (1978) 'Pain rehabilitation and music therapy', *Journal of Music Therapy*, 15, 162–178.

Music in General Hospital / Intensive Care

(no author) (1972) 'In this intensive care unit, the downbeat helps the heartbeats', *Modern Hospital*, 118, 91.

Bonny, H.L. (1983) 'Music listening for the intensive coronary care units: A pilot project', *Music Therapy*, 3, 4–16.

Davis-Rollans, C. and Cunningham S.G. (1987) 'Physiologic responses of coronary care patients to selected music', *Heart and Lung*, 16, 370–378.

Goloff, M.S. (1981) 'The responses of hospitalized medical patients to music therapy', *Music Therapy*, 1, 51–56.

Schuster, B.L. (1985) 'The effect of music listening on blood pressure fluctuations in adult hemodialysis patients', *Journal of Music Therapy*, 22, 146–153.

Music in Oncology / Terminal Illness

Bailey, L.M. (1983) 'The use of live versus tape-recorded music on hospitalized cancer patients', *Music Therapy*, 3, 17–28.

Bailey, L.M. (1984) 'The use of songs in music therapy with cancer patients', *Music Therapy*, 4, 5–17.

Cook, J. (1986) 'Music as an intervention in the oncology setting', *Cancer Nursing*, 9, 23–28.

Cotanch, P. and Strum, R. (1987) 'Progressive muscle relaxation as antiemetic therapy for cancer patients', *Oncology Nursing Forum*, 14, 33–37.

Curtis, S.L. (1982) The effects of music on the perceived degree of pain relief, physical comfort, relaxation, and contentment of hospitalized terminally ill patients. Unpublished master's thesis, The Florida State University.

Gilbert, J. (1977) 'Music therapy perspectives on death and dying', *Journal of Music Therapy*, 14, 165–171.

Maranto, C.D. (1988) 'AIDS: Issues and information for music therapists', *Music Therapy Perspectives.*

Mowatt, K.S. (1967) 'Background music during radiotherapy', *Medical Journal of Australia*, 1, 185–186.

Porchet-Munro, S. (1988) 'Music therapy in support of cancer patients', *Recent Results of Cancer Research*, 108, 289–9.

Presant C.A., Presant, S.N., Kasem C., Friedman, S. and Starble, A. (1988) 'Stress-relieving relaxation audio-tape for supportive care of cancer patients: developmental studies', *Prog. Clin. Biol. Res.*, 278, 151–158.

Sedei, C.A. (1980) The effectiveness of music therapy on specific statements verbalized by cancer patients. Unpublished manuscript, Colorado State University.

CHAPTER 16

Spontaneous Ritualised Play in Music Therapy
A Technical and Theoretical Analysis

Anthi Agrotou

Cyprus

Prologue

This paper aims to trace a connecting link between certain religious rituals, certain ritualisms, certain kinds of ritualisation and ritualised play.

Amidst the vastness, in form and in content, of religious rituals practised among humans worldwide, it is the mourning rituals that will mostly concern our minds here and, in particular, their Easter formalisations. Every spring, Christian communities around the world unite in their celebrations of the death and resurrection of Christ. Their Easter rituals are only an example of a community united in the repetitive actualisation of a common belief. Every Greek Orthodox community, to take but one example, assembles each Good Friday for the collective mourning of Jesus' death. The whole wailing procedure is an elaborate one, amidst which young girls throw flowers at Christ's simulated tomb and people kiss farewell to his image.

Whatever the ornaments and elaborations, every movement occurs in a formulaic manner and within a specified timing, thus reliving in its exact repetitiveness and perfect predictability the relief of timelessness and something beyond.

Rituals of similar content seem to have been carried out since time immemorial. Such was the ritual of Adonis, practised in many places in the ancient world every spring or early summer. Under the name of Osiris, Tammuz or Attis, and whether it was Egypt, Babylon or the Greek lands, the god's death was annually mourned 'to the shrill wailing notes of the flute, with weeping, lamentation and beating of the breast' (Frazer, 1987, p.335).[1] Images of him were carried out as if for burial and then thrown into the sea together with all kinds of flowers; 'but next day he was believed to come to life again and ascend up to heaven in the presence of his worshippers' (ibid).

Similarly, the orthodox communities reassemble the following night to sing of Jesus' victory over death. Amidst the candle-lit atmosphere friends and strangers mingle as they reassure each other, in exactly the same manner year after year, that 'Christ has risen, in truth he has'.

Of course such ceremonial rituals are the result of a complex interweaving of conscious and unconscious phenomena; but here, I wish to propose their observation from a particular small angle, in case that small angle has something to tell us about certain ritualisms manifested in patients who have suffered severe mental and sensory deprivation.

Two such patients will be central in this paper. Annie, born totally blind and with brain injury, would either sit with her head bent down, often in a foetal position, or lie down and cover her head; otherwise she would indulge in the repetitive clapping of her hands in front of her face. It is upon this ritualism of hers that I wish to concentrate.

Alexis, suffering paralysis of the right hand side of his body and severe brain damage, would often retreat to the repetitive throwing away of any object found in his way. If none was there, he would tear his shirt bit by bit and throw it away with a yell, the whole procedure done repetitively until there was no more cloth left on his chest.

At first sight, the only aspect that Annie and Alexis had in common with those people who carry out the afore-mentioned rituals is the periodical repetitiveness of certain actions or movements in exactly the same manner. Unlike the participants of those ceremonial rituals, though, they would remain stuck in their repetitiveness; and the communal element of the rites was totally lacking, as their ritualism retained them in the permanence of their isolation.

There may be further comparisons, but I propose to leave the sacred rituals of mourning here and return to them towards the end of the chapter. I now wish to follow certain aspects of these patients' process in music therapy in search of the deeper meaning of their ritualism, and the part that ritualised communication played in the process of our relationship and in the unravelling of their primal wound.

---

1   Frazer describes in particular the ritual at Byblus which took place in the
      Phoenician sanctuary of Astarte.

The case of Annie

Annie, as mentioned previously, was born totally blind and with brain injury. She has a sister six years older than her, described by her family as highly competent and intelligent. Annie shows developmental delay in most aspects of her life. When I met her, she could utter a few words at random, which she would occasionally use in order to have her wishes immediately met with (for example walk, swing). She would use the second or third person and pronoun in referring to herself.

She was nine years old when we started music therapy: a tall, thin girl with a doll-like face and a gait that would give the impression of uncon-nected limbs. The School for the Blind asked me to take Annie for music therapy, as they felt that there was nothing they could do with her. Her wish to remain isolated in the way I described before dominated the classroom scenes; and on top of that, they said, there was no speech to communicate with.

The sessions began in September 1990 in a school room that offered one grand piano, one cymbal and one tambourine. They lasted 30 minutes and occured once a week during the first school year and twice a week during the second year.

Though lack of speech was reported as one of Annie's fundamental problems, it was speech that Annie first brought with her to music therapy: words and phrases that revealed a girl using all the means at her disposal in order to create a meaning in her world.

Right from session one, she seemed to perceive directly the musical correlations to her sounds. I thus tried to follow her word intonations quite closely, at the same time as putting an affective ambiance according to how I felt she experienced her verbal outputs. The musical working through of the themes she would bring with her words continues to be the focus of our work.

A brief description taken from the first twelve minutes of session two on 24 September 1990 will attempt to convey a picture of Annie in those days, as well as the first implications concerning her ritualism:

> Annie makes her way towards the piano and sits in front of it. I sit on her left. She makes some repetitive vocal sounds which I transfer on the piano. She grabs my hand while I play and explores it by touch. She directs it back to the piano saying 'your sister, yes your touch, your Anthi'[2] while using her hand to explore the piano, my hand and my face. She was, perhaps, trying to connect herself,

---

2   The words 'touch', 'sister' and 'Anthi' sound almost identical in Greek.

through her touch, to her older and able sister and myself. Vocal sounds and laughter sounds follow which I try to put into music. Her posture alternates between upright stillness, while listening attentively to my transformations of her sounds, and stooped head and body while withdrawing into her ritualism of clapping her hands in front of her face – often accompanied by head movements from right to left. Within two minutes of this sequence and while enveloped in her ritualism, she says for the first time the words 'the little eye' in a singing intonation.

Her actual words are 'the little eye, the little e' (in Greek 'to mataki, to mato') the latter being a word that in Greek sounds very like the word 'I stop'. A rough English equivalent might be 'the little eye, I (eye) goodbye (goodbeye)'.

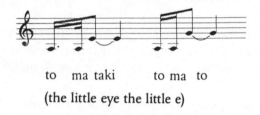

to   ma taki   to ma to
(the little eye the little e)

The four minutes that follow consist of a dialogue between Annie's vocalisations and my responding piano themes that expand these sounds into musical forms. Her vocal output here is an amalgam of 'the little eye' theme uttered in variations and interspersed with indiscriminate sounds and exclamations. It feels like a grey area wherein Annie is exploring the reliability and precision of the piano answers, until she comes out with a clear and musical 'little eye' theme, uttered for the first time outside the shell of her ritualism. Within a few seconds the theme is established as well as the spontaneous and mutual birth of this implied rule: that 'the little eye' theme reappears from my part directly or in variations when she places my hand on the piano and thus indicates it; and that it stops (disappears) when she removes my hand from the piano. Annie's theme sounds something like this:

the little eye

(to ma ta ki)

My substitution an octave higher is the following

In other words, the play between us evolved into a sound 'Peek-a-boo', whereby the word 'the little eye' or a substitute of it would provoke the motif of 'the little eye' to be heard again on the piano. The substitute was her hand placing and withdrawing my hand from the piano, thus doing the job of lifting and putting back the covering blanket.

In a Peek-a-boo play the first episode entails the two players making an explicit contact. In most instances, initial contact is by face-to-face mutual looking. The first episode of mutual looking here is that Annie reiterates 'the little eye' motif in different tempi, as if she wishes to establish it as a theme and test the predictability of my responses.

This is immediately followed by what is parallel to the second round of Peek-a-boo, which is the actual act of hiding and its accompaniments. The format of the play as it gets established is the following:

	Annie	A.A.
Move 1.	Reappearance: Initiates the theme of 'the little eye' by placing my hand on the piano, or by clapping	The 'little eye' motif reappears as I play a substitute theme or variation
Move 2.	Recognition: Laughs and vocalises as soon as the theme reappears	
Move 3.	Disappearance: Pulls my hand from the piano, thus both of us hide 'the little eye'.	

A normal mother–child Peek-a-boo usually follows this format:

> Move 1. Initial contact
>
> Move 2. Disappearance
>
> Move 3. Reappearance
>
> Move 4. Re-established contact.

In both cases, the play shows clear differentiations of participant roles and a structure comprised of moves allocated between the players. The play is repeated on the same sequence of moves, although each move may appear in variation.

Garvey (1986) says that 'what allows a Peek-a-boo play to take place is the willingness of both participants to conform to the agreed procedure – a procedure which involves repetitiveness and predictability within clearly defined roles' (p.103). The latter is the basic characteristic of all ritualised play; Peek-a-boo is merely one good example of it.

Our Peek-a-boo play with Annie lasted for approximately two minutes and consisted of ten rounds containing the three moves listed above. Here is how the tenth round marked the end of the play:

> During the reappearance of the theme Annie slipped her fingers above mine and kept them there so as to encourage repeated reappearances of the theme. While she was giving her characteristic laughter of recognition each time the theme sprang up, it felt as if her lingering fingers above mine were actually touching the object itself; and suddenly, instead of pulling my hand from the piano to hide the theme, she withdrew hers and began her ritualistic clapping in front of her bent face. Laughter and enjoyment was there no more. Perhaps touching 'the little eye' itself proved to be too much for her.

In concluding the 'little eye' Peek-a-boo, I wish to emphasise that this object of disappearance and reappearance (or a close sound substitution of it) is, paradoxically, the very object that annihilated Annie's chances of ever playing a normal Peek-a-boo. It is the eye that said goodbye to the world that her sister and myself enjoy. It is worth remembering that the first utterance of the theme sprang forth from her ritualism. My thesis is that when 'the little eye' became the source of a ritualised play between us, this ritualised play initiated a turning point in our relationship: from then on her trust and hope in the therapist opened up our mutual eye into new paths for exploring the primal wound.

An obscure, dark voice, wherein words and their meanings were hidden, formed Annie's predominant repertoire for the months that followed. I tried to reflect gently that world, a world that seemed threatening, as if it carried with it the image of a primitive black witch. Frequently, the words that laid hidden were 'no, mommy, why and goodbye' – the last two sounding in Greek almost identical.

From the end of January 1991, as the dark voice was beginning to wane, a new theme came up, that of herself being wounded (spoken of in the second person). It is a theme linked with her eyes as can be inferred from the following description taken from a four-minute extract from the session of 20 January 1991:

> Annie and I sit in front of the piano in silence. Annie sits on the chair in a foetal position with her head slightly bent down. Her hand searches for mine and as she gets hold of it she directs it towards her eye and almost allows it to touch her eye, but refrains. Instead, she slowly puts her hand on her eye. A moment of withdrawal and complete stillness follows until she directs my hand on the piano, saying at the same time: 'you've hurt yourself... you've hurt yourself my mommy... you've hurt yourself... we've arrived!' The latter is uttered loudly and dramatically as she lets go of my hand on the piano to do its job.

> In melody and harmony I try to reflect the dramatic affect of her words while following the length and tonal qualities of her phrases. She seems to be listening attentively as her head is turned toward the direction of the sound while her hand is spinning the cymbal on her left.

> My final chord is followed by a few moments of silence and stillness which gradually cause an uneasiness as she says 'come on, come on' together with retreating into her ritualism. In this way she seems to be fending off the tragic events, the awareness of loss. I collude with her need and a lighter music follows to which she repeats her ritualism of clapping hands in front of a swinging face. Suddenly it all stops, and so the music stops as she turns her head towards mine for an 'eye-contact', her blind eyes literally focusing on mine for approximately ten seconds. This comes to an end as she bends down touching her eyes before her hands set off once again for yet another clapping performance.

This excerpt makes me suppose that: first, Annie's ritualism is a way of fending off an awareness of loss of her eyes and she often retreats to it when such an awareness is strongly felt, such as at the end of the extract. This is perhaps why such an awareness springs forth from the same ritualism.

Second, that her blindness might be associated in her mind with a wound, with having hurt herself. Third, that this new level of awareness that we now share allows her to focus the direction of my vision through my eyes in lieu of hers.

Before stating my final conclusions about Annie's case, it may be important to describe one more extract, a step further in the process. It is 27 June 1991, and this is the final session before the summer holidays:

> Annie is sitting in the foetal position once again. She is very quiet and still until she starts clapping her hands in front of her inclined head, this time in a much slower rhythm than before. At the same time she is uttering some indiscriminate vocalisations to which I respond in pitch, while reflecting the sadness of her entire demeanour. Amidst her recurring ritualisms, interrupted by a repeated rubbing of her eye, she takes my hand off the piano to say the following phrases: 'the eyes... it's been hurt... oh my eye!' her voice getting louder towards the end. Having spoken her mind, my hand is directed again by her to play the song of sorrow once more, only that this time it concerned a very specific sorrow over a special kind of loss.

Annie no longer talks of the little eye. It is the eyes, her eye that is being hurt. In between her ritualism once more, the theme of her blindness appears in a much more developed form; for now she has an awareness of both eyes, and of a hurt eye that belongs to her. She is not only closer to the root of her problems, she also has a clearer self-image.

Here I wish to sum up the hypotheses that come to my mind from studying Annie's case: Annie's ritualism seems to be the defense of her psychic apparatus from the pain of blindness. Her ritualism itself points to her eyes, as her clapping hands are bound to create some sensation inside her eyes. Therefore, any awareness of the pain over her lost eyesight comes from within her ritualism, as if that phenomenon inherently covers the hide and seek of the source of her pain; and I restate (at the risk of being ritualistically repetitive) that when such a source of pain becomes the resource of a ritualised play between us, it seems to cultivate intimacy, trust and hope of a new intensity so as to allow a deeper working through of the primal wound and the inflicted sorrow.

Ritualisation – ritualised play

If one lays one's eyes upon the bill-clapping display of a pair of white storks, immersed in their courtship behaviour before breeding, one is impressed by their instinctive synchronicity, the apparent rhythmical form of their mutual repertoire, as they curve their necks backwards and forewards in intimate proximity.

Of course, when it comes to the mating performances of birds in spring, the list of such magnificent ceremonial displays is innumerable, from the cormorant's elegant neck dance to the great crested grebe's head-shaking exchange, culminating in what is known as a penguin dance: each partner speeds towards each other underneath the water and, as they meet, they raise their bodies above the water into an erect position and rest them against each other for yet another series of head-shaking exchanges. Perhaps the most spectacular example of such ceremonies is the one performed by a pair of crowned cranes, wherein the partners attract each other through an exquisite dance: wings outstretched and feet hardly touching the ground, they leap and twist and turn around each other in superb synchronicity.

But what do these ceremonies of the courting bird world share with the vast number of ritualisations performed by humans in their everyday life? Well, they are all encounters carried along some traditional lines, encounters which are familiar through their repetitiveness and predictability (Erickson 1978); yet all these are intermixed with the elements of the seemingly unexpected, with leeway for improvisation; sometimes with the joy of self-expression and the renewal of surprise over recognition – all are possible components of that indescribable concept of playfulness.

Ritualism, on the other hand, also characterised by repetitiveness and predictability, totally lacks any element of playfulness or joy over creativity. Instead, there is a stifled existence and an inescapable isolation.

Human ritualisation[3] means the creative rhythmical formalisation of certain patterns of interaction. Ritualised play is simply an evolutionary form of ritualisation. By definition, it consists of an episode, or a series of episodes of well-organised interaction, in which partners take turns, alternating the same or different behaviours within a predictable regularity of tempo. The resource of ritualised play can be objects, sound or language.

The basic structural characteristics of the play, adapted for a music therapy occurrence, are the following:

1. Each player's output is rather regular in length.

---

3   The definition given here is the psychological use of the term. Ritualisation, as a
     term in zoology, means 'the evolutionary process by which an action or behaviour
     pattern in an animal loses its ostensible function and changes into an effective social
     sign for other members of the species' (The Oxford English Dictionary 1989).

2. Timing of players' output and pauses fall within a predictable regularity of tempo.

3. There is a close relationship between the players' rhythm, tempi, pitch, dynamics and length of phrases.

4. Each player's contribution is called a turn, and if it differs from that of his partner, it does so in ways that can be rather precisely described, i.e., it differs as a substitution of an element or a continuation of the material of the preceding turn.

5. A pair of turns constitutes a round, and rounds are the building blocks of ritualised play.

6. A player uses a particular motif, which is part of a turn, so as to suggest repetition of a whole round.

7. Ritualised play can be interrupted by one of the players when he wishes to correct the procedure.

8. If a player fails to take his turn within the time provided by the rhythm of the episode, the partner will indicate his failure.

9. Through breaking the format, a player can conclude an episode.

Thinking back on 'the little eye' play between Annie and myself, it seems that it followed most of the above characteristics.

Ritualised play appears spontaneously when the setting offers quietness and familiarity. It is often preceded by encounters of ritualisation. Its appearance in the process of Alexis' music therapy further illuminates the implications of its appearance in music therapy.

The case of Alexis

Alexis was referred for music therapy at the age of fifteen because of aggressive behaviour towards his carers in the institution where he had been living since the age of six.

Born in a happy family as a normal and healthy baby, Alexis contracted meningitis on the eighth day of his life, leaving him with severe brain damage and paralysis of the right hand side of his body. He has almost no speech apart from the words 'mother', 'father' 'grandmother', 'water', 'chocolate' and 'shit'.

Unless he was sleeping or sitting motionless with his head bent down, Alexis had the habit of throwing away anything that was found in front of him, or tearing up his clothes and throwing them away bit by bit. Whilst engaged in this activity, his half-paralysed body would often become agitated and full of nervous movement, his outbursts of vocal sounds, intermixed with laughter, only adding to the forcefulness of the entire phenomenon.

We started working together in November 1987 in a special room within the institution where he is living. The instruments included a piano, a big gong, a cymbal, drums and one metallophone. The 30-minute sessions occured in the frequency of twice a week.

It did not take long to discover that it was impossible to place any instrument in front of Alexis or within his left-hand's reach, for the sake of its survival and mine. I soon set up a structure whereby the gong, an instrument big enough to have some holding impact on him, would be near his right-hand side and I would stand behind the gong and sing to him. I would then give him a beater which initially he kept throwing away in such a context of confused and vibrant anger as has been described above; but gradually he began to use it to play the gong for one or two phrases before he would throw it away. Once he threw the beater away, I would remove the gong, only to replace it soon at its habitual location on his right-hand side at the same time as returning the beater to him.

In this way Alexis' ritualism turned into a ritualisation between us, to be repeated session after session. Within our ritualisation, the space and structure was provided, wherein the thrown away objects could return. The context was such that the objects themselves assumed a deeper simulation as they became interconnected with a sounding instrument, a human voice and a pair of eyes. In this way the therapeutic environment provided the predictable return, at the same time as evoking the repetitive reproduction of the traumatic experience as a transference phenomenon.

I say this because it was within this ritualisation encounter that the word 'I had' (Greek 'eha') was born by him while in the act of throwing away the beater, thus giving both of us a deeper sense of his loss – in fact, one abandonment upon another: his health, his mother's breast, his parental home. Perhaps the thrown away objects and the torn bits of his clothing that would leave him half-naked were the bits of himself, the not-yet internalised mother projected on to his clothes and objects and thrown away in abolition.

A second step in the evolution of this ritualisation – which appeared in session 12 on 14 January 1988 – was a vocal interplay of the word 'I had', (eha), wherein the actual throwing of objects is no longer needed. Our understanding and communication here leaves its concrete manifestation and turns into a vocal-sound exchange of 'eha' with its more sorrowful conno- tations: a dialogue, whereby my piano responses were based on Alexis' 'eha' theme in intonation and affective character, evoking an intense and communicative look within which his coherent 'eha' answers were uttered in a soft voice. Soon after the beginning of the piece he grabs his handicapped hand and kisses it tenderly. Then the eyes close and the cheek rests on that lifeless hand, as though in recognition of its loss. It is a gesture that is offered to me to share with and accompany the music.

Three minutes later this ritualisation evolves further through its own momentum into a ritualised play lasting approximately a minute and a half and consisting mainly of two episodes. As the element of playfulness now enters more into our music, it alleviates, in terms of affect, some of the preceding intensity.

Alexis' motif, which has already been established in the ritualisation that preceded is the following, in approximation:

I   had
(e ha)

Through this or a close variant he suggests a repetition of a round. My turn, based on his motif, is actually a continuation of his material.

Every turn of mine is based on this theme, while the initial semitone fall is frequently used by my part so as to suggest a repetition of the round.

Each episode consists of rounds and, like a typical ritualised play, each player's turn falls within a predictable regularity of tempo. This happens more clearly in the second episode, as can be seen in the diagram above. During an episode the length of our turns are roughly regular, Alexis' lasting for approximately 1 second and mine 2–4 seconds in the first episode, and 2 seconds in the second episode. We also follow each other closely in rhythm, tempi and dynamics (v. diagram 16.1). The two episodes are interrupted by some seconds of simultaneous interaction stimulated by Alexis rhythmical turning of his head from right to left. Towards the end of the second episode Alexis fails to take his turn, and I indicate that, through repeating my basic motif in slower tempo. Alexis laughs at having missed his turn. I then try to draw the piece to an end by breaking the format with other motifs and by slowing the tempo. Notes reminiscent of the theme towards the end, though, awaken Alexis' motif in a murmur. I reiterate the message that it is time to finish, slowing the tempo further to ♩=76; when another reminder of the theme occurs, he interrupts with his turn. Slowing the cadenses and reiterating B flat instead of the characteristic semitone fall I indicate to him the very end. He laughs during my turn and, in absolute comprehension of the message, he comes back again with an emphatic restatement of the theme, thus insisting on a repetition of the round.

Diagram 16.1 (Note: Units are in seconds)

	Alexis	Pause or waiting time	A.A
Tempo ♩ = 92	1		1
	1		3
		2	
	2		3
Episode (a)		2	
	1		4
		1	
	1		2
	1		

Tempo speeds up simultaneously to ♩=100   9 ——————————————— 9   = Simultaneous Interaction

	Alexis	Pause or waiting time	A.A
		1	
	1		1.5
Tempo slows to ♩ = 96	1		2
	1		2
	1		2.5
Episode (b)	1		2
	1		2

Alexis	Pause or waiting time	A.A

| | | 9 = repeats the basic motif in slower tempo, thus indicating to him to take his turn. |

Tempo slows further to $\quad$ = 84

| | laughs = for having missed his turn | 10 = brings the piece slowly towards an end by breaking the format. A reminisent of the theme provokes his turn. |

Tempo $\quad$ = 80

| | utters his = 1 turn in a murmur | 5 = further breaking of the format and slowing of tempo Another reminiscent of the theme resounds and he interrupts. |

Tempo $\quad$ = 76

| *interrupts* = *1* with his turn thus suggesting a correction of the procedure. | | 7 = *Slowing the* cadenses and reiterating B flat instead of the characteristic semitonal fall, indicates the very end. |

his turn = 1.5 repeated emphatically so as to cause a repetition of the round.

From session 13 until today Alexis has hardly ever thrown away instruments or beaters or torn bits of his clothes. As his ability to own his grief and his losses grew, so did his ability to own instruments and form relationships. Periods of severe melancholia had alternated with light and playful encounters. On the whole, though, the process has been one of working through grief, wherein Alexis has been, musically, all the more a creative participant. The wildness of the past, together with his violent outbursts of uncouth sound are now abandoned; instead there is a composure within which Alexis' eyes are alive and alert to the content of our shared music. The sounds and silences are now well-organised; rhythm, tempo and dynamics are coherently intermixed as he makes clear and deliberate choices in order to combine the vibrations of the cymbal and the gong with the clarity of the drum's rhythm and the softness of a metallophone's melodic phrase.

With all these instruments situated around him, and with the appearance of a serious young man on the threshold of adulthood, today Alexis' affective messages are far beyond those of rage or anger or even sorrow; rather they seem to lie in that eternal area that oscillates between grief over specific losses and consent over life's offerings, but also over life's multiple deaths.

Epilogue

In conclusion I return to human rituals. Whether religious or not, rituals in general may serve a number of functions, such as (a) the collective adaptation of a community to the laws of nature, (b) the collective mastering of instincts deemed dangerous for the survival of the community, or (c) the channelling of the community's united mind towards what is assumed 'superb and excellent' for that given culture.

However, this chapter aims only to touch upon certain religious rituals from a particular angle: as a continuation of that ritualisation that finds its early beginning in the interplay between the awakening infant and his mother. For it is through the repetitive and predictable appearance of his mother, her shining eyes falling on him and accompanied by the special touch of her holding arms and the texture of her voice that the infant first begins to sense a 'continuity of being' – a term used by Winnicott (1960, 1971). All the daily events of care are similarly grouped into repeatable sequences, in this way arousing in the infant predictable responses and a secure framework within which to develop the core of a self, so that if all goes well enough, the developing infant will have internalised a sufficiently good image of the benevolent mother as to be able to experience his gradual separateness from her without despair.

It seems, nevertheless, to be the lot of humans that affirmation of mutuality and the reassuring presence of another who confirms one's continuity of being are needed, to a certain degree, throughout life. For one's fear of loss, mistrust over abandonment and separation, anxiety over helplessness seem never to be completely overcome.

In this context, the early ritualised play between mother and infant, with its predictable but playfully repetitive patterns, helps to alleviate the infant's mistrust and anxiety and nurtures the growth of trust, and therefore, hope. One may even consider the early Peek-a-boo play as an 'as if' situation where mistrust and anxiety over loss and separation is actually played out, and then compensated for through the repetitive and predictable appearance of the lost one.

From then on, and throughout all the stages of life, ritualisation appears with this function of affirming, through another's presence, one's continuity of being – or, rather, of well-being. The regular exchanges of greetings, the wishes that have to be intercommunicated on special occasions, are just but a few examples.

Perhaps the climax of the beauty, in form and in meaning, that ritualisation – in the psychological sense – can assume is best witnessed in the courtship procedures of all living creatures – humans, animals and birds. One is reminded that they occur to ensure the continuity of being in its very basic manifestation, for, otherwise, the continuation of the species would not have survived; and the lack of the earliest ritualisations is never so painfully seen as in those who have lost all hope of mutual recognition and self affirmation.

Annie and Alexis are examples of such people. Their organic impairment did not allow the space for their mother's face to shine upon them; and to shine predictably and reassuringly.

I have used the music therapy cases of Annie and Alexis – although they are by no means the only ones in my limited experience – to illustrate the following: when the object of their loss, in whatever form they perceive it, becomes the resource of a ritualised communication between us, it cultivates trust and thus opens the way for deeper levels of understanding. For in the context of ritualisation or ritualised play – its further evolved form – that object is given back to them reliably and predictably, whether it was the eye that never witnessed the benevolent mother's presence, or the body that never had enough health and mothering, so that, through the other one, through the therapist, they can begin to own it, to sense it in a way that, at last, allows them to grieve. For it is exactly that, their inability to grieve, through choice or circumstance, for what they felt was the primal cause of their pain, that retained them in their ritualisms.

In other words, they were fixated in movements or actions which, though suggestive of the object of their loss, could nevertheless not allow them the space for any resolution, for any amelioration of inner pain. That space was only granted when their ritualisms evolved into ritualisations through another's presence.

This, then, is the connecting link – or rather the biggest contrast between ritualism and religious rituals of mourning such as those of Christ's or Adonis' death and resurrection. Those rites give the space, under the strength and shelter of the united community, to mourn for all the losses and abandonments, even for that ultimate one of death; and when the community is satiated to its fill with grief – to use a Homeric phrase – it rejoices over its resolution that death has actually been conquered.

This brings to my mind the concept of human helplessness, of smallness; and though I am ending this chapter with another Christian concept, I assure you it is not from a religious motive; it is to illustrate the strength of that earliest of all ritualisations, actualised in the grandest of all rituals of the Christian world; for, half a year round, the Christian communities unite in the rebirth of a new infant that will look up once again for the divine eyes, the divine eyes that will reassure and protect the race for ever, in life and in death.

Bibliography

Agrotou, A. (1988) 'A case-study: Lara', *Journal of British Music Therapy*, 2, 17–23.

Agrotou, A. (1990) 'Chaos and creativity: some aspects of music therapy techniques and processes'. Paper presented at the conference: *Arts Therapies Education – Our European Future*. St Albans, England.

Agrotou, A. (1992) 'Small steps in the darkness: music therapy with a multi-handicapped patient'. Paper presented at the conference: *Mental Handicap: Current Trends and Applications*. Nicosia, Cyprus.

Bruner, J.S., Jolly, A. and Sylva, K. (1985) *Play: Its Role in Development and Evolution*, Harmondsworth: Penguin.

Erikson, E.H. (1978) *Toys and Reasons. Stages in the Ritualization of Experience*, London: Marion Boyars.

Frazer, J.G. (1987) *The Golden Bough. A Study in Magic and Religion*. Abridged edition. London: Papermac.

Freud, S. (1920) S.E. XVIII *Beyond the Pleasure Principle*. London: Hogarth Press.

Freud, S. (1927) SE XXI *The Future of an Illusion*. London: Hogarth Press.

Garvey, C. (1986) 'Play', in J. Bruner, M. Cole, and B. Lloyd, (eds) *The Developing Child.* London: Fontana Press.

Huxley, J. (1968) *The Courtship Habits of the Great Crested Grebe.* London: Cape Editions.

Landsborough Thomson, A. (1964) *A New Dictionary of Birds.* London: Thomas Nelson Ltd.

The Oxford English Dictionary, Second edition, Vol. XIII (1989) Oxford: Clarendon Press.

Whitfield, P. (1984) *Longman Illustrated Animal Encyclopedia.* London: Marshall Editions Limited.

Winnicott, D.W. (1960) 'The Theory of the Parent-Infant Relationship', in J.D. Sutherland (ed) (1987) *The Maturational Processes and the Facilitating Environment.* London: The Hogarth Press and the Institute of Psychoanalysis.

Winnicott, D.W. (1971) *Playing and Reality.* London: Tavistock Publications.

CHAPTER 17

Cultural Aspects of Music in Therapy

Ruth Bright
Australia

The fundamental premise of this paper is that music therapists must be aware of the cultural aspects of both music and human behaviour if they are to provide the maximum benefit to the patient or client through music therapy.

We cannot work through music with clients from a culture different from our own unless we have clear understanding of the expressiveness, style, and emotional meaning ascribed to music in that culture, and also the general cultural relationships and behaviour.

What do we mean by 'culture' and how does it affect music performance

The cliche 'music is a universal language' seems to have been blindly accepted. We have not investigated the influence upon perception of mood in music of such factors as ethnicity, personal experience and psychopathology. Researchers have assessed the perception of emotional content of items of music (Hevner 1937, Wedin 1972), and assigned absolute, or quasi-absolute emotional values to specific items of sounds without discussion of the importance of the listener's cultural background, or of the effects of personal associations with particular items.

Given a population with uniform cultural background, one can forecast that a particular piece will be perceived in a particular way by most listeners (and the papers cited above demonstrate this) but there will be exceptions. This will be discussed further in the second part of this chapter.

Cultural influence has, however, been recognised by some people: Robertson-DeCarbo (1974) referred to the cultural nature of the musical experience and to the influence of learned behaviour as significant in that experience, involving social relationships and behaviour. Bright (1976) discussed the significance of individual associations and how psychiatric illness affects perception of emotional content.

Depending on context, we assign different meaning to the term 'culture':

1. **Ethnic origin**: The person's place of birth and nationality will influence his/her social norms, language and behaviour as well as the musical style or structure with which the person feels at home.

2. **Religious culture**: This may or may not be associated with ethnic culture, but must be considered, as spiritual beliefs affect attitudes towards illness and disability, even when we are apparently working outside any spiritual framework.

3. **Educational, family and social culture**: These strongly influence musical preference, creativity and behaviour, and may override ethnic origin. For example, two elderly patients, both from Estonia and suffering from depression with an early dementing condition, listened to some Estonian folk music. One responded joyfully, smiling and singing, and saying 'Wonderful, wonderful!' The other listened politely and then said scornfully 'O yes, peasant music; my family prefer Brahms and Beethoven.'!

    Families differ in their musical culture, or absence of it. Significance for any given family may lie in: 'Pop' music, themes from radio serials, advertisements, religious music, for example. Practice of music varies: a rock band which practises in the family garage, a chamber music group of family and friends practising in a living room, and so on.

    Attitudes to music are also strongly influenced by inter-generation tensions, or by general attitudes towards school. For many young people school provides their first introduction to serious music.

4. **Chronological age**: This also affects our music behaviour. It is linked with other cultural factors – ethnic origin, education and social class, and the micro-culture of family and peer group – but in itself may have an influence upon which type of music we enjoy.

    The individual personality modifies this, as does the state of cognition. Thus a person who fears newness, or for whom advanced organic brain damage has wiped out most of the capacity for creativity, may cling more closely to the familiar music of the past than does the person who is cognitively intact and who retains a sense of adventure even in old age.

A young person who sees older people as being essentially out-of-date and useless may well reject the music of the past, whereas a young person who has happy relationships with middle-aged or elderly people may be more likely to enjoy participating in music from a decade or so in the past.

5. **Cultural aspects of personal experience**: Our musical behaviour and preference is also strongly influenced by these aspects. For most of us, there are private associations with specific pieces or types of music, whether we are music therapists, professional musicians, patients, clients or casual listeners. These associations have profound emotional connotations, and are a valuable means of communicating with those who are suffering from psychiatric illness, especially those with isolation, denial, substance dependency and suicidal ideation.

6. **Psychiatric illness**: Even if we regard psychiatric illness as being culturally uniform rather than culturally specific, pathology must not be ignored, since we know that, for example, schizophrenia strongly influences people's preferences for musical excerpts (Koh and Hedlund 1969), and we see how projection, thought disorder and delusional beliefs or hallucinations affect the perceptions of the meaning of music.

In summary, music behaviour is strongly influenced not only by the macro-culture of ethnicity but also by the micro-culture of peer group pressures and of the individual family, by psycho-social disturbance and by attitudes and experiences in human life and relationships.

The term 'culture' therefore, when applied to behaviour and preference in music has a wide variety of meaning and implications, all of which must be understood by the music therapist.

Recent cultural changes and implications for music therapists
Throughout history people have moved from one part of the world to another. For example, in Britain we see the influence of the Vikings, the French and the Romans. British people who spent long periods in India have brought to our speech (especially Cockney) such now-familiar terms as 'cha' for a cup of tea, and so on. The same sequence of movement, invasion, adaptation and assimilation occurred in most places throughout the world,

and today we are seeing the effects of even greater movements of population, followed by the same process of assimilation and adaptation, often at a more rapid pace.

In the United Kingdom almost 27,000 people were resettled between 1979 and 1988 as refugees or migrants. At least 67 per cent of the total came from non-English speaking countries (20,500 from South-East Asia) and, since the Americas were dealt with as one category, there would actually be a higher percentage since many of the remaining 33 per cent came from Latin America. Today 'virtually every language under the sun' is now spoken in Britain, to quote the British High Commission in Australia!

In Australia the numbers of migrants and refugees are proportionately even greater, so that, in 1991, 25 per cent of the total population were born elsewhere, and 200 different languages are spoken (including major dialects that differ significantly from each other) (Jamrozik and Hobbs 1989).

In Canada, the most recent census showed that there are over 60 major language groupings, with many variants that are significantly different from each other. Differences in spoken language may well indicate differences (profound or trivial) in social custom, and we must be ready to take this into account in all that we do.

We need to look deeply into cultural influences on music preference. Dr George Duerksen of Kansas has said, 'Music is universal but there is no universal music!' In other words, there is an almost universal interest in some kind of music, but the preferred type of music varies from place to place and from time to time. We can find commonalities such as the pentatonic scale appearing in different cultures, but we find no universality in the way it is used to express emotion.

Nor must we forget those cultures which use music entirely differently, as for example in the micro-tonality of much Indian music. The Indian musician Angadi (1951) described how, having grown up hearing only micro-tonal Indian music, he arrived in the UK and went, unprepared, to a symphony concert. The experience was horrifying because the music sounded, he said, like a cat jumping from place to place, such was his response to the large intervals of tones and semitones.

This factor may diminish as time passes, because, with the ready availability of cassette players, few young people today are unfamiliar with modern popular music, but if our client population includes people from remote areas, or older people who are unfamiliar with or who reject modern western music, we must be willing to take into account their musical preference and experiences from the past.

Cultural differences

As we have already noted, differences in language usually also indicate major differences in social behaviour, taboos as well as permissions.

For example, in Australian aboriginal culture, there are highly complex laws about family and kinship. Any music therapist who attempted to work with traditional aborigines without first learning about their social culture would quickly meet, and cause, disaster. Rules about kinship prevent traditional people from looking at or making eye contact with a person of another 'skin' (family sept). For such people our usual norms about eye contact as an indication of communication are nonsense. Music, too, is involved with cultural norms: some music may be heard only by men and some only by women. Even a music shop in Sydney which sells recordings of genuine aboriginal music has had to observe strict rules about the playing of these recordings to customers, even though the customers are usually non-aboriginal. How much more important such matters are to the music therapist who seeks to create a relationship of trust with a client.

Indo-Chinese migrants and refugees pose other challenges to Australian music therapists. Even if our ultimate aim is clinical improvisation (in which it is perhaps easier to cross cultural boundaries than in other forms of therapy), we must first build a trust relationship. When verbal communication is difficult and achieved only through interpreters, we may achieve this through music. However, the music must be authentic. We generally use recordings because of the difficulty in playing acceptable music on the instruments which are available to us. We must also learn how to work through interpreters, since this is an art which requires specific training for all therapists.

One young man who was referred for music therapy tried in his difficult English to explain how strange it all was. He described how, in his remote East Timor village, meat was obtained by shooting a monkey with bow and arrow. His animist religion led him to believe that the voices he heard were those of the spirits who lived in the trees shouting at him for leaving them behind when he came to Australia. The music he now heard on Sydney TV and radio was so unfamiliar as to be horrible. For him the short-wave radio which enabled us to listen together to the music of his homeland was the only way through to achieving a trust relationship in which 'ordinary' music therapy could then flourish.

Cultural awareness is most important if we attempt to interpret the musical performance of our clients in their improvisations, as their musical behaviour will be strongly affected by their cultural background, and our interpretation may be wrong because it is based upon our cultural norms.

We need also to understand that many refugees and migrants are survivors of torture (in New South Wales there are over 200,000 such victims (Jamrozik and Hobbs 1989), and that their experiences affect their general health and their attitudes to being in an institution. They may be elderly Jews who survived the holocaust and concentration camps (Eaton *et al.* 1982), those who were prisoners of war, people from occupied Europe who lived in constant fear of cruelty and death, or younger people from Asian or South American repressive regimes who survived torture and cruelty (Reid and Strong 1988). This situation is not peculiar to Australia but is found in other countries where refugees and migrants are resettled (Hanen and Williams 1989). In the UK, Professor Isaac Marks, of the Institute of Psychiatry, has worked extensively with post-torture victims (Basoglu and Marks 1988).

Although music therapists may like to see themselves as non-threatening and empathic, for some torture victims the mere fact of our being on the staff of an institution creates distrust. This is especially relevant when there is a psychiatric illness involving fear, depression or delusional beliefs. The music therapist is at an advantage here, since it soon becomes obvious from our tools of trade that we are not about to embark upon systematic cruelty, although, unless we have educated ourselves appropriately, the music we use may be bewilderingly strange – but not (we hope) actual torture.

It is important to know that, in some countries, ideas on rehabilitation are not fully understood, so that occupational and especially music therapy seem to the relatives and patients to be mere recreation and thus a waste of time. The only programmes which are fully acceptable are those such as surgery, prescription of medication (in some countries preferably by suppository or injection rather than by tablets) and physiotherapy. It is hard to convince some clients that music therapy is indeed part of the prescribed programme of treatment.

We need also to understand the taboos about genetic and psychiatric illness. In some ethnic groups anything involving genetic disease or developmental disability is a matter for family shame, affecting marriage prospects and so forth. We notice such family attitudes when our music therapy involves the parents or grandparents. One elderly patient suffered major depression and we found it was caused by the birth of a handicapped grandchild.

Other migrant groups, especially from the Middle East, regard all birth defects as being the fault of the mother with no understanding of the possible genetic responsibility of the father. The wife may be divorced simply on the grounds of having given birth to a defective child. The evil eye may also be seen as a source of deformity. If we know that this may occur, we shall better understand attitudes to disabled children.

In palliative care we must be aware of taboos about death and dying. For Greek patients, for example, we may not use the term 'cancer' to the patient but only speak of the condition, usually in euphemistic terms, to a male member of the family (Health Department of New South Wales 1980). There are difficulties here for those of us who believe that truth is kinder than falsehood and who know that, legally, information about health is the property of the person and not of the family. Clinical team discussion when working in oncology is especially important.

Music therapists need also to be aware of ideas about culture-bound illnesses: are there indeed illnesses which are specific to particular ethnic groups or geographical regions, or are they conditions which are well-known but which are coloured by cultural behavioural features and beliefs (Hahn 1985, Low 1985)?

All these matters are part of our sensitivity to cultural influences in the life of our clients and we cannot say, if we value our integrity, 'I do not need to know about those in order to be a music therapist!'

In summary, whether we follow an improvisational model, a guided imagery technique involving pre-composed music, a music therapy with counselling approach which involves both music and therapeutic conversation, or an activities model, we must be fully aware of the cultural background and needs of our clients.

Applications of cultural awareness to music therapy

Responses to music are influenced by macro- and micro-cultural diversity. Several years ago I conducted a research project which stepped outside the field of pre-composed music to measure the qualities which people perceived in unfamiliar music (Bright 1976). The reasoning behind that research and the research work described here is that our private culture and our personal associations with a particular musical item profoundly influence the emotional responses to that piece. Thus we may in fact respond not to the perceived emotional quality of the music, but to the events of which the music reminds us.

For example, the song 'Danny Boy', because of its words and its harmony, pitch, speed of performance and general structure, is generally perceived as a sad song. In one seminar, however, a participant began to laugh when the song was played. He explained that in his office it was used as a request for someone else to answer your phone whilst you went to the bathroom, based on the line in the song 'The pipes, the pipes are calling'.

On the other hand, the singing of the Australian humorous song about the illegal gambling game of two-up (sung to the tune of 'I'm forever blowing bubbles') caused an elderly man who had been a scaffolding builder on the Sydney Harbour Bridge, a man who prided himself on being tough and strong, to cry bitterly. We found that he associated the song with a friend who had died in a fall from the bridge. While everyone else in the group was amused, he was deeply sad.

If unrecognised, such individual associations alter the reliability of statistical data. (This does not, of course, invalidate such work as Guided Imagery or Counselling with Music Therapy, which frequently make use of the emotional associations with pre-composed music.) They do, however, illustrate the unreliable nature of descriptions of pre-composed music which attempt to assign an absolute emotional value to a composition.

If we are to investigate perceptions of emotional qualities of music, it is essential for statistical validity that the music used is free from existing associations. In 1976 I composed six short pieces and had a number of people aged between 15 and 70 suggest words to describe the mood of each. From their suggestions a random order questionnaire was constructed for the research, comprising the six selected words and two 'dead' words that had no intended application to the items of music.

About 150 subjects listened to the music and used the questionnaire to record their perceptions of the mood of each piece. Statistical analysis of these results indicated that for a population of people familiar with western traditional harmonies and rhythms, there were strong commonalities for the moods perceived in all six pieces. It also showed, however, that, even in a culturally uniform population, there were some whose perceptions of mood were, for some reason, markedly different from the average. This has implications for therapy.

In the 1992 research, three of the pieces from 1976 were used again, so that it was not necessary to establish new norms. In addition, five excerpts of music from Asian countries were selected: music that would be unfamiliar to the subjects. The musical excerpts consisted of wedding music from Thailand and Japan, a traditional 'Happy Song' from China, a happy dancing tune from Indonesia, and a traditional 'happy' flute duet from India. (The cultural attaches of the Embassies and 'Folkways' were most helpful in obtaining the necessary recordings from Java and China.)

Music from Asian countries was chosen for two reasons: first, because it is easier to find unfamiliar music from these places than from European countries, and, second, because it is from Asia that most migrants to Australia come. Thus, the research was especially relevant to music therapy in Australia and to changing cultural attitudes.

Because it was vital that the researcher knew what emotional quality was intended or inherent in each item of Eastern music, the authorities providing the music were asked to ensure that the music was (a) traditional in nature and thus not contaminated by western culture and (b) such that the items were traditionally regarded as being happy in mood. Some other available music had an uncertain mood (described as thoughtful, contemplative, songs of home, etc.) and were open to various interpretations. Because certainty was essential for the results to be statistically viable, these items were not used.

A random order questionnaire was prepared with a word list for each item. The words were the three norms from the 1976 study, together with two 'dead' descriptors. For each piece there was a choice of five pairs of descriptive words: sad/lonely, happy/cheerful, angry/aggressive, meaningless/senseless, stupid/foolish.

After preliminary studies, it was assumed that people would use the 'meaningless' choice as indicating a 'don't know' answer and 'stupid' as indicating a pejorative answer. Discussion with participants after the tests were completed confirmed that this was how the terms had been used.

The choice of descriptors was restricted. In 1976 it was found that to give too wide a choice of terms resulted in confusion and statistical ambiguity. Some people, for example, used the word 'peaceful' as synonymous with 'happy' but some did not. Therefore, only the three terms from 1976 were selected as representing the norms established for those three pieces in that research project.

The eight excerpts, each about 35 seconds in length and instructions from the researcher for performing the test were taped. Each subject heard the items presented in the same way, uninfluenced by the musician's body language. Participants in the test took part in groups of from two to thirty. The total test population was 272: 138 were under the age of 25 years and 134 were 25 or over. All of were of European cultural background.

The results were analysed in order to find out:

1. Whether there were descriptions which were preferred by most subjects for the various excerpts.

2. To what extent the preferred descriptors matched the moods designated by the providers or composer.

3. Whether there were significant differences in choices made by the two age-groups.

4. What percentage of people in each age-group were unable to make an assessment of a meaningful mood.

Those choices which matched the designated emotional content are referred to as the 'correct' answers. Responses were subjected to rigorous statistical analysis, using Chi-square tests, but, in fact, the distributions were so strongly grouped that the results were easily visible to the eye.

The results are summarised in Table 17.1:

Table 17.1

European Idiom – Percentage of 'Correct' Selections

	Under 25	25 and over
Happy	92	89
Angry	90	69
Sad	95	84

Asian Idiom – All Designated as Happy Music by Providers
Percentage of 'Correct' Selections

	Under 25	25 and over
Item 1	37	61
Item 2	7	12
Item 3	0	7
Item 4	30	57
Item 5	10	6

Asian Idiom – Percentage of Failures to Recognise
any Meaningful Mood

	Under 25	25 and over
Item 1	58	23
Item 2	57	28
Item 3	7	4
Item 4	35	11
Item 5	85	73

The tables show clearly that:

1. When listening to music in a familiar idiom most subjects perceived the music in the same way as the composer or provider of the music.

2. In the unfamiliar idiom, there were some descriptions which were strongly preferred, even though they were different from those designated by the providers of the music.

3. The younger subjects were more likely than the older subjects to fail to reach a decision as to a definite mood.

Most important to the music therapist is that, in both the 1976 and 1992 research, there was a substantial number of subjects whose perceptions of mood were markedly different from the average and which were sometimes paradoxical. (A more detailed account of the experiment and the results obtained is given in the Appendix.)

Implications of cultural perceptions in music for music therapy

How important is this for music therapists? Very important indeed, unless we propose to restrict ourselves to a population whose background is identical to our own.

If we are working through music with a range of clients, we must recognise that, not only will some of them have perceptions of music which are different from our expectations, but that they may well express themselves emotionally through music in ways which are different, or even paradoxical, when compared with the normal distribution.

In my own practice, I always 'check things out' with clients, by saying, for example, 'It sounds as if you may be angry (bewildered, in turmoil, sad, or whatever) when you play in that way...', leaving the client to agree or disagree and, if he or she wishes, to discuss the matter further. This non-authoritarian position helps to avoid making false assumptions and generalisations. There is need for still more research in all cultures as to the characteristics in music which lead people to perceive items as happy, sad, or whatever.

We must consider the background of our clients as they first arrive for music therapy. We have to take into account not only their family and educational culture but also their ethnic background, and their possible psychopathology.

In Australia, many music therapists are choosing to study ethnomusicology, so as to equip themselves to work with various migrant groups. I imagine that such study will soon become standard practice elsewhere.

Music therapists everywhere must equip themselves with an ever-increasing bank of information and understanding so as to take their place in this changing world, contributing their very real knowledge and skills in helping people of every cultural background.

References

Angadi, A.D. (1951) *Music 1951*. Harmondsworth: Penguin. pp.17–34.

Basoglu, M. and Marks, I. (1988) 'Post-torture Syndrome', *British Medical Journal*, 297, 1423–1424.

Bright, R. (1976) Perception of Mood in Music. A Statistical Comparison of Two Patient Populations with a Control Group. Conference Proceedings, Australian Music Therapy Association, Melbourne, Australia.

Bright, R. (1986) *Cultural Aspects of Grief, in Grieving*. St Louis, USA: MMB. pp.57–63.

Eaton, W.W., Sigal, J.J. and Weinfeld, H. (1982) 'Impairment of Holocaust Victims after 33 years', *American Journal of Psychiatry*, 139, 773–777.

Hahn, R. (1985) 'Culture-bound Syndromes Unbound', *Social Science and Medicine*, 21(2), 165–171.

Hanen, M. and Williams, A. (1989) 'Life Crises and Ageing People of Non-English Speaking Backgrounds', *Australian Journal on Ageing*, 8(4), 3–6.

Health Department of New South Wales (1980) *Cultural Diversity and Health Care, a Guide for Health Professionals, 4.14–4.17*. NSW: Health Department of New South Wales.

Hevner, K. (1937) 'An Experimental Study of the Affective Value of Sounds and Poetry', *American Journal of Psychology*, 49, 419–434.

Jamrozik, W. and Hobbs, M. (1989) 'Migrants and Medicine. Many Challenges', *Medical Journal of Australia*, 150, 415–417.

Koh, S.D. and Hedlund, C.W. (1969) 'Pair Comparison of Musical Excerpts. Preference Bias of Schizophrenics and Normals', *Arch. General Psychiatry*, 21, 717–730.

Low, S.M. (1985) 'Culturally Interpreted Symptoms or Culture-bound Syndromes. A Cross-cultural Review of Nerves', *Social Science and Medicine*, 21(2), 187–196.

Reid, J. and Strong, T. (1988) 'Rehabilitation of Refugee Victims of Torture and Trauma. Principles and Service Provisions in New South Wales', *Medical Journal of Australia*, 148, 340–346.

Robertson-DeCarbo, C.E. (1974) 'Music as Therapy: A Biocultural Problem', *Ethnomusicology*, 18(1), 31–42.

Wedin L. (1972) 'A Multi-dimensional Study of Perceptual-Emotional Qualities in Music', *Scandinavian Journal of Psychology*, 13, 241–257.

Appendix
Experiment on perceptions of mood in music.

The experiment was based on a similar series of tests carried out in 1976. Six items were composed to test whether subjects were able to distinguish between different moods in music, and whether patients in a geriatric hospital and a psychiatric hospital differed in this ability from members of the public outside either institution. The items were written in the European idiom, and the participants were all of Caucasian stock. The items were written specially for the experiment and not selected from existing works in order to avoid any associations that they might evoke in the participants.

Knowing the reaction of the earlier participants to the items, three of them were selected as points of comparison for this experiment. Five short items from Asian cultures were then selected, on the advice of members of each of the cultures, as pieces of happy music, to determine whether people of Caucasian origin could recognise the mood of each of the items.

The three items of music in the European idiom were:

- a piece readily recognised as happy or cheerful by the previous participants
- a piece similarly recognised as angry or aggressive
- a piece recognised as sad or lonely.

The five items of Asian music included:

- a portion of a piece of dance music from a remote Javanese village
- part of a Chinese folk tune known as 'Happy Song'
- a piece of Thai wedding music

- a portion of an Indian piece recognised as joyous music
- a piece of Japanese wedding music.

Three different groups of people took part in the experiment:

- pupils from two local schools and a number of young people under 25, to represent the student population
- people from various sources, between 25 and 55 years old, to represent the mature working population
- people from other sources, older than 55, to represent the 'ageing' population.

The results of the tests, expressed as percentages of the group participants who made the various choices, are shown in Table 17.2. The results have been subjected to rigorous statistical analysis. They show the levels of discrimination to be highly significant. The significance is so striking that it is clearly visible in the table. However, the differences in response of the two 'adult' groups were not sufficiently different for them to be treated separately, so they were combined in the final comparison with the student group.

In each column of the table, the percentage of 'correct' responses, choices of the mood that the music is meant to represent to people familiar with the idiom, is printed in bold figures.

The table shows clearly that:

- When listening to music in the idiom with which they were familiar, most members of all three groups perceived it in the same way as the composer.
- When listening to music in an unfamiliar idiom, there was discrimination, but far less marked than with music in a familiar idiom.
- A large proportion of the participants, particularly in the student group, failed to recognise any mood in the music; they saw it as stupid or meaningless.
- In one particular case, Item 2, most of the participants perceived it as sad or lonely, despite its being a joyful piece in the ears of people of the culture from which it originated.
- For whatever reason, members of the student group were far less willing to assign moods to the Asian items than were the members of the 'adult' groups.

Table 17.2: Results of Tests
Percentages of Responses in Each Choice 'Correct'
Responses Shown in Bold Figures

Age group: Under 25 – 138 responses.

Responses	European idiom			Happy, Eastern idioms				
	Happy	*Angry*	*Sad*	*Item 1*	*Item 2*	*Item 3*	*Item 4*	*Item 5*
Happy	**92**	1	0	**37**	**7**	**0**	**30**	**10**
Angry	1	**90**	0	0	0	0	0	2
Sad	1	1	**95**	5	34	93	35	2
Stupid	6	4	1	38	24	0	14	60
Meaningless	0	4	4	20	35	7	21	25

Age group: Over 25 – 134 responses.

Responses	European idiom			Happy, Eastern idioms				
	Happy	*Angry*	*Sad*	*Item 1*	*Item 2*	*Item 3*	*Item 4*	*Item 5*
Happy	**89**	3	4	**61**	**12**	**7**	**57**	**6**
Angry	1	**69**	2	3	0	0	1	6
Sad	4	4	**84**	13	60	89	31	15
Stupid	1	6	0	2	4	1	2	23
Meaningless	5	18	10	21	24	3	9	50

Developing Interaction Through Shared Musical Experiences
A Strategy to Enhance and Validate the Descriptive Approach

Jeff Hooper
United Kingdom

Introduction

A recent review of music therapy research was very critical (Radhakishnan 1991). It concluded that literature on music therapy often offered only anecdotal evidence to suggest that change could be detected following music therapy. There were consistent methodological weaknesses, principally the absence of a neutral control and the presence of observer bias. Generally any changes taking place were being recorded and interpreted by the music therapists themselves. The writer summed up by stating that the evidence to support the efficacy of music therapy was not compelling, that the therapeutic value of music therapy was still to be convincingly established.

Perhaps this criticism is too harsh, as valuable quantative research has been carried out (Oldfield and Adams 1990, Bunt 1985, Hooper and Lindsay 1990, Hooper, Lindsay and Richardson 1991). However, the continued predominance of descriptive, philosophical and historical papers in the *Journal of British Music Therapy* would appear to confirm his judgement (Hooper, Lindsay and Richardson, 1991).

In the opening issue of the *Journal of British Music Therapy*, Bunt and Hoskyns (1987) offered a perspective on music therapy research in Great Britain. In this they suggested a number of possible models of research open to music therapists, including the single case study. The single case study which follows combines anecdotal description with an investigation of one aspect of the individual's response.

Background information

Elizabeth (27 years) is a resident of Strathmartine Hospital, and has been since the age of four. She is microcephalic, myopic and a spastic quadriplegic. Elizabeth can walk with one person's help, otherwise she moves about on her bottom. She rarely sits on a seat, preferring to squat. She slides off her chair and under the table during meals. She is much happier sitting facing a corner, either playing with an object, staring at her hands or, when excited, rocking up and down on her knees.

I observed Elizabeth on the ward. She rarely moved, preferring to be alone in the corner engaged in the stereotyped behaviours already described. She did not seem aware of her surroundings and when she did move between corners, she manoeuvred around other people as if they were not there.

Elizabeth was referred to music therapy because of her withdrawn behaviour. The staff were concerned that she was becoming increasingly isolated. They wondered how she would respond to a music therapy session.

The first eight sessions were held weekly in a treatment room on the ward and there was quite a remarkable change in Elizabeth's response. During the first three sessions Elizabeth's behaviour mirrored that observed on the ward. She withdrew into a corner of the treatment room, her head turned away and her back to me. I sang quietly to her for about twenty minutes, lightly tapping a tambourine. Elizabeth remained withdrawn, intently studying her hands.

The fourth session began like the preceeding three – Elizabeth was withdrawn and unresponsive. After about ten minutes, however, she turned her head around, looked at me and smiled. I gently took Elizabeth's hands and began stroking and patting them, singing quietly to her. Elizabeth did not resist and when I introduced the tambourine she smiled and laughed as I shook it.

Elizabeth began the next session withdrawn and avoiding contact. After five minutes she turned round, smiling as before. She took hold of the tambourine and flicked at or pushed over the jangling metal discs. I copied this response and continued to sing quietly, reinforcing her response.

Up to this point Elizabeth had been either squatting on the floor or sitting on a bean bag. The physiotherapist had been using the bean bag; she was working closely with Elizabeth and impressed on me the importance of continuity. Elizabeth's posture had improved with each session spent sitting on the bean bag. She had begun to sit upright and move about less. I decided to encourage her to sit on a chair. She tolerated this happily and did not slip onto the floor. In this new position she acknowledged me almost immediately. I sang a lively greeting song to her. Elizabeth enjoyed this, becoming very animated. She clapped her hands and clapped her hands off mine. When I introduced the tambourine she struck it excitedly. All this time I had been singing, offering encouragement and supporting her responses.

Elizabeth has been attending music each week for eighteen months now. The sessions have been shifted to the music therapy room. Elizabeth was happy to accept this change. During that time our relationship has developed through music and through sharing a cup of tea together. Elizabeth requires the cup to be lifted to her mouth when drinking. Over that time two different volunteers have worked alongside me with Elizabeth. Elizabeth has quickly overcome her apprehension and worked willingly with them. She remains seated throughout each session.

The musical content of the sessions remains simple. Elizabeth continues to enjoy clapping. She is keenly aware of imitation, which motivates and excites her. I spend long periods of the session singing to Elizabeth and responding to her clapping. Often she holds a lengthy musical conversation with me, either clapping her own hands together, or clapping her hands off mine. Elizabeth has begun playing the piano. She plays clusters of notes with her elbows, the palms of her hands or with her fist. Once again she is motivated by imitation, her excitement mounting as each conversation develops.

I have described how over the space of two months a musical relationship developed with Elizabeth, and how that relationship continues to develop. This is the approach that Radhakishnan is criticising. However, I would suggest that you can do more than describe, you can measure as well. Consequently, I also wish to establish whether Elizabeth's response is due to increased individual attention, or to the influence of music therapy. In doing so the paper illustrates a strategy for the development and validation of the descriptive approaches favoured by music therapists and criticised by Radhakishnan.

Design/measures

Elizabeth's response to five music therapy sessions and five control sessions was investigated. The sessions were held weekly, and alternated between the music and control conditions. Elizabeth was videoed during the course of each treatment session. She was also videoed on the ward for ten minutes prior to and immediately after each session.

Elizabeth's response to each intervention was measured on a scale which examined the level of interaction, participation and co-operation; the degree of motivation and the frequency of eye contact (Assessment A). As well as this subjective measure, time sampling was used to give a more objective indication of the level of interaction. A time interval of ten seconds was used, at which point it was noted whether or not Elizabeth was participating in either activity, or interacting through laughing, smiling or engaging eye contact.

Elizabeth's behaviour before and after each session was also time sampled. A time interval of ten seconds was used when it was noted whether or not Elizabeth was involved in any interactions.

Each evaluation was carried out by trained raters, unfamiliar with the purpose of the study. The reliability within one scaled point for Assessment A was 88 per cent. The reliability for the time sampling of interactive behaviour was 87 per cent. The control sessions proved valuable on two counts. They provided a control for individual attention as well as an alternative intervention which could be compared with music therapy.

Treatment

Elizabeth's music therapy sessions were 25–30 minutes in duration. In each session Elizabeth responded to a sung greeting song and was encouraged to play the tambourine and piano.

The control sessions were 15–20 minutes in duration. In each session Elizabeth was encouraged to play with equipment designed for sensory stimulation. In particular, a mirror box and a carousel hung with discs which were bright plastic on one side and mirrorised on the other. This equipment was recommended to me by Elizabeth's Occupational Therapist. In the course of her work Elizabeth had responded particularly well to these items.

Results

Table 18.1 details Elizabeth's response to the five music therapy and the five control sessions. It shows the results of the time sampling as a percentage of the total time engaged in interaction, before (1), during (2), and after (3) each session. It gives the total score (out of 20) on the assessment scale (4).

From the results, it would appear that both treatment conditions produced an increase in interaction. Both the time sampling and the subjective assessment produced considerably higher scores for the music therapy sessions. In each case the lowest score for music therapy exceeding the highest control session score. The total of the scores for the five sessions

Table 18.1 Subject's Response to Treatment Sessions

Session Number	Music Therapy Sessions				Control Sessions			
	(1)	(2)	(3)	(4)	(1)	(2)	(3)	(4)
1	0%	54%	0%	18	0%	32%	0%	9
2	0%	65%	0%	13	0%	27%	0%	5
3	0%	46%	0%	14	0%	39%	0%	9
4	0%	70%	0%	16	0%	25%	0%	3
5	0%	79%	0%	15	0%	42%	0%	7
Total	0%	314%	0%	76	0%	165%	0%	33

– Percentage of time engaged in interaction before (1) during (2) after (3) eah session
– Total score (out of 20) gained on the assessment scale (4)

suggest that music therapy was twice as effective as the control condition in encouraging interaction.

Discussion

Both the treatments have something to contribute as part of a range of non-aversive approaches available for the client. The control condition should not be discounted as a possible form of intervention. The equipment used – carousel and mirror box – develops hand functioning, and if this aspect of the client's response had been measured the results may have differed considerably. Nevertheless, in this instance, with the emphasis on developing interaction, the results of the study suggest that while Elizabeth will respond to the increase in individual attention offered by the control condition, music therapy exerts a greater influence over this particular aspect of her behaviour.

A possible explanation is offered by Nordoff and Robbins (1976) and Schulz (1987). Both have described, and illustrated with case histories, how the music therapist is not primarily concerned with eliminating stereotyped behaviours, rather with helping the individual gain alternative and worthwhile experiences through an externalisation of the stereotypies.

A closer observation of Elizabeth's behaviour confirmed that many of her stereotyped behaviours were being incorporated into our musical interactions. In particular, her hand clapping, which we had developed into imitative conversations; her often repeated slapping of the floor, walls, or work surfaces, which Elizabeth had translated into striking the tambourine and playing the piano; her rocking and her excited vocalisations which both influenced the tempo and the content of my own singing. In this way each behaviour was being actively used to communicate with Elizabeth, breaking down the barriers they would normally have built up around her.

Conclusion

Music therapists recognise the need to establish an interaction through a shared musical experience (Pavlicevic 1991). This case study establishes the impact of music therapy on Elizabeth's behaviour and confirms the value of such an approach.

References

Bunt, L. and Hoskyns, S. (1987) 'A perspective on music therapy research in Great Britain', *Journal of British Music Therapy.* Vol.1(1), 3–6.

Bunt, L. (1985) Music Therapy and the child with a handicap: Evaluation of the effects of intervention. Unpublished Ph.D thesis. Department of Music, The City University, London.

Hooper, J. and Lindsay, B. (1990) 'Music and the mentally handicapped: The effect of music on anxiety', *Journal of British Music Therapy*, Vol. 4(2), 19–26.

Hooper, J., Lindsay, B. and Richardson, I. (1991) 'Recreation and music therapy: an experimental study', *Journal of British Music Therapy.* Vol.5(2), 10–13.

Nordoff, P. and Robbins, C. (1976) *Creative Music Therapy.* New York: John Day.

Oldfield, A. and Adams, M. (1990) 'The effects of music therapy on a group of profoundly mentally handicapped adults', *Journal of Mental Deficiency Research,* 34, 107–125.

Pavlicevic, M. (1991) 'Music Therapy in Scotland: An Introduction', *Health Bulletin,* 49(3), 191–195.

Radhakishnan, G. (1991) 'Music Therapy – A Review', *Health Bulletin,* 49(3), 195–199.

Schulz, M. (1987) 'Stereotypic Movements and Music Therapy', *Journal of British Music Therapy,* Vol.1(2), 11–16.

CHAPTER 19

Autistic Children and Music Therapy
The Effects of Maternal Involvement in Therapy

Pierrette Müller and Auriel Warwick

United Kingdom

The primary aim of this research study was to investigate whether music therapy has effects on autistic children and whether the involvement of mothers in the therapy enhances these effects and facilitates generalisations. The second aim was to gain detailed information about patterns of interaction between mothers and their autistic child, such as the ambiguity of avoidance and approach behaviour, and the role of stereotypic behaviour.

It has long been suggested that autistic children respond well to music (Applebaum *et al.* 1979, Thaut 1988) and music therapy. It has also been speculated that certain communicative skills they developed in the session could generalise to everyday life (Alvin 1978, Benenzon 1976, Nordoff and Robbins 1977). Unfortunately, these claims rely largely on anecdotal observations and their tentative statistics did not fulfil the requirement of good evaluation.

Thus, better planned and systematic observations to evaluate the effects of music therapy are still needed and were the subject of this study. The study was based in certain hypotheses:

> **Hypothesis 1**: Over a series of music therapy sessions, autistic children's communicative behaviour during sessions will improve, measured by increases in *imitation, imitation* and *turn-taking*, and a decrease in *avoidance* and:

Hypothesis 2: Music therapy will lead to enhanced results in mother-child interaction in the play situation.

It has often been found that behaviour changes in autistic children are strongly linked with the person with whom, and settings in which, learning occurs (Lovaas *et al.* 1974, Koegel and Koegel 1988, Schreibman 1988). Thus clinical researchers have suggested that parents should occupy a central place in their child's treatment (Wahler 1969, Lovaas *et al.* 1973, Rincover and Koegel 1975, Hemsley *et al.* 1978, Howlin *et al.* 1973, Howlin and Rutter 1987, 1989, Schopler *et al.* 1987, 1988) in order to maintain these changes outside the therapeutic situation.

This project examines the effectiveness of music therapy under what might be regarded as optimum conditions – when the mother participates in her child's therapy, which is the objective of:

Hypothesis 3: Involving the mother in the music therapy will facilitate and reinforce the generalisation to non-therapy settings, which will show greater change than when the mother is not involved.

Although the efficacy of parents as co-therapists for their autistic children has been evaluated in previous research (Wahler 1969, Lovaas *et al.* 1973, Hemsley *et al.* 1978, Howlin *et al.* 1973, 1987, 1989, Schopler *et al.* 1984, Schopler and Mesibov 1985, Schreibman *et al.* 1988), only a few studies have assessed parental attitudes towards the autistic child and changes in interaction before and after intervention (Howlin and Rutter 1987, Schopler *et al.* 1984). Thus it was expected that, as a result of the mother's involvement in therapy, her perception and attitude towards the autistic child will change gradually.

Hypothesis 4: While the mother is involved in therapy, her perception of the child will become more accurate and her attitude towards the child will change towards a greater understanding.

To do so, a time budget analysis measured the amount of interaction between family members and the autistic child during the day. Maternal assessments of the child's behaviour and their attitudes and constructs were gathered at various stages of the project. Although fathers' contribution was desired as 'controls', since they were not actively involved in therapy, these question-naires could not be evaluated, because only three fathers participated con-sistently throughout the study. Teachers were asked to complete a child behaviour problem checklist and a school report. A list of the questionnaires used is presented in Table 19.1.

Table 19.1: Questionnaires

I. Parents

Tests	Content	Purpose
EE (5 minute free description)	subjective description of the autistic child	to see differences between mother's and father's view and possible changes later
CBL (1983; Achenbach)	Child's Behaviour Problems list	provides a description of the child's specific problem (profile)
Problems in family social life	Restriction in family social life, e.g. going out with child, as a couple, visiting friends...	to localise stress-factors in families having an autistic child
Communications' Questionnaire	concentrates on the child's communication	to obtain information about child's ability to communicate and to build up relationships
Time Budget	Time spent at home with the child	to evaluate the proportion of time parents spend with the autisitic child and together
Self-Concept (Orlik 1979)	Constructs taken from own self-perception	to localise the autisitic child and significant others in parent's own self
Musical Behaviour	musical habits in the family	previous musical knowledge and attitude towards music therapy

II. Teachers

- CBL: Teacher's Report Form of Achenbach's Child's Behaviour Checklist
- Teacher's Report about child's school ability and aims

Conceptual and methodological approaches

Design of the study

In ten sessions the music therapist interacted with both child and mother involved, whereas in the other ten sessions the child was with the therapist alone (see Table 19.2).

Two blocks of music therapy one, (10 sessions) with and one without the mother in counterbalanced order, was delivered by an experienced music therapist. Although the structure was roughly the same for each child (introduction with a 'hello' song, free improvisation and finally a 'goodbye' song), the therapy was tailored to the child's individual need and ability.

For fifteen minutes immediately before and after music therapy, the child was engaged in a play activity with the mother. Both mother and child could choose from a range of activities. Some toys, puzzles, building bricks, books, crayons and paper were provided by me (identical each week), some others were selected by mother or child from the child's own possessions. No advice was given to the mother about how to behave, except that both she and the child should stay in the room during these sessions. This procedure allowed me to evaluate short-term carry-over effects by comparing interactions before and after music therapy. Long-term changes could be examined by comparing early and late stages of the twenty weeks of therapy. All sessions were filmed. A range of social interaction behaviours, such as approach, requesting and negative behaviours by mothers and children were assessed, as well as avoidance and stereotypic behaviour by the children.

During the play sessions the music therapist was waiting in another room, out of the child's sight. No instrument belonging to the therapist was available at that time. To keep the conditions as constant as possible, all the sessions were filmed at the child's home by myself. I avoided any direct contact with the child and mother, unless directly spoken to.

Subjects

Nine autistic children between 3 years 4 months and 14 years 7 months, varying in linguistic and intellectual handicap, received music therapy in their own homes.

First, ten children diagnosed as 'autistic' according to Rutter's criteria for autism were chosen by headteachers from Oxfordshire special schools for autistic children. There were eight boys and two girls. Two groups of five children each were formed considering the following criteria: sex, age, previous experience in music therapy, language development and holding therapy. However, two children dropped out from the project for personal reasons. Only one child was replaced, which caused a number and age imbalance in the groups (means ages were 9.8 and 7.7). Nevertheless, the children could be matched satisfactorily on the other factors (see Table 19.3).

Table 19.2: Research Design

(DURATION of STUDY →)

1. Questionnaires and Interviews to parents:			
Problems	• Child Behaviour Checklist (Achenback 1983) • Problems in family social life		
Attitude	• Communication questionnaire • Free description of the autistic child • Orlik's Self-Concept		
Family musical activities			
Time budget			
Teachers:	• Child Behaviour Checklist (Achenbach 1983)		
→ *Time within session* →			
2.	*Before* *15 minutes*	*Music therapy* *10 to 30 minutes*	*After* *15 minutes*
1st term 10 sessions	play with mother Groups *WM* and *MW*	*MW*: with mother *WM*: without mother	play with mother Groups *WM* and *MW*
3. Questionnaires and interviews to parents and teachers: as in 1.			
4. → 4 weeks holiday break →			
5.	*Before* *15 minutes*	*Music therapy* *10 to 30 minutes*	*After* *15 minutes*
2nd term 10 sessions	play with mother Groups *WM* and *MW*	*MW*: without mother *WM*: with mother	play with mother Groups *WM* and *MW*
6. Questionnaires and interviews to parents and teachers: as in 1.			

Data analyses of the 'before' and 'after' videotapes

The second and third sessions of each condition were chosen to reflect the 'baseline' stage of each therapy block. The ninth and tenth sessions were chosen to represent the end of each block, to assess change due to the different conditions or the passage of time.

Table 19.3: Description of the Children

Name	Age	Group MW	Group WM	Name	Age
GR male	11.6	no Music Therapy no Holding Therapy no Language Mental Handicap	no Music Therapy no Holding Therapy no Language IQ undetermined	TH male	3.4
TO male	6.11	Music Therapy Holding Therapy no Language IQ undetermined Fragile X Chromosome	Music Therapy Holding Therapy no Language IQ Undetermined	JU female	8.11
CL female	10.1	Music Therapy Holding Therapy Language Able	no Music Therapy Holding Therapy Language Able	CH male	6.9
JO male	6.0	no Music Therapy Holding Therapy repetitive Speech Able Fragile X Chromosome	Music Therapy Holding Therapy repetitive speech Able Fragile X Chromosome	ST male	11.8
GO male	14.5	no Music Therapy no Holding Therapy echolalic Speech Mental Handicap 3 days home week			
4 boys 1 girl		**Mean Age: 9.8**	**Mean Age 7.7**	**3 boys 1 girl**	

Summary

Group MW	Group WM
3 no Music Therapy 2 Music Therapy	3 no Music Therapy 2 Music Therapy
2 no Holding Therapy 3 Holding Therapy	1 no Holding Therapy 3 Holding Therapy
2 no Language 1 repetitive Language 1 good Language 1 echolalic speech	2 no Language 1 repetitive Language 1 good Language
2 Mentally Handicapped 1 IQ undetermined 2 Able	2 IQ undetermined 2 Able
2 Fragile X Chromosomes	1 Fragile X Chromosome

To code the interactions between mother and child in the play sessions, behaviour descriptions derived from previous studies in this area (Dowdney *et al.* 1984, Mash *et al.* 1982, Howlin *et al.* 1973) were taken, and acceptable inter-observer reliability for these behaviours was established.

The multiplicity of behaviours coded had to be grouped in a functional way to build up global categories relevant to the hypotheses. To validate the categories, correlational analyses were carried out. Once the categories were satisfactorily defined, ANOVAs (Analysis of Variance) were carried out to investigate possible changes in the child and mother. The categories were: positive social behaviour, positive response, social (neutral) activity, social request, negative social behaviour and looking (at other, at object, away). In addition, the categories avoidance and stereotypic behaviour were formed for the children only (see Table 19.4).

Table 19.4: Behaviour of Mother–Child Interaction in Play Settings

Fifty-five behaviours for the child and 35 for the mother were observed and coded. The descriptions of those behaviours derived from definitions in previous studies in the area (Howlin, Mash, Lovaas and Richer).

Cohen's Kappa Test was calculated for each behaviour to measure inter-observer's agreement. The results ranged from 0.63 to 1.0.

After the coding was completed, the behaviours were grouped into categories relevant to the hypotheses and validated through corellations analyses.

The following categories were formed:

- Positive Social Behaviour
- Positive Response
- Social Activity (more neutral)   for both mothers and children
- Social Request
- Negative Social Behaviour
- Looking (at other, at object, away)

- Avoidance   for children only
- Stereotypic Behaviour

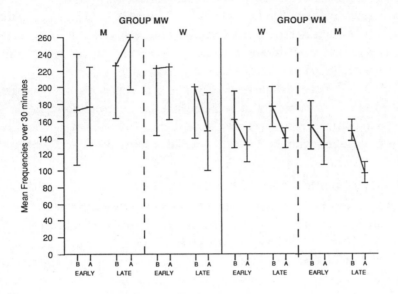

Figure 19.1: Mother's request behaviour in play sessions

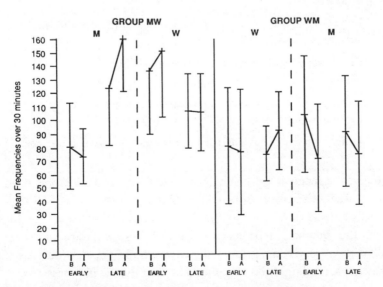

Figure 19.2: Children's avoidance behaviour in play sessions

Some categories of behaviour showed little evidence of change across the various phases; however, significant changes were found in mothers' request behaviour and children's avoidance (see Figure 19.1 and 19.2).

When mothers participated in therapy in the first phase of this study, their requests increased strongly, but when withdrawn from therapy, they decreased such requests. Mothers who were involved in music therapy in the second phase decreased their requests over time, especially during the 15 minutes after therapy. Children's avoidance behaviour in the two groups varied in a similar pattern to their mothers' requesting.

Exploratory sequential analyses suggested that this is because mothers' demands elicit avoidance by the child. Under some conditions, mothers involved in music therapy may become over-demanding, which suggests that careful preparation with mother and/or child is advisable.

Evaluation of music therapy videotapes

Unlike the before and after interactions, the musical interaction was evaluated in a more conventional way. A variety of social and musical aspects of child-therapist-mother interaction were recorded and the children's avoidance and stereotypies measured. The definitions of these categories of behaviour were derived from previous research work on other forms of social interaction, especially by Sigmund *et al.* (1986) and Mundy *et al.* (1986)

Table 19.5: Interaction in Music Therapy

The categories were:

- Initiation, in form of request behaviour and initiating a musical activity.

- Response, which always followed a request by the other, such as compliance, rejection or no response.

- Other positive behaviours, e.g. joining in a musical activity, turn-taking, imitating.

- Other negative behaviour, such as non-acceptance or avoidance.

Inter-observer agreement on behaviours coded in the dyadic and triadic interactions was satisfactory (Cohen's Kappa test, 1960).

An analysis was done on the dyadic (therapist–child) music sessions, examining the therapist's requesting and the child's avoidance and stereotypy, allowing direct comparison with corresponding behaviours in the immediately proceeding/following mother–child dyadic play sessions.

M   =   Condition M
EARLY = Sessions 2–3
B   =   Before Therapy
A   =   After Therapy

W   =   Condition W
LATE = Sessions 9–10
M   =   Music therapy

Standard Error

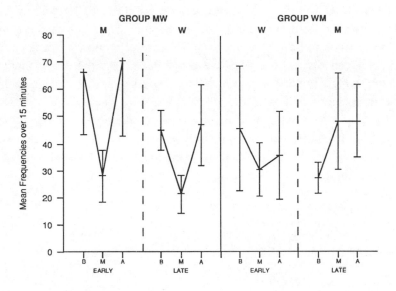

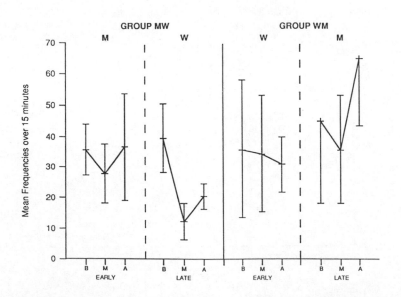

Figure 19.3: Children's avoidance and stereotypic behaviour in play and music

Children's avoidance and stereotypic behaviour

The results were not quite as expected. Though children's stereotypic behaviour was less during music therapy than in adjacent play sessions, their avoidance was not (Figure 19.3).

A closer look at the events diary which families, the music therapist and researcher kept, could provide an explanation for the increase of avoidance in music therapy. It was due to one particular child: for some reason the timetable of JU was changed. Unfortunately, school staff as well as JU's mother forgot to inform the child about the change. Although she could accept the 'improvised' free play setting, which was familiar to her since the family enjoyed playing together, she could not accept the music therapy situation, which broke her routine. Thus JU resisted strongly during the whole intervention session. Although this single event seemed to 'spoil' the data (causing a marginal significance, p=.056), it can be affirmed that taking the data out from the analysis would only suggest that avoidance behaviour did not differ from the free play situation. In addition, there were no changes due to conditions and to time.

⊥ Standard Error for child and therapist

M = Condition M   W = Condition W
EARLY = Sessions 2–3   Late = Sessions 9–10

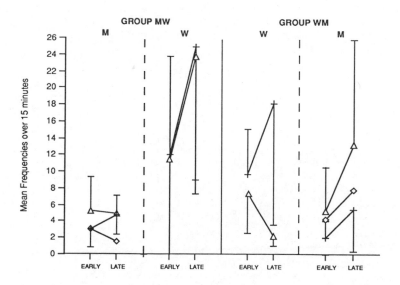

Figure 19.4: Children's turn-taking

Turn-taking

However, over the course of therapy there were some increases in children's turn-taking (regardless of mother's presence in music therapy). Turn-taking is seen as a precursor of language development (Trevarthen 1974, Wimpory and Chadwick 1990), so this result may be important (Figure 19.4).

Initiation

The analysis of Initiation showed that mothers and therapist initiated significantly more in group WM than in group MW (Figures 19.5a,b). However, although Figure 19.5c showed the reverse in child's initiation (less by WM than by MW), the difference was not significant. This may have been due to the 'type' of mothers in each group: in group WM there were two over-intrusive mothers, whereas in group MW there was only one, but two quite passive mothers. The reason why the therapist tended to initiate more in group WM than in MW is not clear.

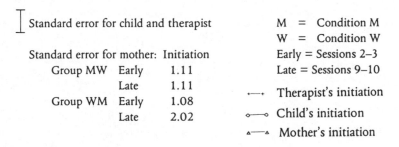

I Standard error for child and therapist

Standard error for mother: Initiation
Group MW Early 1.11
          Late   1.11
Group WM Early 1.08
          Late   2.02

M = Condition M
W = Condition W
Early = Sessions 2–3
Late = Sessions 9–10

•—→ Therapist's initiation
∘—∘ Child's initiation
▵—▵ Mother's initiation

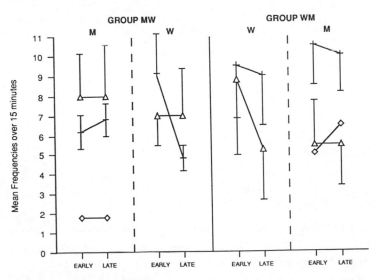

Figure 19.5: Therapist's mother's and child's intiation

Duration of musical play and attention

When mothers were involved in therapy, the duration of the child's musical activity was similar in both groups (Figure 19.6). The increase of children's musical activity by group MW in condition W (mother not participating), while group WM seemed to 'stagnate', suggest that the dyadic interaction (child/therapist) facilitated the child's concentration, whereas sharing the activity with both adults prevented a further increase (group WM started with condition W; group MW with condition M). However, it is reassuring that no deterioration occurred in group WM. They seemed to accept this more demanding situation (no decrease/increase of musical activity between early and late session).

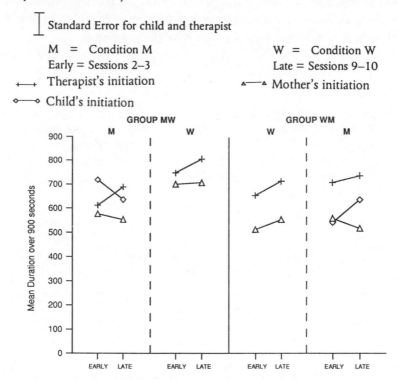

I Standard Error for child and therapist

M = Condition M   W = Condition W
Early = Sessions 2–3   Late = Sessions 9–10
⊢——⊣ Therapist's initiation   ▲——▲ Mother's initiation
○——○ Child's initiation

Figure 19.6: Musical Activity

Mothers' attitude change

Two techniques were used to assess parental attitudes towards their autistic children over the course of music therapy. Orlik's Self-Concept Grid (Orlik 1979) attempted to compare views about a number of important people in the mother's life, including the autistic child. This allows comparisons to be made between her descriptions of members of her social network. It was found that, over the course of music therapy, mothers appeared to become more accepting of the child's handicap.

Two interesting questions arose from this part of the study:

1. Is the way mothers described their autistic child on the Self-Concept-Grid specific to autistic children, or do similar patterns to these emerge for handicapped children generally? Are the patterns different from 'normal' children and if so, how?

2. When mothers are involved in therapy other than music therapy, do they show the same effects?

To resolve these issues, the questionnaire should be administered to other matched families. This is intended after the completion of the thesis.

The second technique used was to collect a 'free description' of the autistic child by the mother, using a technique developed by Magana (1985). A content-analytic system devised by Symlog-Bales (Symlog-Bales and Cohen 1979) was applied to the descriptions. An inter-rater reliability test on the Symlog system showed high agreement between an expert user of the coding system and myself.

This technique showed that mothers tended to describe the target child in a more positive light over the course of therapy. However, there was no evidence that these changes were due to mothers' involvement in music therapy; they occurred across time in both stages of the project. The children 'improved' over time, in the sense that they were perceived initially as being withdrawn, to become more active, positive and task-oriented six months later. But these optimistic results could not be attributed to music therapy, since the effect of passage of time could not be isolated. To overcome this problem, control groups not having music therapy are needed. As with the Self-Concept-Grid, further studies are planned after the thesis is completed.

Summary of the results

Increase in turn-taking and some increase in musical activity, as well as a decrease in stereotypic behaviour could be demonstrated in music therapy sessions. Mothers' participation did not have a particular influence on their children's behaviour. No carry-over effects in the free play session nor changes in mother–child interaction (with the exclusion of mothers' request and children's avoidance) could be measured in this short time of treatment. This is not surprising since autistic children have particular difficulties in generalising learned behaviours across situations and persons with whom they interacted. However, a sequential analysis suggested that the increase of children's avoidance by group MW in the free-play situation was due to mothers' increased request behaviour. There may be two reasons why mothers tended to be more demanding when they participated in music without being given any instruction:

1. When mothers could observe how differently their autistic child responded to music from the way they responded to play, they may have been over-optimistic, trying to elicit the same kind of response in the free play sessions; and/or

2. Understanding that the researcher will compare the interactions in music with the free play at the end of the project, mothers may have felt pressured and in competition with the music therapist.

Because mothers in group WM could not observe their children's activity in the music sessions, they may have been less anxious about performing well. Their late involvement in the intervention may have allowed them to be more realistic about the child's ability. Nevertheless, these mothers decreased their demands consistently after therapy. This suggests that they responded sensitively to their children's behaviour.

Due to their participation in music therapy, mothers seemed to see their children in a more realistic light. Over time, they described their children as being more active, positive and goal-oriented.

The implication of these results suggest that mothers can gradually learn to perceive their autistic children more realistically. However, it is the task of the therapist to monitor mothers' as well as the children's behaviour. Mothers are as vulnerable as their children and need time to learn and experience new ways of communication with the child.

The therapist's experience: A subjective view

The mothers were not given any instruction in music therapy techniques before the research began. This was an added burden at the time and although it was difficult for both the mothers and me, I am convinced that it was necessary to measure the results from this basis of inexperience. We could not be certain that this instruction might not have some inhibiting factors, such as the mother feeling that she might have to teach rather than explore and share common ground with her child. We had to learn 'on the job'. With hindsight, this was an essential learning experience for me, giving valuable insight into the problems of the mother–child interaction and the difficulties of the family relationships. Since the therapy took place in the family homes,

Pierrette and I were not on our own territories. We had to be very sensitive to what might seem like an intrusion until we were accepted.

Being a partner in such research as this has been an excellent discipline. When music therapists experience an important step forward during a therapy session with a client, we feel warmed and boosted by the sense of achievement and progress. This is a very natural and human response to a therapy that aims to build or to restore relationships, but there is a danger that the therapist may read too much into the event, making an interpretation that reveals more about the therapist than the client. It can be difficult to stand back and to be objective about an experience when a sudden and exciting development in musical and personal communication has taken place. It is easy to believe that more has happened than actually has. For this reason, having the research done by an independent psychologist left me free to be the therapist and to get along as best as I could in that role.

As a therapist, it was a privilege to have the opportunity of observing and sharing part of the family interaction, that between mother and child in the family home. There was pain, guilt and often a sense of hopelessness; negative feelings which could and did change, even if briefly, when a mother realised that her child could respond positively through music. I, too, felt guilt when a child seemed to respond to me more than to mother, even though I was aware that it was probably because I was the musical 'expert', whereas mother had to cope with a new means of communication and had to learn how to use it. The greatest joy for me was when a mother began to interact musically with her child on equal terms, able to accept and respond to the child's challenges. Another achievement was for an over-intrusive and anxious mother to realise that her child could and would approach her more when she was prepared to wait, rather than when she tried to goad the child into action. Naturally, when pressure was felt, the child resisted.

The over-intrusive mothers provided the greatest challenge and so, after consultation with Pierrette's supervisors, we decided that I should give these mothers three instructions:

1. Avoid eye contact

2. Do not touch your child unless he comes to you spontaneously

3. Avoid any physical attempt to involve the child – it doesn't matter if he appears not to be actively participating

These mothers were intelligent and highly motivated and, although they understood intellectually what I was telling them, they found it extremely difficult to carry out the instructions during the sessions and the research period was too short for any major intervention. At that point we could not undermine the mother's confidence, which fluctuated enough at the best of times.

Fortunately, the problem could be resolved for one of these mothers who asked if she and her child could continue with me privately after the research period was over. Two other mothers also asked for further sessions. Sessions requested by the first mother continued on a weekly basis, apart from school holidays, for almost four years. The opportunity to extend time for working with these three families was valuable and allowed me to make the necessary interventions, helping the mothers more directly to relate musically to their children, and letting this time for increased experience enhance our relationships. All three mothers expressed great relief at the absence of the video camera. They felt more at ease to express themselves and it was within this more relaxed atmosphere that relationships grew closer and the children seemed less avoiding. If only we could have had a hidden camera of which none of us had any knowledge to record this new progress.

Of these three mothers, the first was a good, sensitive musician who had formal music training; the second was an untrained but natural musician who enjoyed improvising with both instruments and voice while the third felt she had no musical abilities whatsoever (untrue as it turned out), but she believed that music was the only positive force in her very disturbed daughter's life, therefore important for both of them to share. It took the first mother a further eight to nine months to free herself from her training enough to improvise with enjoyment and confidence. She was also less anxious that her son had to be participating all the time and learned to enjoy playing and singing with me, or just being quiet, waiting for the boy to join us again. As soon as the pressure of expectation was relieved, he began to approach his mother spontaneously. Mother could begin to play the major role while I became the co-therapist.

The second mother was a single parent with two children, the mildly autistic boy being the elder child. She was young, out-going and attractive, with all the attendant problems of coping with the needs of her family and her own life. She began to use the sessions to express her own needs through some very poignant melodic improvising. The breakthrough came in a session in which she cried and her son was able to comfort her. At the time, he was curled up on the settee, quietly watching us. Normally, he was determined to be the dominant member of the trio. Mother and I were improvising together, modally, on glockenspiel and chime bars when I noticed the tears on her cheeks. The child also realised that she was sad. He got up and in a very matter-of-fact way went across to her, saying, 'When you cry, you need a tissue.' He retired to the kitchen to collect the box of Kleenex.

The third mother had always felt herself to be a failure, despite the fact that she was an attractive person with a stable marriage and, seemingly, most things she could wish for. Her difficult daughter with her sudden mood swings and chronic anxieties confused and worried her. It took a long time to convince her that she could express her own feelings through her music-making and that I was there to give support and to encourage a spontaneous relationship between her and her musical child. She began to answer her daughter's musical challenges, matching dynamics and style of playing which daughter was able to recognise. The turning point for them was when they could relax and enjoy music-making together.

During the additional music therapy sessions with these mothers and children, I felt very close to them emotionally. We laughed and cried together, experiencing similar feelings of joy and frustration. Overall, I realised the importance of working within the family. A poised and confident parent is more ready to cope with children who have such unpredictable behaviour as those with autistic features. It is vital that these parents feel cared for and supported.

My feelings about being involved in this research were mixed: on the one hand, excitement at the prospect of a new and different venture, while, on the other, trepidation at taking part in a previously unexplored area and strong sense of responsibility towards the mothers and children with whom I would be working. I had already worked with some of the children in their schools and had built relationships with them through interactive music-making. Now their mothers were to be involved as well and I had misgivings about how they should be introduced into a very different and possibly, to them, alien means of communication using musical instruments and voices. It was also important that the confidence of the participants should not be undermined. However, my belief in the value of helping and enriching mother–child interaction overcame the niggling fears. To produce a dramatic and miraculous breakthrough, however, was highly unlikely and I had to accept the possibility of failure.

I would like to conclude this section of the chapter with the following words, written by one of the mothers:

> 'These sessions have been an opportunity, not to be missed, to share in the opening out of my son as a person and to develop a unique relationship with him. For him it is the one time in a busy week when he and I are alone together for an hour, sharing something which means a great deal to both of us.'

As it can be seen, this project had its advantages and disadvantages. The rigidity and demands of the design (cross-over design, play before and after therapy, which demanded long-time attention), as well as the constant presence of the camera may have had strong inhibiting effects. In addition, the small sample size does not allow generalisation over the autistic population and the results cannot be attributed to music therapy specifically. Nevertheless, by using the same design, other therapies can be evaluated and compared.

The benefit of this project was to develop a system of evaluating quantitatively and qualitatively effects due to intervention and time. This project demonstrates that, although change is a slow process in autism, factors which inhibit the effectiveness of therapy could be identified in this short time. We are now at the stage of setting up a programme concentrating on the elimination of those factors, to test whether we can accelerate change.

References

Alvin, J. (1978) *Music Therapy for the Autistic Child.* Oxford: Oxford University Press.

Applebaum, E., Egel, A.L., Koegel, R.L. and Imhoff, B. (1979) 'Measuring musical abilities of autistic children', *Journal of Autism and Developmental Disorders*, 9, 3, 279–285.

Benenzon, R.O. (1976) 'Music therapy in infantile autism', *British Journal of Music Therapy*, 7, 2, 10–17.

Donwdey, L., Mrazek, D. Quinton, D. and Rutter, M. (1984) 'Observation of parent–child interaction with 2–3 year olds'. *Journal of Child Psychology and Psychiatry*, 25, 3, 397–407.

Hemsley, R., Howlin, P., Berger, M., Hersov, L., Holbrook, D., Rutter, M. and Yule, W. (1978) 'Treating Autistic Children in a Family Context', in M. Rutter and E. Schopler (eds) *Autism: a Reappraisal of Concepts and Treatment.* New York: Plenum Press.

Howlin, P., Marchant, R., Rutter, M., Berger, M., Hersov, L. and Yule, W. (1973) 'A home-based approach to the treatment of autistic children', *Journal of Autism and Childhood Schizophrenia*, 4, 308–336.

Howlin, P. and Rutter, M. (1987) *Treatment of Autistic Children.* New York: John Wiley & Sons.

Howlin, P. and Rutter, M. (1989) 'Mothers' speech to autistic children: a preliminary causal analysis', *Journal of Child Psychology and Psychiatry*, 30, 6, 819–843.

Koegel, R.L. and Koegel, L.K. (1988) 'Generalised Responsivity and Pivotal Behaviours', in R.H. Horner, G. Dunlap, and R.L. Koegel (eds) *Generalistion and Maintenance: Lifestyle Changes in Applied Settings.* Baltimore, MA: Paul H. Brookes.

Lovaas, O.I., Koegel, R.L., Simmons, J.Q. and Long, J.S. (1973) 'Some generalization and follow-up measures on autistic children in behaviour therapy', *Journal of Applied Behavior Analysis,* 6, 131–166.

Lovaas, O.I., Schreibman, L. and Koegel, R.L. (1974) 'A behaviour modification approach to the treatment of autistic children', *Journal of Autism and Childhood Schizophrenia,* 4, 2, 11–129.

Magana, J. (1984) *Coding Expressed Emotion from the Five-Minute Speech Sample.* Los Angeles: UCLA Family Project.

Mash E.J. and Johnston, C. (1982) 'A comparison of mother–child interactions of younger and older hyperactive and normal children', *Child Development,* 53, 5, 1371–1381.

Mundy, P., Sigmund, M., Ungerer, J. and Sherman, T. (1986) 'Defining the social deficits of autism. The contribution of non-verbal communication measures', *Journal of child Psychology and Psychiatry,* 27, 5, 657–669.

Nordoff, P. and Robbins, C. (1977) *Creative Music Therapy. Individualized Treatment for the Handicapped Child.* New York: John Day Books in Special Education.

Orlik, P. (1979) 'Das Selbstkonzept als Bezugssystem sozialer Kognitionen'. *Zeitschrift für Sozialpsychologie,* 10, 167–182.

Richer, J. (1976) 'The Partial Non-Communication of Culture to Autistic Children – An Application of Human Ethology', in M. Rutter and E. Schopler (eds) *Autism: A reappraisal of concepts and treatments.* New York: Plenum.

Rincover, A. and Koegel, R.L. (1975) 'Setting generality and stimulus control in autistic children', *Journal of Applied Behavior Analysis,* 8, 235–246.

Rutter, M. and Schopler, E. (1978) *Autism: A Reappraisal of Concepts and Treatment.* New York: Plenum.

Schopler, E., Mesibov, G.B., Shigley, R.H. and Bashford, A. (1984) 'Helping Autistic Children through their Parents', in E. Schopler and G.B. Mesibov (eds) *The Effects of Autism on the Family.* New York: Plenum Press.

Schopler, E. and Mesibov, G.B. (1985) *Social Aspects of Communication in Children with Autism.* New York: Plenum Press.

Schreibman, L. (1988) 'Parent Training as a Means of Facilitating Generalisation in Autistic Children', in R.H. Horner, G. Dunlap and R.L. Koegel (eds) *Generalization and Maintenance: Lifestyle Changes in Applied Settings.* Baltimore, MA: Paul H. Brooks.

Schreibman, L., Koegel, R.L., Mills, D.L. and Burke, J.C. (1984) 'Training Parent–Child Interactions', in E. Schopler and G.B. Mesibov (eds) *The Effects of Autism on the Family*. New York: Plenum Press.

Sigmund, M., Mundy, P., Sherman, T. and Ungerer, J. (1986) 'Social interactions of autistic children mentally retarded and normal children and their care givers. Journal of Child Psychology and Psychiatry, 27, 5, 647–656.

Thaut, M.H. (1988) 'Measuring musical responsiveness in autistic children: a comparative analysis of improvised musical tone sequences of autistic, normal and mentally retarded individuals'. *Journal of Autism and Developmental Disorders*, 18, 4, 561–571.

Trevarthen, C. (1974) 'Conversation with a two-month old'. *New Scientist*, May, 230–235.

Wahler, R.G. (1969) 'Setting generality: some specific and general effects of child behavior therapy', *Journal of Applied Behavior Analysis*, 2, 239–246.

Wimpory, D.C. and Chadwick, P.D.J. (1990) 'Communication Therapy with Music Support for Autistic Children: an Evaluative Case Study'. 'Facilitating Possible Precursors to Theory of Mind: a Case Study in Autism'. 'Experimental Psychology and the Autistic Syndromes'. Collected Papers from Conference Organized by NAS and Sunderland Polytechnic's Autism Research Unit. University of Durham, April.

CHAPTER 20

Research in Practice in the Music Therapeutic Treatment of a Client with Symptoms of Anorexia Nervosa[*]

Henk Smeijsters and José van den Hurk
The Netherlands

Introduction

Research into music therapy is often obstructed by the fact that researchers and music therapists are sceptical about one another, instead of joining forces. The music therapists, who have usually not been trained in research, are suspicious of the researcher and lack sufficient understanding of what a researcher actually does. Perhaps they regard research as a threat to their practical work. The researcher, coming from an academic background where standards such as objectivity and detachment are in force, goes off into the research field of the music therapy with a bag filled with research methods, terrifying the music therapist even more.

The gap that exists between the music therapist and the researcher could be overcome by training every music therapist in the standard methodologies and methods of data processing. The music therapist and the researcher would then speak the same language. However, it remains to be seen whether this would solve the matter in a satisfactory way. Apart from the practical problem of whether the training to be a music therapist leaves time for the academic training in methodology and statistics, another question arises. Is the subject of research done sufficient justice by traditional research methods? It is possible that, even if the music therapist and researcher harmoni-

---

[*] Translation by Marie-Anne van der Veer, M.A.

ously apply traditional methods of research, it may eventually turn out that they have come to a dead end. The methodological errors of research in music therapy listed by Tischler (1983) are partly a result of the fact that the research methods do not match the subject of research. The conventional experimental research methods do not always turn out to be the research methods most suitable for the research into therapies (Petermann 1977, Soudijn 1986, Soudijn and de Zeeuw 1986, Kazdin 1986, Harm 1986, Tüpker 1990). In experimental research the researcher tries to reduce the variability in order to gain insight into the causal relations of individual variables. A treatment situation, however, is no laboratory setting; the number of variables of the client, the therapist and the treatment is unlimited. The mere realisation of a homogeneous experimental group and control group confronts the researcher of therapies with almost insurmountable problems (Schagen 1983). The research of practice situations, where the variability cannot be artificially reduced, requires therefore other forms of research (Doets 1981, van Strien 1986, Soudijn 1986, 1988, Soudijn and de Zeeuw 1986, Grauenkamp 1988, de Graaf 1990). An additional factor is that one should look for descriptive strategies in the research of music therapy that do sufficient justice to the musical process. Alternative research methods have also been developed for the research into music therapy (Ferrara 1984, Forinash and Gonzalez 1989, Tüpker 1990).

The research in practice at the Music Therapy Laboratory at Nijmegen is a research method in which the gap between research and practice and, in line with this, the gap between researcher and music therapist, is reduced to a minimum. The treatment situation is affected as little as possible. Underneath follows an outline of the method of research in practice, illustrated by means of a case study.

Research method

The research question of the research in practice is subdivided into two parts, requiring that the first part be answered before the second one. These parts are:

1. How can the problem of the client be described by means of research?

2. How can the treatment by the music therapist be described and developed by means of research?

By answering the first question, the research makes a contribution to the music therapeutic observation and diagnostics. The description of the client's problem is composed of processing the reports by the music therapist, the self reports by the client and the audiovisual recordings – together making up the 'raw material' – into focus points by the researcher (Soudijn 1988). In the definition used by us, a focus point is a description of part of the client's problem, comparable to the 'sensitizing concept' of Glaser and Strauss (1967). It consists of a title and a brief characterisation of the title and arises from an iterative process of comparing and correcting the description by the researcher and the music therapist, using new raw data (Greenberg 1986). The client's problem is mapped by means of several focus points, until a saturation point is reached (Glaser and Strauss 1967): the new raw data fit into the existing focus points. The saturation point does not occur until the treatment has already been started. Characteristic of this method of research and treatment is that the focus points are adjusted in the course of the treatment.

The aims, the therapeutic approach and the action plan are formulated, following the provisional concept of the focus points. The formulation of aims and objectives results from the interaction between researcher and music therapist in which various sources of information are drawn on. The music therapist introduces her own know-how, skills and experience, whereas the researcher contributes relevant information based on the existing literature in the field of clients' problems, literature on the therapeutic approaches and the music therapeutic methods. In a process of critical reflection the music therapist and the researcher select the possible aims, therapeutic approaches, work situations and techniques. By a process of selection and development, the treatment matches the client optimally. Then the music therapist starts the treatment.

When, after some time, it turns out that the newly gathered material no longer fits into the existing focus points, when a turning point has been reached, new focus points are described. A turning point can occur when the client's problems change as a result of the treatment, or because events outside of the therapy have an effect on the client. The new focus points continue in new aims, new therapeutic starting-points and a new action plan. The regulative cycle (van Strien 1986) of complaint, professional diagnosis via focus points, the drawing up of the action plan, intervention and evaluation, is passed through several times. At the end, the various phases of the treatment are put in line with one another in the final evaluation.

During the treatment there is a process evaluation in which side effects, disturbances and catalysts are taken into consideration. A side effect (Grauenkamp 1988) is an unintentional consequence of the treatment by the music therapist. A positive side effect contributes to the effect of the treatment, a negative side effect harms the effect of the treatment. A disturbance (Soudijn 1982, 1988) is an external influence on the music therapy, counteracting the treatment. A catalyst is an external influence on the treatment influencing and/or accelerating the treatment in a positive way.

The final product of the research is, besides the treatment of this client, also a set of guidelines (Grauenkamp 1988, Soudijn 1988), alternatives for treatment with similar problems and for dealing with negative side effects and disturbances.

The research in practice is a mixture of the case study and the experimental research. Similarities with the case study are the complexity of the variables, working with a single client and the aim of treatment. Similarities with the experimental research are the search for new information and the intersubjective search strategy. The interaction between the music therapist and the researcher guarantees a larger degree of reliability and validity of the information than is the case with a case study (de Graaf 1980).

The method of working of music therapist and researcher has been schematically described in Figure 20.1.

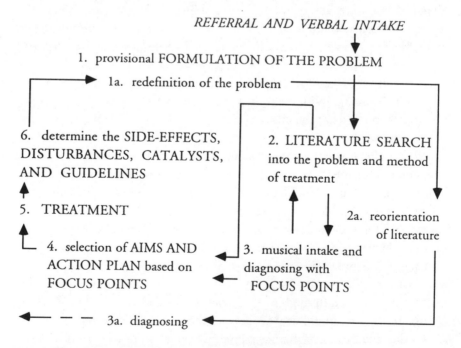

REFERRAL AND VERBAL INTAKE

1. provisional FORMULATION OF THE PROBLEM

1a. redefinition of the problem

6. determine the SIDE-EFFECTS, DISTURBANCES, CATALYSTS, AND GUIDELINES

2. LITERATURE SEARCH into the problem and method of treatment

5. TREATMENT

2a. reorientation of literature

4. selection of AIMS AND ACTION PLAN based on FOCUS POINTS

3. musical intake and diagnosing with FOCUS POINTS

3a. diagnosing

Figure 20.1. The regulative cycle of the research in practice

The music therapeutic treatment of a client with symptoms of Anorexia Nervosa

Background information

The outline on the method of research in practice is followed by a practical illustration of the treatment of a client with symptoms of anorexia nervosa.

The client was a 23-year-old woman who, with the help of the Bureau Slachtofferhulp (Agency for Aid to Victims), found her way to a psychotherapist, who thought it wise to use music therapy alongside psychotherapy. The client had been going steady with a boyfriend who used to beat her and force her to have sex with him against her will. Yet, whenever she had tried to end the relationship, she had always agreed to carry on. When she had finally put a stop to it, the young man had continued pursuing her. This pursuit had had a tragic ending when the young man shot the client's new boyfriend, a married man, dead.

The client was referred to music therapy on the basis of undealt with feelings of mourning, guilt and anger. When entering music therapy she was on sick leave and lacked energy to take up hobbies, too. Although she had suffered from anorexia nervosa in the past, there were no clear symptoms when she entered.

As a result of the referral and the initial interview between the client and the music therapist, the researcher started with an initial study of the literature on the basis of the suspicion that it could be a matter of a post-traumatic stress disorder, dealing with feelings of mourning and a dependent personality. Music therapeutic approaches that could match these problems were listed. This produced a large range of methods (Morrison 1978, Willms 1979, Priestley 1982, Jordan 1984, Schwabe 1986, Canakakis 1989, Jochims 1990, Strobel 1990).

Since a large number of music therapeutic methods, which can lead to a positive effect within a fair period of time, are applicable to the suspected problem, a provisional indication for music therapy was decided upon.

Treatment process

FIRST PHASE

The verbal introductory session was followed by a musical induction consisting of five sessions. On the basis of the information from the verbal and musical session, the following focus points were formulated for the time being:

1. *Feelings of sorrow, guilt and anger.*
   The client felt sad over the loss of her (second) boyfriend and
   guilty, because she thought she had given him too little love. She
   had feelings of anger towards her ex-boyfriend and the people
   around her who reproached her.

2. *Breaking down.*
   By turning on the volume knob and beating hard on the
   instruments, she came to a great development of dynamics and
   intensified her feelings of sorrow and anger, which repeatedly
   became visible in intensive fits of weeping. She indicated that she
   was frightened and that if she was not stopped she would smash
   everything to pieces.

3. *Feelings of uselessness and weakness.*
   She said she did not feel like doing anything, that she had the
   feeling that she did not exist and that she would rather be dead. At
   moments when she strongly felt this uselessness she made a dull
   impression.

4. *Social seclusion.*
   She felt alone and thought that other people did not understand
   her anyway. Her confidence in others was therefore not great.
   Besides, she felt that she should not burden others with her
   problems. During the music therapy her social seclusion became
   visible, among other ways, by the fact that when she expressed her
   anger during the musical play, she would not allow the music
   therapist in on it.

5. *Eating problems.*
   At the beginning of the music therapy she indicated that she was
   dealing with her problems by literally throwing up food.

The aims formulated as a result of the focus points at the first phase of
treatment were (1) going through the mourning process, (2) looking for
means of expression which the client could control, in order to prevent her
from breaking down, (3) making contact and admitting trust.

During the first phase the first two aims in particular were adopted in the
treatment. The action plan to realise these two aims consisted of the
following techniques:

Stimulating release

- have the client select an instrument that made release possible. Techniques that were used by the music therapist to bring this about were: pacing, intensifying (Bruscia 1987).

- have the client perform symbolic improvisations with which emotions were evoked, deepened and dealt with. The techniques used by the music therapist were: symbolising, projecting, analogizing, reflecting, holding (Bruscia 1987).

Checking release

- offering an instrument that prevented release and calmed down the person.

- techniques with which the music therapist could withdraw the client from the trance of breaking down, such as: rhythmic grounding, introducing change, differentiating, modulating, calming (Bruscia 1987).

EFFECTS

The first phase of the treatment consisted of eight sessions and one evaluation session. One of the effects of the first phase was that the instruments got a different emotional charge. While beating the gong, the client became extremely angry. The vibraphone made her peaceful and calm, but also lonely. The cymbals became the sign of resistance against her being well-adjusted.

Initially, the client's playing increased with great vehemence, during which she fell into some sort of a trance and did not keep her expression within bounds. She released her anger in powerful and vicious playing, often accompanied or followed by fits of weeping. Whenever the music therapist tried to guide the musical releases by introducing peaceful sounds, she was wiped out by the client.

With the intention of checking the release, the music therapist incited the client to change the instrument, since influencing her by musical means proved to be impossible. By changing instruments, however, it did become possible to influence the client's musical playing in a musical way, which made her play in a more peaceful and softer way, admitting the other person more and more into her playing. While the musical contact increased, the client's feeling of anger changed into a feeling of tenderness and poignancy. By means of this new feeling she could slowly feel liberated from the past, which she eventually expressed by saying that she had said farewell to the past. Verbally she expressed it as follows: 'The past is over, I am a free human being who will not allow herself to be influenced by others'.

Although she had not been able to control herself on her own, the music had apparently given her a chance, after the interference of the music therapist, to let go of old feelings. She was liberated from the past and the accompanying feelings that had had a grip on her. As she was able to abandon the preoccupation with herself, room was created for someone else, room that she had not granted formerly.

Outside the music therapy she said goodbye to her past by performing a ritual. She burnt the diaries of the past period, lighted a candle in a chapel and placed a rose and some poems by herself on the altar. The first signs of an increase in energy outside the music therapy became visible in her decision not to go into a psychiatric home, in taking up hobbies such as playing squash and needlework classes and by starting work again.

With the disappearance of the mourning problem, the contact problem became more prominent. It is true that her attention to the music therapist had increased, but her ability to make contact still proved to be limited. She played without much variety, fleetingly, restless and fast, with constantly the same volume, without taking any notice of the music therapist's playing.

SECOND PHASE

Although the first phase had had several focus points and aims, going through the mourning process and the release of emotions had been focused on in particular. When the feelings of sorrow, guilt and anger had disappeared into the background, it was time to reconsider the focus points.

With the help of the material that had become available at the end of the first phase, the following new focus points were formulated:

1. *Unable to draw the line*
    In the first phase it proved to be difficult for the client to keep her behaviour under control when breaking down. That phenomenon could be regarded as a symptom of the incompetence to draw the line for herself, an incompetence that was expressed both in individual and social respect. In the music therapy it was very difficult for her to define the playing and to conclude it. Outside the music therapy she was not able to put an end to activities she no longer wanted, nor did she have the strength to break off relationships.

2. *Have difficulty in making contact, admitting intimacy, emotionality and equality into the relationship.*
   Against the inability to break off contacts there was the inability to make contact. The client exhibited two extreme conducts; she either devoted herself completely to a contact without drawing the line anywhere, or kept well away from it. Apparently, she did not have access to the central area of making contact without her losing control over it. She lacked the balance between restraint and freedom. Whenever she handed herself fully over to her partner, there was no equality, because she lost control over herself. At moments when she completely secluded herself, she cut herself off from intimacy and emotionality in contact.

3. *Lack of insight as to whether or not making contact.*
   The client did not have a clear understanding of how she acted in contacts. Sometimes she felt she had (musical) contact, when the other person did not feel the same way. On the other hand, there were times when she gave the impression of an invitation, while she was not aware of this.

In response to these focus points, literature search was carried out. In relation to the contact disturbances, the work by Perls (1985) was taken as a guideline. Following Perls, Frohne-Hagemann (1990) defines 'negative confluention' as the inability to draw the line. The music therapeutic methods, taken from the gestalt therapy, that raise the matter of this contact problem (Hegi 1986, Petzold 1988, Frohne-Hagemann 1990) are about discovering the right balance between being melted together with the other person and being independent.

As the client showed a number of symptoms of anorexia nervosa, such as 'throwing up' food (phase 1) and the fact that her period had failed to occur (amenorrhoea), the thought of anorexia nervosa remained a factor in the treatment, the more so since the anorexia nervosa problem can be related to a disturbed balance between symbiosis and individuation (Loos 1986, 1989). The lack of 'knowing where to draw the line', (Maler 1989), characteristic of both anorexia and bulimia nervosa clients, is shown in ways other than excessive eating or not eating at all and the period failing to occur, it is also apparent in the complete melting together with someone or the complete ignoring of the other person, the behaviour of breaking down and of not admitting the peaceful and well-formed. Many of these symptoms were more or less present with the client.

The cause may lie in a traumatic 'core experience' which has led to an irrational negative view of one's own self, making the person give up her own wishes. Anorexia nervosa is sometimes also regarded as a rebellion against the situation of one's life which has led to this irrational view. A treatment is often selected in which first the core experience is corrected by way of regressive melting. This can be denoted as a 'corrective emotional experience' and meets the client's existing wish for melting and all-embracing care without there being anything in return (Balint 1988), but apart from this need for uninhibited melting, there is also a fear of melting.

The focus points led to the following aims:

1. Enable the client to experiment in the central area between strong control and no control at all.

2. Give the client the opportunity to make contact and to break it off.

3. Enable the client to make appropriate and intimate contact, so that there is an interaction of action and reaction and an emotional experience.

The action plan consisted of the following work situations and techniques:

Balance between freedom and restraint

- the client could, for instance, choose the dynamics or the tempo, determine the duration and select the instruments.

- work situations in which the main thing was the acquisition of a free rhythm within a fixed metre.

- assignments that allowed a reaction, as seen fit, on the music therapist.

Making and breaking up contact

- assignments which put the client in charge, who had to make and break off contact by means of developing or concluding musical tension.

Equality, intimacy and emotionality

- the music therapist used empathic techniques and techniques of intimacy, so that having contact could be experienced as a positive feeling, and contact as something one could rely on. Techniques: imitating, synchronizing, incorporating, making spaces, interjecting, sharing instruments and giving (Bruscia 1987).

- A game of questions and answers, started by either the music therapist or the client, based on the selection of a musical element by the music therapist or the client. Techniques: receding, experimenting, playing back, reporting (Bruscia 1987).

EFFECTS

In the course of this phase, which lasted for six sessions, the client learned to improvise with rhythmic motifs and to conclude the improvisation. She could play both staccato and legato, using a lot of dynamics and many different rhythms without breaking down. Each time she was able to conclude the play. She said she could conclude a musical play without feeling wretched. This shows that breaking off relationships had given her a wretched feeling in the past, a feeling of guilt because of wronging the other person, which points to a limited ability to guarantee one's own interests. Her increased ability to conclude musical contacts became visible in situations outside music therapy. She now dared to fend off men's advances.

While listening more and more to the playing by the music therapist, the client experienced that there were other ways of making contact. She said it surprised and bewildered her, that she felt good about it, but that she did not understand what was happening to her, because she felt she had never experienced this before. For the time being, however, she was not able to respond to this in an equal way. This inability first led to feelings of worthlessness, but the harmonious music which the music therapist would play for her made it clear to her that others apparently considered her worthwhile.

Gradually, she was able to play with the music therapist on the same instrument. When playing the piano the client responded, according to herself, 'slowly and sensitively', with high notes following the base chords of the music therapist. The client's verbal reactions during the subsequent discussion with reference to this playing together were '...it is the most beautiful, most important thing for me. I want to feel worthy. It sounds good, not frightening, I do not want to escape...'

THIRD PHASE

As early as the second phase of the music therapy the music therapist realised instinctively that the fact that she was a woman was an important ingredient of the therapy. The third phase started when both the music therapist and the researcher had the suspicion that the client might have a deeper underlying sexual problem in relation to men. Already, during the verbal introductory session, vague memories of sexual incidents from her childhood had surfaced. In one of her later reports the theme of sexual abuse suddenly came up again. The new focus points were:

1. *Sexual abuse and sexual relationships with men*
    The client felt abused, raped and filthy, reduced to a sex object in the presence of men. She suspected that when she was a child one or two things had happened sexually, but could not (yet) remember this specifically.

2. *Little self-respect*
    In her report she wrote that she had been pestered as a child because she had been fat and had had protruding ears. At an early age she had taken steps to get rid of her fatness and protruding ears. She had adhered strictly to diets and had had her protruding ears changed by plastic surgery. She looked upon her family as a family without love, which prevented her from feeling worthwhile, despite everything.

3. *Loneliness*
    The lack of self-respect led her to seclude herself during her puberty. It was a period when she was very lonely, did not feel at home with either her family or her friends and boyfriends, played music a lot all by herself and would then live in a fantasy world. At as early an age as ten she had played music with lyrics about loneliness.

Against this background, an additional literature search was carried out. The vagueness she had in relation to her sexual experiences in the past could point to repression. In her stories her father continually turned up, which raised the suspicion that her sexual problems, the possible projections, were connected with this relationship (Freud, S. 1972, Freud, A. 1982). It was possible that sexual experiences with her father were transferred to the relationships with male friends. However, it could not be ruled out that it was not so much a matter of personal negative experiences, as of a negative colouring of the personal sexual experiences due to the assumed problematic sexual relationship between her parents. The black-and-white image the client had of heterogeneous sexual relationships was interpreted as a symptom of 'splitting' (Klein 1983).

She had little self-respect as a result of the fact that she had been pestered because of her appearance, and had never thought that she could still be worthwhile, despite her looks (Rogers 1961). Her attempts to be appreciated by others had not had the desired effect. She had, therefore, withdrawn herself into her fantasy world since her childhood. Here, music was an 'Ersatz' for her (Freud 1980, Schumann 1982), listening to music took the place of making contact with people. Both the lack of self-respect and the escape into a (musical) daydream are found with anorexia nervosa clients. The tensions between the parents are also present (Loos 1986).

The direction the music therapy could take was threefold. First of all, attention could be paid to having her awaken repressed experiences and go through her relationship with her father. Music therapies with a psychoanalytic background that work either receptively or actively with symbols or themes that can start the process of association were put forward (for example Leuner 1974, Priestley 1982, Bonny 1989). Aims that matched the first strategy were: (1) locating the repressed material, in particular in relation to her father, (2) releasing aggressive feelings in relation to sexual abuse, (3) transforming the aggressive reactions, (4) going through and providing insight into the transformation.

As there was still uncertainty about whether or not the client's releases would lead to new understanding, it was decided that should no new memories emerge after a few sessions, the first strategy would have to make way for a second one, aimed at integrating parts of her personality. The second strategy was chiefly of a gestalt therapeutic nature, working at bringing out and integrating emotions and conduct, which were regarded by the client as not being a part of herself (Perls 1985). Aims with this strategy were: (1) re-introjection of projections and thus gaining insight into both one's own verbal and non-verbal behaviour, (2) the integration of different emotions and conducts in one's own personality.

As well as the second strategy, there was a third strategy following from the second. Based on the techniques from the client-centered therapy and the gestalt therapy, such as, empathy, unconditional positive regard and confrontation (Bruscia 1987, Smeijsters 1991b), the aim was to have the client experience so much confidence and self-respect in contact with people that she would no longer avoid these contacts and would learn to deal with these contacts in an adequate way. Aims in the third strategy were: (1) the reduction of secluding oneself, (2) the increase of confidence and self-respect in relationships, (3) experimenting with contacts, (4) standing up to confrontations.

The action plan of the different aims consisted of the following items:

Repressed experiences

- the client's search for and listening to music that was somehow connected to periods of her life during which the sexual problems had occurred. These listening assignments were followed by active work situations in which a theme had to evoke associations:

> 'Concentrate on the period when you were 0 to 10 years old and try to express it in sounds.'

Integration

- thematic improvisations in which contacts from the client's life were acted out.

Confidence and self-respect

- improvisations in which the music therapist followed and confronted the client musically. The music therapist would select instruments that did not at all match the client's instruments, pursue her own course dynamically and create long silences.

- symbolic improvisations in which experiences that had emerged while searching for repressed experiences were used as a theme.

EFFECTS

The effects of the third phase, 12 sessions and one evaluation session, were different in nature, corresponding to the different strategies. Listening to music which she had selected herself (for example Michael Bolton: 'When I'm back on my feet again'), evoked a tremendous aggression within her. It was, however, characteristic of this phase that she was now able to control this aggression better. The volume knob was turned on less far and Bolton's music was alternated with music by the Carpenters, music that made her calm and relaxed.

One memory that surfaced, when listening to music she had brought along herself, was about the time when she had been playing as a child and had constantly been undressed and fingered by her friend's little brother, while she had been shaking her head. The picture of the game as a child was for her the frame of reference for other relationships, such as the relationship between father and mother and her relationship with male friends. Both tolerating and shaking her head at the same time symbolised an inner conflict: grant someone a favour you do not really want to give. This ambivalence also characterised her later behaviour. Thus, she repeatedly allowed her ex-boyfriend to make love, although it made her feel very unhappy afterwards.

In one of her reports she wrote: 'I feel like I always have to earn the attention. Men cannot love me without any reason. I have to earn this love.' This 'motto' was apparently the core experience which determined her entire life. Allowing herself to be used as a sexual object was looked upon by her as the price that had to be paid for being accepted as a person. The moment she became aware of the lack of freedom and realised that she did not really want this conditional contact and this conditional acceptance, aggression came over her. Perhaps the former anorexic disturbance was an unconscious revolt against the situation she saw herself faced with.

In front of her father she had constantly felt 'exposed', but it was not very likely that real sexual abuse had taken place. The negative picture she had of her father's sexual relationship with her mother had possibly added a sexual connotation to her own relationship with her father. In order to avoid the feeling of exposure, she had escaped to her own room.

An aspect of integration was the client's discovery of her own role in the interaction. At first she would express herself in sentences such as 'Other people do not make any contact'. An effect of the music therapy was that, as a result of a thematic improvisation about her childhood years, she recognised that she had secluded herself and become inaccessible during that period. Her secluding herself manifested itself during the improvisation when she was playing the temple blocks and once moved to the chinese bars, although returning to the temple blocks right away, as though she was trapped and unable to break out. She beat the gong so hard that it drowned out the sound produced by the music therapist. Further on in the session she played an ostinato rhythm on the vibraphone, of which the small-ranged melody ended in a repeating tone, played softly in the high register. She interpreted this as 'sinking into myself'. Her comment was: 'People could not get through to me, I rejected contact myself'. Since she noticed that she herself fenced off the musical contact during the improvisation, she recognised the detached attitude to be her own conduct. It was a matter of re-introjection of former projected behaviour.

The integration was expressed by the music during one of the last sessions of the third phase. Following the theme 'Express how you feel at this moment', the client came to a musical improvisation which was characterised both on a large and small scale by repetition and variation, a balance between the familiar and unfamiliar. On the large scale there was the rondo form with an ostinato on the temple blocks; the A-part was each time alternated with different B-parts. The B-parts were described by her as sensitive intermezzi, restricted by the surrounding ostinato (part A). She had discovered a musical way to vary and control her feelings. Apart from the variation being expressed by the use of the B-parts, this also happened within the parts themselves. The ostinato was not inflexible when there was a variation and acquired an a-b-a-b-a structure, since a new rhythm had been inserted.

The various elements of form were each concluded very clearly, and the conclusions themselves were also varied by, at one time making use of a repetition, at another of a ritardando, a decrescendo or by intonating and reverberating a single note. The reverberation of the tone was interpreted by her as a symbol of the 'Sense of self-respect'.

It appeared from her piano playing that she was able to drift within a structure. Her left hand consisted of a 'question motif' of two quavers, the right hand played an 'answer motif' of a dotted semi-quaver rest, a demisemiquaver followed by a dotted semi-quaver, a demisemiquaver and a minim. This rhythmic structure remained almost intact, but the motifs drifed across the whole keyboard. It was striking that it was also the first time she was experimenting with harmonies.

Initially, the confronting techniques of the music therapist had made the client try to follow her, but gradually she went her own way. The self-confidence appeared, amongst other ways, from her comment that she did not feel comfortable any longer when she overdid the 'dolling herself up' in her everyday life. Instead of the urge of having to offer herself and make a sexually attractive or sweet impression, there was this urge to be herself.

A remarkable physical effect during the third phase was the return of her period, as she had not had a period since of age of 11 or 12.

Suddenly, during the third phase, memories of her mother surfaced. She once said: 'My mother was far too busy'. Due to the summer holidays, there were no music therapy sessions for seven weeks during this phase. The sudden lack of the intimate contact which the client had found in the music therapy resulted in her understanding that this had always been missing in her relationship with her mother.

FOURTH PHASE

The fact that the early relationship with the mother is of overriding importance with an anorexia nervosa client has been concluded before (Maler 1989). If the mother insufficiently confirmed the child's individuality, the child may develop feelings of guilt when demanding more room for herself as a result of the natural urge to break away. In the case of the client, breaking away had never taken place, because of the bad conscience that had been developed. By means of visits, the client had tried to redeem her guilt, while neglecting her own needs.

The music therapist had successfully adopted a compensating role of a caring mother and had given the client what she understood to have missed with her mother. Parallel to breaking off the relationship with her mother, the music therapy and, connected with this, the relationship with the music therapist, were broken off in the fourth phase.

The focus points of the fourth phase were:

1. *The ambivalent relationship regarding her mother.*

   The still existing ambivalence towards her mother was shown in the concealed aggression towards her, her simultaneous feeling of guilt and her smoothing over her mother's conduct. Her dissatisfaction with the fact that her mother never came to visit her nowadays was thus repressed. She dared only face her mother's lack of love in the past.

2. *A lack of independence.*

   Although the client had indicated at the end of the third phase that she thought the therapy need not last much longer, and that she was able to handle her loneliness better, there was still an alternating feeling regarding independence. Despite the fact that she had somewhat renounced her mother during the holidays, she still visited her on a regular basis. It made her feel constrained, but she was not yet ready to distance herself completely.

The following aims corresponded with the focus points: (1) going through the relationship with her mother by means of the re-introjection of the qualities projected on the mother and the integration of the various qualities of the mother, (2) being able partly to give up her mother and to stand up for herself, (3) take leave of the music therapy, because there was the danger of the client regarding the music therapy as a situation in which she could continue to correct her former experiences. She had to find the strength to develop satisfying relationships outside of the music therapy.

Work situations of the action plan were:

- act out the mother herself.
- act out different sides of the mother.
- act out different sides of oneself.

The work situations during this phase were of a concrete nature. This means that the theme 'distance-nearness' was interpreted as relating to her mother. The role of the substitute mother which the music therapist had adopted unconsciously in the client's eyes, was now referred to as such. Gradually, the music therapist gave up this role.

Techniques used:

- referential techniques (Bruscia 1987): symbolising, projecting.

- discussion techniques such as: summarising, interpreting, meta-processing.

- procedural techniques: receding, playing back.

EFFECTS

The fourth phase of the treatment included six sessions and one evaluation session. During one of the first sessions after the summer holidays, the client's playing was interpreted by herself as looking for contact with her mother. While playing 'the mother' with an ostinato on the temple blocks and symbolising 'her own call for attention' by playing the triangle, the inflexibility of the play on the temple blocks made her angry, which she released on a cymbal. The vibraphone, on which one hand played 'the mother' and the other hand symbolised 'my call for attention', did not bring about any contact either. On the piano the client called with her left hand for her mother (the right hand) which, as though unaware of the intensive calling, continued its playing. Whenever the left hand came near the right hand, the latter would escape to the high register.

In the next session, the stubborn ostinato returned. On the temple blocks ('the mother') resounded an uncompromising ostinato with one hand, on the vibraphone ('the client') resounded alternating fast lines going up and down between both hands. The musical theme symbolised that the client was once again looking for contact, but again 'her mother' would not change her playing, which made the client angry again, to which the mother also responded with anger. This was followed by a period of silence, indicated by the client as a short 'truce', followed by a play consisting of fewer tones in a slower tempo. This changed into a more varied playing on both the vibraphone and the temple blocks, which indicated to the client that the ice was beginning to break and that new forms of contact became possible.

The client began to understand that each penetrating attempt on her part to make contact had caused her mother to avoid the contact. If, on the other hand, she was more reserved when approaching her mother, the latter would come nearer. This taught the client an alternative behaviour in the musical improvisation.

Especially by playing the piano, the client showed how she tried to reduce the distance between two musical themes. If, at first, legato and staccato, high and low were defiantly opposed to one another as provocation and reaction, afterwards the hands would creep towards on another and play close together, even entwined in each other. Yet the tension remained, as the harmony was particularly characterised by dissonants (small seconds). Her verbal reaction in the subsequent discussion illustrated what had happened: 'Making contact is difficult for both sides. At times there is, nevertheless, contact. It can be nice, yet it is also frightening'.

From her written comments it appeared that the relationship with her mother was passing through remarkable changes. The anger as a reaction to her feeling of frustration had disappeared completely. There remained a feeling of pity for her mother who, according to the client, could not very well express love to her in a clearly visible way. Due to the increase of her self-strength it was now possible for her to accept her mother the way she was. The client was no longer dependent on her mother's love for her feeling of strength. She accepted her mother and with it integrated qualities of her mother which she had repressed in the past. She could now see her mother as someone with both positive and negative qualities, someone who was worthwhile even if she was not the way the client had hoped her to be. As the client regarded herself as being worthwhile, she also considered her mother – despite her shortcomings – to be worthwhile.

Outside the music therapy it was striking that she went away on a holiday alone for a week and a half and enjoyed being all by herself. This confirmed that she had conquered room for herself and had stepped out of the tight relationship that had held her in its grip. She no longer felt wretched being home alone.

The musical farewell to the music therapy was characterised by a musical play on the piano by the music therapist and the client, during which a similar transformation as in the previous sessions became audible. Fast rhythmical music containing many mezzoforte staccato tones changed into music with fewer tones in a slower tempo and with soft dynamics (mp-p). The rhythmical element disappeared, the melody changed in arpeggios and the music therapy was concluded in an harmonious way.

This session was followed by another one, at which the music therapist, the psychotherapist and the client were present and said goodbye to each other musically.

Side effects, disturbances and catalysts

During the course of the treatment, a large number of side effects, disturbances, catalysts and guidelines were collected. The most important ones are listed below.

SIDE EFFECTS

Negative

- a negative side effect of being actively engaged in music was that the client did not know where to draw the line and would break down completely.

- a negative side effect of the receptive music therapy was that the client could avoid contact and withdraw into her own fantasy world.

- a negative side effect was that the client was in danger of becoming dependent on the music therapy.

Positive

- since the dependence was initially increased and the client's obedience was confirmed, it was possible to make her undergo new musical experiences.

DISTURBANCES

- a disturbance which occurred at the beginning of the therapy was the client's arriving too late.

- the amount of insight on the part of the client drew the line as for digging deeper into and interpreting her problem.

- a disturbance that occurred when the therapy was well advanced arose when others became interested in the method of treatment and research. This jeopardised the privacy and the relationship based on trust between the music therapist and the client.

CATALYSTS

- the motivated attitude and lack of scepticism towards the music therapy on the part of the client, stimulated the music therapeutic experience.

- certain situations outside the music therapy, for example encounters with men, made the client understand that she needed help and had to work at her problem.

- the accidental interruptions of the music therapy, such as the summer holidays, clearly showed how far the client had come and which problems still remained.

- an important catalyst was the fact that the client was treated by a female music therapist.

GUIDELINES

In the case of the guidelines, only those guidelines are mentioned which were prominent and related to specific problems.

Guidelines for Working at Repressed Experiences

- provide favourable circumstances (for example a female therapist).
- start with safe work situations (for example the client brings her* own music).
- try to sense if someone is ready for it.
- work gradually towards less secure, confronting situations in the way of active music therapy and play-off periods, situations, feelings by means of thematic improvisations.

Guidelines for Working at the Various Emotions that Occur with Mourning

- select instruments and musical elements that can articulate the emotions from the various phases of the mourning process.
- continue exploring these emotions until they have become musically less intense and are less expressed in the report.
- stimulate the client to bid farewell symbolically, in a musical way in the music therapy and in a non-musical way outside the music therapy, for example by performing a ritual.
- have the expression of emotions depend on the fact whether the client has had too little opportunity to express emotions in the past.

Guidelines to Encourage or Check the Expression of Anger

- continue the release until the anger has 'worn off', which means that its vehemence is passing over – audible in dynamics, rhythm and tempo – and that a balance between musical tension and relief develops after not too long a period of time (at any rate within one session).
- in case the vehemence does not pass over, and one can expect the released anger to escalate and degenerate into uncontrolled regressive behaviour, this release should be stopped by guiding the musical play into another direction. Should this fail, then have

---

*   Guidelines are regarded as being applicable to more clients. Whenever the feminine form is used, the masculine one is also meant.

the client stop playing the instrument concerned and offer another one.

- after the process of release, stimulate the client in 'knowing where to draw the line'. This is releasing oneself without having an uncontrolled breakdown, by keeping one's own playing within bounds. For this purpose, offer work situations that include elements of structured release. Work situations in which elements of form, characterised by musical tension and relief alternate with each other.

- stop using release if it does not increase the understanding in relation to experiences and feelings (if the release does not produce new material).

Guidelines for Working at Feelings of Uselessness and Worthlessness

- express the feelings musically. If the music therapist does this both for and together with the client, he/she uses empathic techniques or empathic counter-transference.

- if necessary, present the client with a musical gift by using musical means that affect the client emotionally. This way it also creates an entrance for working at other matters.

- adopt symbolically the role of the very first guardian. Give up this role in time by pointing out the transference to the client, or by shifting the client's attention to the person who originally filled the role. The next step is to work at integrating the various feelings of the client regarding the originally failing guardian and with it the acceptance of the various sides of that person.

- try to compensate the feelings by structuring the musical improvisation in such a way that the client realises that a personal contribution is necessary, that the ensemble cannot do without her.

Guidelines for Learning Where to Draw the Line

This means that one should learn not to continue doing activities against one's own will:

- do not start working at this until conceivable existing emotions, tensions, for example, as a result of mourning, have been dealt with.

- use work situations in which the curve of tension has to be both developed and concluded.

- have the client experiment with various degrees of control with the help of variations in the material that has to be formed, and by securing some musical elements and letting go of others.

Guidelines for Encouraging a Balanced Human Contact

This means, drawing the line in the contact and experiencing equality:

- enable the client to make musical contact and to conclude it by means of different conclusions.

- make use of work situations that enable the client to experience equality and intimacy in the interaction.

- give the client verbal feedback about the degree in which contact has or has not been made.

In relation to situations outside of the music therapy:

- first work in a more abstract, that is, not interpreting, way at relations by means of musical interactions.

- restrict the interpretation to what happens during the music therapy. Illustrate the interaction patterns between client and music therapist by the musical play.

- meanwhile, express one's own feelings that have come up in the contact (empathic counter-transference).

- use video recordings to teach the client to watch her own social role self-consciously.

- have the client gradually find herself the connection with situations outside of the music therapy.

Guidelines to Increase the Self-Confidence

Apply the following order:

- support the client musically in such a way that the client's play becomes an important ingredient of the music.

- allow the client in time to take initiatives and adopt a leading role.

- confront the client with deviant musical material after she has repeatedly been confirmed in her choices.

Guidelines for Encouraging Integration

- stimulate the client in the improvisation of forms consisting of different elements.

- encourage the client to the variation of motifs.

- include isolated expressions of the client, for example, releases, in a form.

- have the client act out persons to whom perhaps parts of the client were projected. In particular, have the various sides of the mother acted out. Record these improvisations on video and have the client interpret her own musical play.

- encourage the client to improvise several unknown or impenetrable parts of herself.

- select instruments that enable demonstration of opposite behavioural patterns and expressions of emotion.

Discussion and conclusions

The method of research ensures a great openness in relation to the client's problem. On the basis of the information which was available at a certain time, the music therapist and the researcher formulated, by means of critical reflection, focus points that described different areas of the psychic disturbance. These descriptions do not constitute a final diagnosis on the basis of which fixed aims are formulated. Both the descriptions and the aims are only provisional and are continually adjusted by means of new raw information from the treatment and information gained by study of the literature. The procedure can be regarded as a falsification process during which the existing hypotheses regarding the psychic disturbance, the derived aims and work situations are constantly brought up for discussion. The cyclical process of reformulation and treatment that is thus created guarantees that the treatment matches the client's problems optimally, since the diagnosis, the aims, the sequence of the phases of the treatment and the work situations are flexible.

In the treatment of this client it becomes apparent how both the description of the individual focus points and the sequence in which the focus points occur, take shape. One focus point is developed during the research and is given priority, whereas the other one retreats into the background or disappears. Initially, the focus point relating to mourning, in particular, found expression in the therapy. The more the treatment progressed, however, it appeared that some focus points, which had already been formulated at the start, became more important. The contact problems in particular came more and more into prominence and were constantly adjusted. The eating problems, which had merely been briefly indicated at the start, were given more emphasis during the further course of the treatment – not because it was still really a matter of anorexia nervosa, but because more and more information pointed in the direction of problems connected with anorexia nervosa. Due to the openness of the diagnosis and the treatment, insight into the problem could develop and it became clear that some steps in the treatment were conditional for other ones. Whenever dropping focus points, aims or work situations, one would look at why a focus point had become less important, what period of time could be regarded as being worthwhile for working at an aim and why a certain work situation was no longer satisfactory. Thus, the situation arose, for instance, the focus point dealing with mourning becomes less important when emotional intensity declines and the client has said farewell in the form of a ritual. In relation to working at repressed sexual experiences, it was determined that working at this aim would only be advisable if repressed material becomes available within a previously fixed period of time.

Because of the inventory of side effects and disturbances, a work situation with undesired side effects could be stopped in time and attention could be paid to a disturbance that made working at an aim impossible. Thinking about the question of what work situations could lead to negative side effects, and how to deal with disturbances, was an essential element of the research. The guidelines in relation to working with release and receptive work situations were formulated as a result of this. Integrating disturbances guarantees that whatever the music therapist does will indeed match the experience of the client.

The openness that existed about determining the disturbance, the selection of aims and work situations, also existed with regard to the therapeutic angle of approach. From the raw material therapeutic methods were composed that seemed to match the psychic disturbance best. If the focus point and the aim changed, so did the therapeutic orientation. This meant that at one moment the matter was looked upon from a gestalt therapeutic frame of reference and at another moment from a psychoanalytic one. It was not the music therapist's preference that determined the therapeutic angle of approach, but the client's psychic disturbance.

The most striking aspect of the treatment of this client was, first of all, the fact that, looking back, many focus points could be placed against the same background and, second, that it was a matter of analogy between the behaviour outside and in music therapy (Smeijsters 1992).

In the course of the music therapy it turned out that much of her musical and non-musical behaviour was connected with anorexia nervosa. Symptoms such as throwing-up food and not having a period immediately pointed in this direction, but also her inability to 'draw the line' – visible in the lack of balance between order and chaos, not being able to stop activities, the inability either to break off relationships or to realise a balance between restraint and freedom in relationships – her feelings of inferiority, the adjustment to her mother, the daydreaming and the existence of a negative 'motto' that marked her life, showed a connection with anorexia nervosa.

These behavioural qualities were expressed during music therapy in an analogous way. The client could not check herself when playing an instrument. She could not vary the tempo, the dynamics and the musical motifs, was not able to conclude her play and could not develop and conclude a worthy musical contact. This behaviour was influenced by musical work situations. The treatment focused on finding the central area between the extremes of order and chaos, the melting and detachment in human contacts. Afterwards, it was possible to look for the origin of the contact problem with the help of symbolic improvisations.

At the same time, integrating the various aspects of her personality were included in the therapy. Not just the integration of her breaking down was important, but also her fending off the contact which she had projected on others.

The outcome of the musical work situations was that the client could bend her musical release towards peaceful sounds, that she could invent musical forms in which opposite musical elements were merged into a unity, that she could conclude a phrase with various musical means. She was able to make musical contact and to conclude it, she could face the confrontation in the musical contact and adopt a role of equality. The client learned to take initiatives, to imitate and to distance herself from matters. She found an equilibrium between being together and being at a distance and found a balance in it. Playing musical instruments made her discover new ways of making contact, after she had acted out the existing relationship with her mother.

The analogy between the general and the musical behaviour resulted in the fact that changes in the musical behaviour gave rise to changes outside music therapy. After some time, the client appeared to be able to fend off undesired contacts, to adopt a more independent attitude towards her mother and to make contact in a different way. She also integrated the positive and negative sides of her mother, by analogy to her musical play in which she connected opposite musical elements.

As for the process, it can be said that the treatment changed from a more abstract level to a more concrete level; abstract not in the sense of theoretical, but in the sense of lacking concrete interpretations. Almost from the start, the music therapist adopted, in a musical way, the part of the caring mother. During several sessions there were constantly moments when the client would arrive at a 'corrective emotional experience' in the music therapy. The concrete relationship between the client and the mother was not formed until the end of the music therapy. While the music therapist did not go beyond interpreting the musical behaviour and the musical interaction within the present, the client made concrete connections in the end between what happened in music therapy and her relationship with her mother.

Likewise, the deficient understanding of the client of her own functioning in relationships dawned on her for the first time while reflecting her musical play. Working at contacts in a more abstract way was a condition of coming within the mother's range of vision.

Characteristic of the process was also that passing through the mourning process was a condition for penetrating the real problem. The vehemence of her emotions had to be expressed first, be it within certain bound, before energy could become available for working at the contact problem.

References

Balint, M. (1988) *Die Urformen der Liebe und die Technik der Psychoanalyse*. München: DTV.

Bonny, H.L. (1989) 'Sound as symbol: guided imagery and music in clinical practice', *Music Therapy Perspectives*, 6, 7–10.

Bruscia, K.E. (1987) *Improvisational models of music therapy*. Springfield, Illinois: Charles C. Thomas.

Canacakis, J. (1989) 'Gongschwingung und Gongklang in der Trauerarbeit', in H. Petzold (Hrsg) *Heilende Klänge*. Paderborn: Junfermann Verlag.

Doets, C. (1981) *Praktijk en Onderzoek*. Amersfoort: De Horstink.

DSM-III-R (1989) Amsterdam/Lisse: Swets en Zeitlinger.

Ferrara, L. (1984) 'Phenomenology as a tool for musical analysis', *The Musical Quarterly*, 355–373.

Forinash, M. and Gonzalez, D. (1989) 'A phenomenological perspective of music therapy', *Music Therapy*, 8, 1, 35–46.

Freud, A. (1982) *Das Ich und die Abwehrmechanismen*. München: Kindler.

Freud, S. (1972) *Abriss der Psychoanalyse*. Frankfurt am Main: Fischer Taschenbuch Verlag.

Freud, S. (1980) Analyse der Phobie enes fünfjährigen Knaben. 'Der Kleine Hans'. Frankfurt am Main: Fischer Taschenbuch Verlag.

Frohne-Hagemann, I. (1990) (Hrsg) *Musik und Gestalt*. Paderborn: Junfermann Verlag.

Glaser, B.G. and Strauss, A.L. (1967) *The Discovery of the Grounded Theory*. Chicago: Adline.

Graaf, H. de (1990) 'Levensecht toegepast onderzoek', *Intermediair*, 16, 44.

Grauenkamp, F.J. (1988) *Onderzoek in de praktijk*. Dissertatie, Universiteit van Amsterdam.

Greenberg, L.S. (1986) 'Research strategies', in L.S. Greenberg and W.M. Pinsof (eds) *The Psychotherapeutic Process. A Research Handbook.* New York: The Guilford Press.

Hanser, S.B. (1987) *Music Therapist's Handbook.* St Louis, Missouri: Warren H. Green.

Harm, T. (1986) 'Grenzen der musiktherapeutischen Forschung?', *Musiktherapeutische Umschau,* 7, 303–308.

Hegi, F. (1986) *Improvisation und Musiktherapie.* Paderborn: Junfermann Verlag.

Hoog, R. de, e.a. (1980) *Veranderen door onderzoek.* Meppel: Boom.

Hurk, J. van den and Smeijsters, H. (1991) 'Musical improvisation in the treatment of a man with obsessive-compulsive personality disorder', in K.E. Bruscia (ed) *Case Studies in Music Therapy.* Phoenixville: Barcelona Publishers.

Jochims, S. (1990) 'Krankheitsverarbeitung in der Frühphase schwerer neurologischer Erkrangungen', *Psychotherapie Psychosomatik und medizinische Psychologie,* 40, 115–122.

Jordan, C.S. (1984) 'Psychobiology of structural imagery in post-traumatic stress disorder', *Journal of Mental Imagery,* 8, 4, 51–66.

Kazdin, A.E. (1986) 'The evaluation of psychotherapy: research design and methodology', in S.L. Garfield and A.E. Bergin (eds) *Handbook of Psychotherapy and Behavior Change.* New York: John Wiley and Sons.

Klein, M. (1983) *Das Seelenleben des Kleinkindes.* Stuttgart: Klett-Cotta.

Leuner, H-C. (1974) 'Die Bedeutung der Musik in imaginativen Techniken der Psychotherapie', in W.J. Revers, G. Harrer and W. Simon (Hrsg) *Neue Wege der Musiktherapie.* Düsseldorf: Econ.

Loos, G. (1986) *Spiel – Räume. Musiktherapie mit einer Magersüchtigen und anderen frühgestörten Patienten.* Stuttgart: Gustav Fischer Verlag.

Loos, G.K. (1989) 'Anorexie – eine Frauenkrakheit – eine Zeiterscheinung', *Musiktherapeutische Umschau,* 10, 105–131.

Luteijn, F. en Ouborg, M.J. (1986) 'Toewijzing aan behandelingen', in A.P. Cassee, P.E. Boeke and C.P.F. van der Staak (Red) *Psychotherapie de Maat Genomen.* Deventer: Van Loghum Slaterus.

Maler, T. (1989) *Klinische Musiktherapie.* Hamburg: Verlag Dr. R. Krämer.

Morrison, J.K. (1978) 'Successful grieving: changing personal constructs through mental imagery', *Journal of Mental Imagery,* 2, 63–68.

Perls, F. (1985) *Gestalt-Wachstum-Integration.* Paderborn: Junfermann Verlag.

Petermann, F. (1977) (Hrsg) *Psychotherapieforschung.* Weinheim bei Basel: Heltz Verlag.

Petzold, H. (1988) *Integrative Bewegungs und Leibtherapie.* Paderborn: Junfermann Verlag.

Priestley, M. (1982) *Musiktherapeutische Erfahrungen.* Stuttgart: Gustav Fischer Verlag.

Rogers, C.R. (1961) *On Becoming a Person.* Boston: Houghton Mifflin.

Schagen, S. (1983) *Het effect van psychotherapie.* Deventer: Van Loghum Slaterus.

Schumann, C. (1982) *Musiktherapie und Psychoanalyse.* Freiburg: Schumann- Gehrmann Verlag.

Schwabe, C. (1986) *Methodik der Musiktherapie und deren theoretische Grundlagen.* Leipzig: Karl Barth.

Smeijsters, H. (1991a) *Methoden van onderzoek in de muziektherapie en andere kreatieve therapiën.* Nijmegen: Hogeschool Nijmegen.

Smeijsters, H. (1991b) *Muziektherapie als psychotherapie.* Assen/Maastricht: Van Gorcum.

Smeijsters, H. (1992) 'Indicatie en analogie. Kan muziektherapie beschouwd worden als een vorm van psychotherapie?', *Tijdschrift voor Psychotherapie,* 18, 2, 88–101.

Soudijn, K.A. (1982) *Kwaliteit van psychotherapie.* Meppel: Boom.

Soudijn, K.A. (1986) 'Explicitering van ervaringskennis bij psychotherapeuten'. *De Psycholoog.* XXI/3, 115–119.

Soudijn, K. (1988) *Vraag het aan de wetenschap.* Amsterdam/Lisse: Swets en Zeitlinger.

Soudijn, K. and Zeeuw, G. de (1986) 'Drie vormen van psychotherapie- onderzoek en hun beperkte functies', *Kennis en Methode,* 99–111.

Strien, P.J. van (1986) *Praktijk als wetenschap.* Assen: Van Gorcum.

Strobel, W. (1990) 'Von der Musiktherapie zur Musikpsychotherapie', *Musiktherapeutische Umschau,* 11, 313–338.

Tischler, B. (1983) 'Ist Musiktherapie empirisch begründbar?', *Musiktherapeutische Umschau,* 4, 95–106.

Tüpker, R. (1990) 'Wissenschaftlichkeit in kunsttherapeutischer Forschung', *Musiktherapeutische Umschau,* 11, 7–20.

Vandereycken, W., Hoogduin, C.A.L. and Emmelkamp, P.M.G. (1990) (Red) *Handboek psychopathologie dl 1.* Amsterdam/Houten: Bohn Stafleu Van Loghum.

Wester, F. (1987) *Strategieën voor kwalitatief onderzoek.* Muiderberg: Coutinho.

Willms, H. (1979) 'Musiktherapie: Behandlungsmethode der Arbeit im therapeutischen Vorfeld', *Musik und Medizin,* 39–47.

CHAPTER 21

The Guitar Doesn't Know This Song
An Investigation of Parallel Development
in Speech/Language and Music Therapy

Julie Sutton
Northern Ireland

The professional work of a music therapist demands constant and detailed enquiry. We frequently ask questions for which there are no neat answers and, inevitably, in all our detective work, we uncover more questions.

In *Last Chance to See* (1991) Douglas Adams describes eloquently the evolution of the Baiji dolphin as being 'written' in the developing embryo. As the foetus grows, the evolutionary stages are revealed – a huge time span encompassed within a few months. In Adams' words, 'It's a sort of action replay' (p.147). Although we rely largely on verbal language for day-to-day communication, in evolutionary terms language is new to us. What came before words? Did anything? Did music?

This chapter describes a musical journey, seen in relation to evolving speech and language. The journey is travelled by me and Paul, a five-year-old boy with a complex speech and language impairment. Could there be identifiable parallels in speech and language development and in the development of musical responses within music therapy sessions? Could we indeed be seeing part of an Adams-type 'action replay' as we watch the process unfold?

I believe that patterns emerging in the timing and spacing of sounds in sessions were closely linked with Paul's speech and language development. Two years of work will be reviewed, during which Paul moves through concrete and then abstract levels of language. I am indebted to Paul, his parents and his speech and language therapist for permission and support in telling his story.

When we first met, Paul was five years old. Small and blond, the thinness of his wiry legs was interrupted by two knobbly knees peering out from below his shorts. He was slightly ungainly (but not clumsy) in his movements, restless and energetic. He looked both vulnerable and inquisitive.

He was born three and a half weeks early, and was a small baby weighing approximately $4\frac{1}{2}$ or 5 pounds. He was hospitalised for the first five weeks of his life, operated on at birth for a diaphragmatic hernia and ventilated continuously for three weeks due to heart failure. He developed a chest infection with further heart failure, causing him to be ventilated intermittently over the following two weeks. After such a shaky start, Paul flourished, although 'global developmental delay' relating to his speech and language was observed. An Electroencephalogram (EEG) carried out when he was four years old was identified as 'abnormal'. Frequent sharp wave discharges were recorded focally and independently from both hemispheres; however, Paul has apparently had no convulsions. This was not clinically significant, although his consultant paediatrician described Paul as being 'wired up wrong', a colourful but nevertheless apt phrase. A report from the audiologist described unusually narrow ear canals, which may well be related to the history of intermittent hearing loss.

A slow feeder, Paul did not babble until after he was two years old. At two and a half he began weekly speech and language therapy, also attending a playgroup and then a local nursery from this time. He said his first words at three years – and in the same year contracted chickenpox.

Some months before his fifth birthday Paul attended the assessment clinic at a school offering specialist educational provision for speech and language impaired children from all over Northern Ireland. Ten significant aspects relating to his difficulties were recorded during this assessment:

1. Paul had severe attention and concentration difficulties.

2. Co-operation was 'difficult'.

3. The assessors had to use informal procedures, thus ensuring that any results were unreliable.

4. Paul was apparently functioning at 12–18 months below his chronological age of four years two months.

5. There were two-word utterances with one or two three-word utterances, suggesting that syntax (i.e., rules for sentence-building) was beginning to develop.

6. His speech was only partially intelligible and then only when the context was known.

7. His expressive vocabulary was limited; the receptive vocabulary was not tested.

8. Motor skills were 'fair to good', apart from catching a ball – it is likely that Paul revealed immature motor skills.

9. He showed 'reduced motivation' for verbal communication and relied heavily on gesture.

10. His areas of greatest need and difficulty included expressive language and vocabulary.

A diagnosis was made describing the areas of language that posed difficulty for Paul. These included problems with the rules governing sentence-building and access to the vocabulary necessary for self-expression. This is termed *Lexical Syntactic Deficit Syndrome* (Sloan and Levinson 1980).

Paul began attending the specialist school soon after his fifth birthday. He was restless and did not find it easy to be part of a group. He struggled to hear, listen to, process, assimilate and categorise auditory information. It took over six weeks to complete the usual two-session speech and language assessment. After one term Paul was referred for music therapy.

Clinical material

This overview, covering two years, records the main features of both the music therapy and the speech and language development. I am aware that a major aspect of the music therapy – the developing relationship between child and therapist – does not feature significantly in this overview; this was central to Paul's therapy but is not concentrated on here.

In the following clinical examples links can be seen between speech and language development and some aspects of music therapy. I have divided the examples into four main areas: discovery, play, fears and the verbal world.

Discovery

In the early sessions Paul chose to play the drum and cymbal loudly and energetically, his sounds rushing and tumbling out. There were very few quiet periods and these were short-lived; brief rests before continuing sound. I found myself drawn into the whirlpool where Paul's rate of playing kept changing every 3–5 seconds. His auditory processing difficulties (hearing, processing, assimilating what he heard and reacting to it) and the emotional effect of trying to filter successfully his sounds and my sounds – these were presented so quickly that this was possible for only a few seconds before he became confused – were integral to his music.

In his third session he lifted his drumstick from the drum head and glanced at me as I simultaneously lifted my hands. He dramatically, slowly brought the stick back to the drum head until it touched it softly, now looking directly at my hands as I quietly played a single chord. These few seconds encompassed his discovery of a link between his sounds and mine, a stretching out of the interaction that was usually so rushed and the longest period of silence we had experienced together.

Over the next few months Paul discovered a sense of shape in our music, changing his playing from constantly changing outbursts to forming energetic phrases, creating and experiencing a beginning, middle and end to his groups of sounds. Soon after this he began spontaneously to construct his first simple sentences.

Play

Apart from using the instruments, Paul had rarely vocalised during music therapy. His speaking voice had a forced, strident, mechanical quality that echoed his anxiety in understanding and being understood in a world of words. Now he chatted to me at the beginnings and particularly the ends of sessions, drawing his own boundaries to our music making in this way. One day I brought two kazoos to the session. Paul organised us with one each and we held prolonged conversations of expressive babble, accompanied by exaggerated gesture. I was stunned by the ease with which he entered into this interaction and afterwards found myself wondering if he had had the opportunity to play vocally and explore at any other time, outside our sessions. I discovered that his speech and language therapist had begun to work towards expanding his spoken phrases and preparing for syntax (the word level in sentences).

Just as Paul had discovered a sense of musical structure before speaking his first simple sentences, so his experience – and need for – vocal play marked expanding phrases in speech.

Fears

I had begun work with Paul in the January and we were now meeting after the summer holiday that same year. While on holiday, Paul had slept apart from his parents for the first time away from home and had been frightened. He brought much anxiety to his session, talking about a 'scary monster', wanting me to play 'scary music' and to 'make a scary film'. As the tension in my music increased, Paul told me to 'stop the music!' and ran around the room, playing the instruments strongly in a disorganised way, reminiscent of our first sessions. He shouted 'go away!' to the monster, together with me and – standing close to me – on his own. Was he beginning to meet this fear, trying to make sense of it or to distance himself from it in words? Did using the words supported by the music help him to contain and safely express these frightening feelings?

Later, Paul spotted the piano dustsheet at the side of the room and crawled under it, becoming the monster and scaring me. I had to tell Daddy and Mummy that the monster was scaring me, as I underpinned the drama with music.

We are accompanied by the monster into the second year of music therapy. Paul and I exchange roles and I am the monster; he trusts the space and time offered by the therapy to express feelings and moods in a way that, for him, words cannot. His playing becomes freer, less disorganised and more sophisticated in that he is aware of component parts of the music – he finds short rhythm patterns, sustains ostinati and some melodic rhythm as he sings his words.

In a sense, he has used his sessions to bring his internal world out into the therapy room and the outside world; his fears are voiced musically and verbally as he liberates some of his tension. As a result, he seems open to more of the world, his music becomes freer and he is aware of musical detail.

At this stage his speech and language therapist is able to work with the grammar of his speech and language (syntax). This would seem to parallel Paul's musical responses, which now reveal awareness of the detailed make-up of phrases – the underlying pulse and recurring pattern within this.

The verbal world

During the remainder of the second year of music therapy, Paul is confidently organising his sessions. It is clear that the chaos he experiences as he tries to make sense of the verbal world is still in evidence (yet this very experience is now familiar and less overwhelming) and he uses his therapy space as a link between his inner self and this world.

He makes a 'concert', narrating to the imagined audience the music that will be played, much as had happened some weeks previously at his local church. He picks up the guitar and begins to sing the song 'Jesus Loves Me', strumming the open strings while I add the accompanying harmony with quiet piano chords. Paul finishes, then sings directly to me with his solo guitar accompaniment. After a few phrases he stops, looks at the guitar, then at me and announces, 'the guitar doesn't know this song'. Paul knows that he wants to hear the changing harmonies of the guitar yet cannot link such sounds with his playing – the guitar does not make the expected sounds, the guitar cannot know the song.

On another occasion, Paul came to the session with a worried, fretful expression on his face. He arranged all the drums he could find around him and sat, ready to play; I remained poised, near the piano, waiting to see what would happen. Paul began to tell me about his dog, who had clearly died recently, punctuating much of our dialogue with playing instruments (see Transcript). Here he was controlling, ordering and using his therapy time for expressing anxieties about the unexpected loss of his dog and the inevitability of the passing of time. For all children the concept of time is not easy to grasp – how much more difficult this must be for Paul, who does not seem able to use the abstract sense of words. In the loss of the dog, as well as in the loss of his parents when sleeping apart from them on holiday, there may well be echoes of the loss of close parental contact during Paul's traumatic first weeks of life; perhaps by his music he can reclaim some of these feelings and then find words for them?

At this stage in his speech and language therapy the work was centred around the move from concrete to abstract levels of language. As Paul revealed his needs through his musical responses and growth in music therapy, so the development began in his speech and language.

Conclusions

From the beginning Paul brought tremendous energy and humour to the sessions, anticipating our meetings with enthusiasm as if hungry for music. Over the next two years the shape of the music therapy emerged, as Paul moved from discovery through haphazard, chaotic playing, to play in his vocalising, until he began to express and then meet some of his fears with music and words. Eventually, he confidently used his sessions as a link between himself and the outside world. Within this overall shape other patterns emerged that formed an unexpected link with his speech and language development.

What happens when we express ourselves in words? Our intense emotional experiences are difficult, if not impossible, to 'put into words'. We struggle to express intense feelings as we feel them, yet in time words may help us to gain perspective. Paul cannot rely on words in this way.

When Paul played the guitar for the first time he wanted to sing 'Jesus Loves Me', associating the instrument with seeing it being played in his church. He began, but stopped as the six open strings did not give him the simple harmonic structure of the song. He looked at the guitar, then at me. He said, 'the guitar doesn't know this song'. His observation – and the way he expressed it – characterises for me his struggle with the world of words. We apparently know more about the auditory processing of speech sounds than those of music. Existing literature illustrates the wide contrasts in the analysis of speech sounds, language and music. We know relatively little about the child's processing of music, but we do know that, unlike language, we can react to, appreciate and process music without knowledge of its rules and structure. Perhaps it is this accessibility that was such an important feature of Paul's music therapy. At the end of the two years Paul's sounds are still to some extent disorganised (for his auditory processing difficulties are still there), but he now has a wider sound vocabulary – he can use his sessions as he needs and he is relating this experience to the outside verbal world.

There is something about spontaneous music-making that links us all with our early development, part of which is our emergence into a verbal world. Journeys in music therapy tell this story again and again. *Last Chance to See* (1991) is a book describing a search for endangered species. A close encounter with a gorilla prompts Douglas Adams to ponder:

> 'I watched the gorilla's eyes again, wise and knowing eyes, and wondered about this business of trying to teach apes language. Our language. Why? There are many members of our own species who live in and with the forest and know it and understand it. We don't listen to them. What is there to suggest we would listen to anything an ape could tell us? Or that it would be able to tell us of its life in a language that hasn't been born of life? I thought, maybe it is not that they have yet to gain a language, it is that we have lost one.' (pp.77–78)

Adams is not, of course, the first to reflect on the relative youth of homo sapiens. I began this paper by recognising the detective work that is part of music therapy; it is fitting that the last word should go to Sherlock Holmes:

Holmes: Do you remember what Darwin says about music? He claims that the power of producing and appreciating it existed among the human race long before the power of speech was arrived at. Perhaps that is why we are so subtly influenced by it...

Watson: That's rather a broad idea. (Conan Doyle, 1887)

References

Adams, D. (1991) *Last Chance to See.* London: Pan Books.

Altman, S.A. (1987) 'Primate Communication', in B.M. Mayer and A.K. Pugh (eds) *Language, Communication and Education.* Milton Keynes: Open University.

Bishop, D.V.M. (1989) 'Autism, Asperger's Syndrome and Semantic-Pragmatic Disorder: where are the Boundaries?', *British Journal of Disorder of Communication,* 24, 2, 101–121.

Bruner, J. and Watson, R. (1987) 'From Communication to Talking', in B.M. Mayer and A.K. Pugh (eds) *Language, Communication and Education.* Milton Keynes: Open University

Conan Doyle, A (1887) *A Study in Scarlet.* London: Grafton Books.

Fridman, R. (1973) 'The First Cry of the Newborn: Basis for the Child's Future Musical Development', *Journal of Research in Music Education,* Vol.21, 264–9.

Moog, H. (1976) *The Musical Experience of the Pre-School Child.* (Translated by C. Clarke). London: Schott and Co.

Nolte, J. (1988) *The Human Brain.* St Louis, Missouri: CV Mosby Co.

Shuter-Dyson, R. and Gabriel C. (1981) *The Psychology of Musical Ability.* London: Methuen and Co.

Sloan, C. and Levinson, P. (1980) (eds) *Auditory Processing and Language: Clinical and Research Perspectives.* New York: Grune and Stratton.

Sutton, J.P. (1991) The Parallel Development in Speech/Language and Music in a Group of Children with Speech and Language Impairment. Report of a project funded by 2-year DHSS Medical Research Award, Belfast, N. Ireland.

Trehub, S.E. and Sheider, B. (1985) (eds) *Auditory Development in Infancy, (Advances in the Study of Communication and Affect Series, Volume 10).* New York: Plenum.

Transcript

The dog that died (words in brackets = music therapist)

Paul: When I was in Class 1 did you bring me on Monday? (Yes) Now you bring me a Thursday? (Yes) Will you bring me um Wednesday when I'm Class 5?

Paul: My dog is a dead very dead dog, so she is. (Is your dog dead?) Yeh. (How did that happen?) Ah, she was very old, 'bout ninety. (Oh...) She was quite a wee dog. (Right, so she lived a long time...) Yeh. (Right) She was younger when she was born – (She what?) She was born when she was about one years old. She was only wee puppy. (Oh right) That height grew up, she was about that height. (Right) Now... she was a very old dog

now, (she was... when did she die then?) Cough; yesterday, ah
yesterday. (Did she?) Yes. (Gosh... what was her name?) It was
Kim. (Kim, ah – do you miss her?) Um... she never see again.
(She didn't?) No. (Well, not if she was dead, no – but it was
probably time for her to die if she was very very old, wasn't it?)
Is it near time when you're dead? (For me?) Yeh. (No, I've got a
long time yet, I'm still quite young!) See – in – what age are
you? (I'm 34, I'll be 35 in September – that's not 90 is it?) I got
one more year and a, to go, one more year to go and d-d-d-d
juniors. (Oh right, so how old are you?) Uh, 'bout eight. (Oh
right) I nearly nine (Right)... (So you're younger than me and
I'm younger than your dog)... Oh yes, are you older than –
what age were you when I was in Class 1? (In Class 1... how old
were you in Class 1?) Um, I was bout five... one, two foot. (How
old in years?) Two foot. (Yeh, but how many years old – you
weren't two feet old – ?) I was two feet old (No, you were two
feet tall; you must have been taller than that...) But I was three
foot, I was three foot in Class 2. (Right)... (Let me see) I was
four foot in Class 2, Class 4... (I was 32 years old...) Let's get
started –

plays instruments

Paul: You know what happened to my dog? (What?) Uh, she was
             very very old... Uh, let's get back –

plays instruments

Paul: You know what's wrong with my dog? My dog DIED. She
             was about ninety (Yeh) Uh, uh and she uh, had to die. I – um,
             longer than Kim. (Uhu?) Yes.

*Transcript from a session towards the end of the second year of
music therapy. Paul needs to talk about his dog who has died. He struggles
with the concept of time, of ageing.*

CHAPTER 22

Observational Techniques in the Analysis of Both Active and Receptive Music Therapy with Disturbed and Self-Injurious Clients

Tony Wigram
United Kingdom

Introduction

The questions that often have to be answered, particularly in order to justify the value of music therapy in both health and educational practice, revolve around whether a particular intervention or method of work can have a successful and reliable outcome, and also what components in both the musical elements and the therapist's use of a medium contribute or are influential. So, perhaps in the wrong order, we are concerned to find out 'Does it work?', and 'What causes it to work?'. Analysing the process of music therapy requires detailed investigation to look at both the musical contribution of the therapist and the client, and to consider such important factors in a session as critical moments, musical texture and structure, and the significance of the interplay between those involved in musical conversations, improvisations and interactions. Such analyses can tell music therapists a lot about the way they are initiating and then responding to musical activity, the significance of intervals, chord structures, modulations, modalities and many other elements, including variety, volume, pitch, rhythm and tempo that can affect the engagement and emotional interaction taking place (Lee 1989, 1990b, Pavlicevic 1990).

Predominantly, though, we have spent our time researching the outcomes of music therapy, looking at its effect on the client and seeking reliable and measurable changes. A recent and growing area of interest has been the physiological effect of music, and the clinical application of music therapy in the general medical field. Maranto (1991) has documented studies undertaken in America and Europe, looking at conceptual and historical applications of music in medicine, physiological applications, clinical applications and applications of performing arts medicine. In Germany, Spintge (1991) has investigated the neurophysiology of emotion and its therapeutic applications in music therapy and music medicine, and looked at music's function as an emotional and aesthetic stimulus in cognitive/verbal activity, vegetative/physiological activity and non-verbal, psycho-motor behaviour, including gesture, expression and behavioural patterns. Looking at the healing power of music, Clynes (1986) described various processes that have been researched. The de-stressing effect relies on three elements that are also pivotal in music therapy process. First, as a pleasant and social activity, causing the cathartic effect of releasing repressed emotion; second, as a means of contacting memories and associations; and third, generating empathy, a feeling of belonging and connectness with other life, or with the universe. For neuro-chemical and immune system reactions, the release of both positive emotions such as joy, love and sex, as well as negative emotions, such as grief, anger and hate, is beneficial, particularly as repression of the latter emotions can cause harm to the person. Clynes cites Guillemin, Cohn and Melnuchuk (1985), who have explored the effects of emotion (and implicitly of music) on the level of functions of the immune system. The neuro-motor and exercise effect of making music is helpful to the healing process, as they are caused by harmonious, controlled and sometimes effortless movements.

In some studies, the specific style of music used seems to be unimportant to the research. For example, in one study in Japan, on the effects of anxiolytic music on endocrine function in surgical patients (Oyama et al. 1986), no specific type of music used was stated, and yet in another study (Taniuka et al. 1986) on patients during surgical operations under epidural anaesthesia, non-specific mention is made of the use of 'soft popular music, Japanese folk songs or Japanese popular music'.

One aspect of my work recently has involved a close look at the physiological effect of sound, in particular, of low-frequency sound and sedative music, in reducing the level of self-injurious behaviour in clients with learning difficulties. The use of this passive modality therapy, but with specific physical effect, is already documented from research studies and treatment programmes over the last ten years (Skille 1982, 1986, 1989,

Skille and Wigram 1993, Wigram and Weekes 1989, Wigram 1991) and has been widely applied to a variety of conditions, illnesses and disorders in the normal population and in the field of mental health and learning difficulty. Research into self-injurious behaviour has frequently involved very small sample groups, and often only a single study design is used. Self-injurious behaviour (SIB) is considered to be any behaviour initiated by the individual, which directly results in physical harm to that individual (Murphy and Wilson 1985).

Clinical Material

The first client involved in this study is a 27-year-old who self-injures by consistent slapping of his face with one or both hands. When not slapping, he can also be in a state of arousal and tension resulting in hand activity on his body or hand plucking. SIB was particularly noticeable with this young man during any form of intervention, when his anxiety levels seem to rise. Subject two is a 31-year-old man who also self-injures by banging his head with one or both hands and also by rubbing his head until the hair falls out. In this subject there is no clear evidence of a reliable antecedent to SIB, which in itself causes distress for the carers. Subject three was an extremely disturbed young lady of 26 years, whose SIB consisted of banging her head against walls, floors and objects. She would also pick at her skin, and her head was so damaged that a large part of the left-hand side of her skull and the rear of her skull were very pulpy. In addition to SIB, this subject also had extremely difficult behaviours, including kicking patients and staff, biting and scratching, pinching and grabbing, and was in need of almost continuous restraint. The design that was used for this study was to treat each subject four times a week over three weeks, using a within-subjects design. The music chosen for the study included a series of 'cello pieces with orchestra on a tape of classical 'cello music:

Bailero from *The Songs of the Auvergne*	
'Softly awakes my heart' from *Samson and Delilah*	Saint-Saens
Elegie	Faure
Bachianas Braxileiras No 5	Villa Lobos
Arioso	J.S. Bach
'Serenade' from *Hassan*	Delius

Treatment sessions involved the clients lying on a specially constructed chair with speakers built into it, through which the pieces of music were played, also incorporating a low-frequency pulsed tone of 41 Hz, pulsed over a 10 second cycle. These sessions were randomly interspersed with placebo sessions, during which the subjects sat in the same chair, and the same music was played without the low-frequency tones, through ordinary stereo equipment.

The method of monitoring change in the clients is one that has been employed by music therapists in other investigations involving changes in observed behaviour (Bunt 1987) and involves recording through a multi-channel event recorder the incidence of the behaviours, their frequency and duration. The following behaviours were recorded for each of the subjects:

Subject 1

U = Unrestrained
R = Restrained
1 = Slapping face while unrestrained
2 = Slapping face while restrained
3 = Attempting to slap face while restrained
4 = Sleep
D = Disaster
5 = Gentle hand stroking
6 = Frenzied hand clasping

Subject 2

U = Unrestrained
R = Restrained
1 = Slapping head while restrained
2 = Slapping head while restrained
3 = Attempting to slap head while restrained
4 = Sleep
D = Disaster
5 = Rubbing head on back of chair
6 = Slapping elsewhere

Subject 3

U = Unrestrained
R = Restrained
1 = Banging head while unrestrained
2 = Banging head while restrained
3 = Attempting to bang head while restrained
4 = Sleep
D = Disaster
5 = Resisting restraint
6 = Aggressive behaviour after breaking restraint

The observers recorded a D (Disaster) if one of the subjects became so self-injurious that they were forced to stop recording while they calmed down the subject, or otherwise dealt with the situation.

Results

The results of these trials showed fairly clearly that Subjects 1 and 2 responded positively to VA and there was a reduction in their self-injurious behaviour during the session, and, in the case of Subject 1, after the session, whereas Subject 3's difficult behaviours and aggression towards the staff made it impossible to be clear about the effect of this treatment on her.

Table 22.1: Mean Duration of Positive and Negative Behaviours (in seconds) in the Two Conditions

Subject 1	With VA	Without VA (Placebo)
Negative Behaviour		
R + Beh.1 + Beh.3	656.50	807.75
Total	**656.50**	**807.75**
Positive Behaviour		
Beh.5	1010.75	800.00
Beh.4 (sleep)	0.00	0.00
Unrestrained – Beh.1 + 6	1193.87	989.00
Total	**2204.62**	**1789.25**

Table 22.2: Mean Duration of Positive and Negative Behaviours (in seconds) in the Two Conditions

Subject 2	With VA	Without VA (Placebo)
Negative Behaviour		
Beh.1	14.5	90.00
Beh.6	21.62	32.75
Positive Behaviour		
Beh.5	917.25	578.25
Beh.4 (sleep)	148.75	0.00

The results show that in a 30 minute (1800 second) session, there was a proportion of both positive and negative behaviours. Subject 1 indicates that, on average, when we were using VA therapy, the accumulated mean scores of· restraint, Beh.1 and Beh.3, which we have put together as a total result for negative behaviour, are occurring for less time than when we didn't use VA. Correspondingly, there is more positive behaviour, in particular Beh.5.

When Subject 1 wasn't being restrained, and we took away the scores accumulated in Beh.1 and Beh.6, we counted this as the positive time period during the session and this also was better when we were using the VA treatment than when we were using the placebo.

Subject 2 gives a correspondingly encouraging result. In Table 22.2, Beh.1 (face-slapping behaviour) is markedly less with VA, on average, than without, and Beh.6 is also less. His positive behaviours were improved during VA, and there was one occasion when he slept for a large proportion of the session.

Subject 3 had such diverse results, due to the confusion over her aggressive behaviour which was very prevalent throughout the session, that VA had no significant effect on her self-injurious behaviour.

Discussion

Overall, we find the results going in the right direction with both Subject 1 and Subject 2. With Subject 1, we also received anecdotal reports from the ward of a reduction in his self-injurious behaviour on the ward during the period of the trials, and the staff recorded many less incidents of having to use restraint with him. They also recorded that the effect of the relaxation was to improve his bowel movements and reduce the number of times they used enemas. Although one can see some worthwhile effect, the problem of precisely identifying the causes and antecedents to SIB in each of these subjects present uncontrollable variables. The researchers found the problem of having to tolerate more SIB in the placebo trials lessened as the trials progressed, giving some evidence that the environment of the trials was also influential, and as the subjects became more familiar with the treatment, their behaviours lessened. From this we can get an indication of the need for some further studies on the subjects who have self-injurious behaviour. Why the treatment had this particular effect is still, to some extent, an unknown quantity. We are aware of its relaxation effects but relaxation alone may not prevent self-injurious behaviour. It is possible that with these subjects, where the stimulatory effect of continuous face/head slapping is replaced by a more powerful effect, this could explain the results we were getting and the value of continuing with further investigation.

At the same time as I was undertaking this study, I was involved in a period of individual therapy with a blind, disturbed lady on one of the locked wards at the hospital. I was working with a colleague, and we were attempting to find a way of reaching Marion through frequent, but short, music therapy sessions. Marion's response to anyone trying to make contact with her was to try to bite them or scratch them, grabbing for hands, clothes and hair anywhere near her. My colleague, Lucy Melluish, worked from the piano, providing a musical foundation through improvisation and structure for the session, and I worked with Marion, vocalizing and introducing her to instruments. Typically, our session involved a welcoming song, a period of vocalizing, the introduction of the following specific instruments: a guitar, a tambor and a beater, an amplifying microphone and a cymbal. It seemed that the best way of attempting to evaluate the changes that were occurring for Marion during these sessions was to video her, and then employ the same method of analysing events in the sessions as had been used in the study on self-injurious behaviour. The use of the event recorder was impractical during the session, but, on watching the videos, it was possible to record in seconds the positive and negative ways in which she was responding to the interventions we were making.

We were particularly concerned to find out how she could cope better with physical contact and with physical closeness, in an effort to move through the therapy towards her active participation in music-making, both vocally and manually. Consequently, the events we recorded of positive response from Marion were as follows:

> Z Allowed hand to be touched
> X Tolerated stroking
> C Clapping her own hand or the hand of the therapist
> V Allowing hand to play instrument
> B Spontaneous playing/singing
> N Put her legs on the floor and broke foetal position
> M Moved towards and cuddled therapist.

The negative behaviours we recorded in the sessions were as follows:

> 1 Biting therapist's hand
> 2 Biting therapist's body
> 3 Pulling therapist's hair
> 4 Biting herself
> 5 Head or chest banging
> 6 Folding arms
> 7 Hands on face
> 8 Pushing instruments or hands away
> 9 Obsessive vocalizing/talking.

By looking at the progress Marion made over the weeks we saw her for therapy, we were able to see that, during the first sessions, Marion was defensive and aggressive, given any form of contact. During some very gentle, generally based, improvised music, I would gently touch her hands and arms, before introducing her to any instruments. In the early sessions I also sang to her, often quite close to her ear. As the weeks progressed, Marion began to take her hands away from her eyes and ears, into which she dug her fingers, and let me tap my hands on hers or even clap them with my own. As we moved into the therapy, we found that she responded to guitars and drums, and after five months she began initiating the musical interaction by reaching out for the guitar or vocalizing with the piano improvisation. Following this, she began to allow us to help her use a beater, and played instruments with large, excited and rhythmical beats. The analysis of the video material is still incomplete, but, by adding up the increases or decreases in events of positive and negative behaviours, and by totalling the amount of time she demonstrated these responses, we will be able to give a very accurate picture of the changes that occurred throughout the therapy process with Marion. We will be able to see which particular musical influences, such as which instruments we used or the vocally improvised parts of the session were more effective.

Conclusion

The cases described above illustrate how one can use observational analysis either during a session or following a session to research the effect of music therapy, and also the effect of the therapist's intervention. During vibroacoustic therapy, because of the passive nature of the treatment, it is possible to record information while the session is going on. In the therapy work with Marion, one cannot be distracted or influenced during the session when trying to sustain a therapeutic relationship, but subsequent video analysis of the processes and responses is very revealing, particularly as one can look in close detail at exactly what is happening.

References

Bunt, L.G.K. (1987). Music Therapy in the child with a handicap: Evaluation of the effects of intervention. Ph.D Thesis (unpublished). City University, London.

Clynes, M. (1986). 'On music and healing', in R. Spintge and R. Dron (eds) *Musik in der medizin*. Berlin/New York: Springer Verlag.

Guillemin, R., Cohn, M. and Melnuchuk, T. (1985) (eds) *Neural modulation of immunity*. New York: Raven Press, pp.258.

Lee, C.A. (1989) 'Structural analysis of therapeutic improvisatory music', *Journal of British Music Therapy*, Vol. 3, No.2, 11–20.

Lee, C.A. (1990a) 'The efficacy of music therapy for people living with the virus Aids', *The Journal of Humanistic Psychology*.

Lee, C.A. (1990b) 'Structural analysis of post-tonal therapeutic improvisatory music', *Journal of British Music Therapy*, Vol. 4, No. 1, 6–21.

Maranto, C.D. (1991) *Applications of music in medicine*. Washington, D.C.: National Association for Music Therapy Publications.

Murphy, G. and Wilson, B. (1985) (eds) *Self-injurious behaviour*. London: BIMH Publications.

Oyama, T., Sato, Y., Kudo, T., Spintge, R. and Droh, R. (1986) 'Effect of Anxiolytic music on endocrine function in surgical patients', in R. Spintge and R. Droh (eds) *Musik in der Medizin*. Berlin/New York: Springer Verlag.

Pavlicevic, M. (1990) 'Dynamic interplay in clinical improvisation', *Journal of British Music Therapy*, Vol. 4, No. 2, 5–10.

Pavlicevic, M. and Trevarthen, C. (in press) *Music therapy in the rehabilitation of chronic schizophrenics*.

Skille, O. (1982) 'Musikkbadet – anvendt for de 1 svakeste'. *Nordisk tidsskrift for spesial pedagogikk* nr 4 s. 275–284.

Skille, O. (1986) 'MUBS – ein diagnostisches Hilfsmittel', in R. Spintge and R. Droh (eds), *Musik in der Medizin*. Berlin/New York: Springer Verlag.

Skille, O. (1989) 'Vibroacoustic Therapy', *American Journal of Music Therapy*, Vol. 8.

Skille, O., Wigram, A. and Weekes, L. (1989) 'Vibroacoustic Therapy: The therapeutic effect of low frequency sound on specific physical disorder and disabilities', *Journal of British Music Therapy*, Vol. 3, No. 2, pp.6–10.

Skille, O. and Wigram, A. (1993) 'The effect of sound and vibration on brain and muscle tissue', in A. Wigram, R. West and B. Saperston (eds) *Music and the Healing Process: A Handbook of Music Therapy*. Chichester: Carden public- ations.

Spintge, R. (1991) 'The Neurophysiology of Emotion and Its Therapeutic Application to Music Therapy and Music Medicine', in C. Maranto (ed) *Application of Music in Medicine*. Washington, D.C.: NAMT Publications, p.59–72.

Stillman, B. (1970) 'Vibratory Motor Stimulation', *Australian Journal of Physiotherapy*, XVL, 118–123.

Taniuka, F., Takazawa, T., Kamata, G., Kudo, M., Matsuki, A. and Oyama, T. (1986) 'Hormonal effect of anxiolytic music in patients during surgical operations under epidural anaesthesia', in R. Spintge and R. Droh (eds) *Music in der Medizin*. Berlin/New York: Springer Verlag.

Wigram, A. (1991) 'Die Wirkung Von Tiefen Tonen und musik auf Den Muskel-Tonus und die Blutzirkulation', OBM. *Zietschrift des Osterreichiscren Berufsverbands der Musiktherapeuten*, Vol. 2–91, 3–12.

Wigram, A. and Weekes, L. (1989) A project evaluating the difference in therapeutic treatment between the use of low frequency sound (LFS) and music alone in reducing high muscle tone in mentally handicapped people, and oedema in mentally handicapped people – Paper presented to the Internasjonale Bruker-seminar Omkring Vibroakustisk Behandlingsmetodikk in Steinkjer, Norway.

The Contributors

Anthi Agrotou trained in London at the Roehampton Institute of Higher Education. She is a registered music therapist of the British Association of Professional Music Therapists; a member of the Music Therapy European Research Group; an associate member of the Association for Psychoanalytic Psychotherapy in the National Health Service. She is founder and President of the Elikas Foundation of Friends of People with Special Needs, and works as a private practitioner.

Giuseppe Berruti, Giovanni Del Puente, Roberta Gatti, Gerardo Manarolo and Caterina Vecchiato constitute a work group interested in research about receptive music therapy at the Institute of Psychiatry of the University of Genoa. They are now developing a listening test, a psychometric tool aimed at assessing personality elements from a psychodynamic point of view. Giuseppe Berruti and Gerardo Manarolo also lead active music therapy groups in psychiatric services in the community. Caterina Vecchiato and Giovanni Del Puente are researchers at the Institute of Psychiatry.

Massimo Borghesi is a psychiatric nurse and graduate of the Cittadella Four Year Music Therapy Course.

Ruth Bright was born in the UK and educated at Queen Anne's, Caversham; she graduated Bachelor of Music at the University of Melbourne, Australia, in which country her work in music therapy has been developed. Her work over some 32 years has covered a diversity of clinical fields, including stroke rehabilitation and geriatrics in general, developmental disability, psychiatry, substance abuse, and grief counselling facilitated through music therapy. Her teachings and writings (known throughout the world) have reflected this diversity of interest and her books are used in many educational establishments as well as forming a valued part of individuals' book collections. She has served in the Australian Music Therapy Association and has also held office as President of the World Federation of Music Therapy for a three-year term. She is President of the Gerontology Foundation of Australia and a Director of Maranatha, a group home for developmentally disabled young adults. She enjoys bush walking and home music-making, is much involved with her local Anglican Church, and was recently awarded Membership of the Order of Australia for services to Music Therapy.

Jos De Backer studied in Music Education, Leuven (Belgium) and Music Therapy, Vienna (Austria). He is Professor, at the Higher Institute of Music 'Lemmens Institute' (Louvain), of music therapy and Co-ordinator for the training course for Music Therapy, Louvain. He is also head of the Music Therapy Department at the University Psychiatric Centre, Kortenberg and head of the Music Therapy Department of Voluntas (Advice, Consultation and Training Centre for Helpers and Parents of Handicapped Children).

Denise Erdonmez studied music therapy at Michigan State University, USA. She holds a Master's degree from the University of Melbourne, and is presently working towards a PhD. She has completed advanced training in Guided Imagery and Music, and has a small private practice. She is Senior Lecturer in Music Therapy at the University of Melbourne, and is Chair of the Commission on Education and Training of the World Federation of Music Therapy.

Claire Flower trained as a music therapist at the Guildhall School of Music and Drama. She subsequently worked in Manchester, establishing music therapy services at Prestwich Hospital and the Gardener Unit. She returned to London in 1991, and now divides her time between work with children, with adults in mental health settings, teaching music therapy, and being married.

Brigitte Flucher is a community worker and graduate of the Cittadella Four Year Music Therapy Course.

Gianluigi di Franco M.D. is a musician (vocalist), psychiatrist, and Freudian group psychoanalyst. He is founder of CRM and School Director. He is also the European Music Therapy Committee's member for Italy and was a member of the Scientific Commission for the VIIth Music Therapy World Congress, Vitorio, July 19–23 (1993).

Loredana Guida is a community worker and graduate the Cittadella Four Year Music Therapy Course.

Margaret Heal is the Senior Music Therapist for the Forest Healthcare Trust, London (England) and clinical supervisor at the Guildhall School of Music and Drama, London. She was born in Portage La Prairie, in Canada. After obtaining a Bachelor of Arts and Bachelor of Music at Queens's University (Canada) she moved to London to complete postgraduate training in music therapy at the Guildhall School of Music and Drama. She has a special interest in psychoanalytically-informed music therapy with clients who are learning disabled, and publishes and lectures in this area.

Jeff Hooper qualified as a music therapist from the Guildhall School of Music and Drama in July 1985. Since then he has been employed by Tayside Health Board and has worked in the field of mental handicap. He is based at Strathmartine Hospital, Dundee, and is Senior Music Therapist for the Dundee Mental Health Unit.

José van den Hurk, R.M.Th. is a music therapist at the Music Therapy Laboratory, Nijmegen (The Netherlands). She is lecturer and supervisor of the music therapy programme at the Hogeschool Nijmegen. Together with Henk Smeijsters she presented a case in *Case Studies in Music Therapy* (1991) edited by K.E. Bruscia.

Hanne Mette Kortegaard is Research Fellow at Aalborg University, Denmark. Since 1984 she has taught in the Music Therapy Programme, Aalborg University. She is attached to Aalborg Psychiatric Hospital as a full-time researcher, and has established a research clinic as a co-operative project between University and Hospital. She is Former Chairman of Musikterapeutforeningen (Ass. Prof. Music Therapists) and is a member of the European Music Therapy Committé, DISC-coordinator (Worldwide Data Communication and Information Network), Denmark. She has published several articles on music therapy and schizophrenia, and music therapy research.

Marzia Mancini is a music teacher and graduate of the Cittadella Four Year Music Therapy Course.

Cheryl Dileo Maranto PhD, RMT-BC is Professor and Coordinator of Music Therapy, Temple University, Philadelphia, PA, USA. She is a Past-President of the National Association for Music Therapy, Inc. (USA) and is a Council Member and Chair of the Commission on Ethics and Research of the World Federation of Music Therapy. She is the author/editor of numerous books and articles on music therapy, the most recent of which is *Music Therapy: International Perspective*, and is a consulting editor for three professional journals. She is a frequent international lecturer, and her clinical and research interests include professional ethics, music therapy education and training, and music in medicine.

Pierrette Müller has a background of nursing, psychology and counselling training, and has a great interest in children with special needs, particularly those on the autistic continuum. Her interest in music therapy developed over a period of 12 years, soon after she arrived in England. This interest led to a dissertation on the effects of music therapy for her MSc degree and the present study which she has now completed for her PhD from Reading University.

Piera Nocentini is a physical education teacher and graduate of the Cittadella Four Year Music Therapy Course.

Amelia Oldfield has worked as a Music Therapist in the fields of mental handicap, child development and child and family psychiatry for the past 13 years. She completed a five year music therapy research project in 1986. She is an approved supervisor and a past Chairman of the APTM. She has given numerous workshops and lectures on music therapy, both in Great Britain and abroad, and has published many articles and chapters on the subject. She is co-author of the book *Pied Piper – Musical Activities to Develop Basic Skills*, which was published in October 1991.

Dr Pier Luigi Postacchini was born in Bologna on May 9, 1950. He took his degree in Medicine and Surgery, specialising in Psychiatry and Infantile Neuropsychiatry. He now practices as a psychotherapist on a psychoanalytical basis. Since 1980 he has been professor of the Music therapy four year course at Assisi University. He has published on music therapy. He plays the clarinet and the saxophone. He is president of APIM (Associazione Professionale Italiana Musicoterapeuti/Italian Musicotherapists Vocational Association), a group of Assisi graduates which supports the vocation and training of Italian Music therapists.

Josée Raijmaekers obtained degrees in 1971 and 1975 in both musical and therapeutic training. In 1984 she specialised in Receptive Music Therapy, in 1988 in Neuro Linguistic Programming. Since 1974 she has worked as a music therapist in a psychiatric hospital in the Hague (The Netherlands). In addition, she is author and co/author of several articles on music therapy, and gives workshops on music therapy.

Fiona Ritchie has been a music therapist for six years. She started working at a hospital for people with learning difficulties and gradually set up the Music Therapy Department for North Warwickshire. She now works for North Warwickshire NHS Trust as a Community Day Services Manager. She has always been an active promoter of music therapy and has been a member of the Executive Committee of the Association of Professional Music Therapists.

Dr. Clive Robbins CMT/RMT-BC is Co-Director of the Nordoff-Robbins Music Therapy Center at New York University. His pioneering collaboration with Paul Nordoff, D.Mus., 1959–1976, contributed substantially to the development of musical improvisation as a therapeutic modality. Through his clinical work, demonstrations, writings and teaching, he is internationally recognised for his commitment to creativity and musicianship in the practice of music therapy. With Paul Nordoff, he co-authored: *Therapy in Music for Handicapped Children, Music Therapy in Special Education, Creative Music Therapy*, and many books of musical activities for children. With his wife, Carol Robbins, he has co-authored: *Music for the Hearing Impaired – and Other Special Groups*.

Laura Rubin is a social worker and graduate of the Cittadella Four Year Music Therapy Course.

Sergio Santoni is a music teacher and graduate of the Cittadella Four Year Music Therapy Course.

Anne Sloboda is Head Music Therapist at St Bernard's Wing, Mental Health Unit, West London Healthcare Trust, and Senior Music Therapist at Addenbrookes Hospital Psychiatric Unit. She is Clinical Tutor on the Music Therapy Training Course at the Guildhall School of Music and Drama. She is currently the Chairperson of the Association of Professional Music Therapist (APMT).

Dr. Henk Smeijsters PhD is a music psychologist and researcher at the Music Therapy Laboratory Nijmegen (The Netherlands), lecturer in the music therapy programme at the Hogeschool Nijmegen and co-ordinator of and lecturer in the music therapy programme at the Conservatory of Enschede. He has written several papers in journals and is the author of *Muziek en psyche* (1987) and *Muziektherapie als psychotherapie* (1991). He is a member of the editorial board of *The Arts in Psychotherapy*.

Julie Sutton was born in Cornwall. She obtained a Bachelor of Music honours degree from Royal Holloway College, London University. She then qualified as a teacher and in 1982 completed music therapy training at the Nordoff-Robbins Music Therapy Centre, London. She worked in London for five years before moving to Northern Ireland. She has worked with a wide range of clients, including children and adults with special needs in the areas of physical, mental, sensory and emotional impairments. She has undertaken research with people with Parkinson's Disease and speech and language impaired children. Currently writing her M.Phil thesis, she is also engaged in research work with girls with Rett Syndrome in Belfast and Dublin.

Esmé Towse was born and educated in Scotland. She then studied at the Royal College of Music and at the Guildhall School of Music and Drama. She has worked in Manchester since 1980, with the elderly and in psychiatry, and is an approved music therapy supervisor. She is approaching completion of the North West Regional Diploma in Dynamic Psychotherapy training. She is senior music therapist at Withington Hospital and has a private psychotherapy practice.

Auriel Warwick has worked with children with special needs, specialising in autism, for the Oxfordshire Education Authority for 21 years. She has been Chairperson of the British Society for Music Therapy and is now one of its Vice-Presidents. Her work also includes lecturing, both in Britain and abroad, examining for the Music Therapy course at the Guildhall School of Music and Drama and she is an approved post-diploma supervisor for the Association of Professional Music Therapists.

Tony Wigram is Associate Professor in Music Therapy, University of Aalborg, (Denmark), and Head Music Therapist at the Harper House Children's Service. He took an honours degree in Music at Bristol University, and more recently a qualifying degree in Psychology at London University, where he is currently researching his Doctoral thesis in Psychology. A former Chairman of the Association of Professional Music Therapists, Churchill Fellow of 1985, and Music Therapy Advisor to the Department of Health, he is currently Chairman of the British Society for Music Therapy and Coordinator of the European Music Therapy Committee. He is on the Council for the World Federation for Music Therapy, and is a member of the ISME Research Commission for Music Therapy and Music in Medicine. He has published extensively in his clinical specialisms of child and adult developmental disability, autism and vibroacoustic therapy. He has lectured in many European countries, North and South America, Australia and New Zealand, and regularly teaches and examines on Music Therapy courses in Spain and Italy.

Subject Index

References in italic indicate figures or tables

Author Index

*References in italic indicate
figures or tables*